Management Science Applications in Tourism and Hospitality

Management Science Applications in Tourism and Hospitality has been co-published simultaneously as *Journal of Travel & Tourism Marketing,* Volume 16, Numbers 2/3 2004.

Management Science Applications in Tourism and Hospitality

Zheng Gu
Editor

Management Science Applications in Tourism and Hospitality has been co-published simultaneously as *Journal of Travel & Tourism Marketing,* Volume 16, Numbers 2/3 2004.

First published by

The Haworth Hospitality Press®, 10 Alice Street, Binghamton, NY 13904-1580 USA

The Haworth Hospitality Press® is an imprint of The Haworth Press, Inc., 10 Alice Street, Binghamton, NY 13904-1580 USA.

This edition published 2012 by Routledge

Routledge
Taylor & Francis Group
711 Third Avenue
New York, NY 10017

Routledge
Taylor & Francis Group
2 Park Square, Milton Park
Abingdon, Oxon OX14 4RN

Management Science Applications in Tourism and Hospitality has been co-published simultaneously as *Journal of Travel & Tourism Marketing,* Volume 16, Numbers 2/3 2004.

© 2004 by The Haworth Press, Inc. All rights reserved. No part of this work may be reproduced or utilized in any form or by any means, electronic or mechanical, including photocopying, microfilm and recording, or by any information storage and retrieval system, without permission in writing from the publisher.

The development, preparation, and publication of this work has been undertaken with great care. However, the publisher, employees, editors, and agents of The Haworth Press and all imprints of The Haworth Press, Inc., including The Haworth Medical Press® and The Pharmaceutical Products Press®, are not responsible for any errors contained herein or for consequences that may ensue from use of materials or information contained in this work. Opinions expressed by the author(s) are not necessarily those of The Haworth Press, Inc.

Cover design by Jennifer M. Gaska

Library of Congress Cataloging-in-Publication Data

Management science applications in tourism and hospitality / Zheng Gu, editor.
p. cm.
"Management science applications in tourism and hospitality has been co-published simultaneously as Journal of travel & tourism marketing, volume 16, numbers 2/3 2004."
Includes bibliographical references and index.
ISBN 0-7890-2518-3 (pbk : alk. paper)
1. Tourism–Management. 2. Hospitality industry–Management. I. Gu, Zheng, 1947- II. Journal of travel & tourism marketing.
G155.A1M249 2004
910'.68–dc22

2004007836

Management Science Applications in Tourism and Hospitality

CONTENTS

ABOUT THE EDITOR

Zheng Gu holds a PhD degree in Finance from the University of Central Florida. Before he joined the faculty in 1991, he taught tourism at Hangzhou University in China, and Financial Management at the University of Central Florida. As a visiting professor, Dr. Gu also taught courses and conducted research at Institut De Management Hotelier International (sponsored by ESSEC and Cornell University), France.

Dr. Gu's research interests are financial management and operation analyses for the hospitality, tourism and gaming industries. Currently his research focuses on destination capacity optimization, U.S. and European casino operations comparison, hospitality firm bankruptcy prediction, casino industry mergers and acquisitions, and tourism markets in the Asian/Pacific region. Dr. Gu has about 70 articles published in academic and industry journals. He has won a series of awards for his research papers.

Preface

Management science is an approach to problem solving and decision making using scientific methods that involves extensive use of quantitative analysis. It has been widely applied in the service industries. Recent years have seen an increase in applications of management science in tourism and hospitality operations. To keep readers abreast with new developments in its tourism and hospitality applications, this special volume features eight articles with an emphasis on data envelopment analysis (DEA) and forecasting, two important topics of management science.

DEA is a performance evaluation technique based on linear programming that involves weighted outputs and inputs. Unrestricted by any assumptions of its operational form, DEA is a nonparametric method that can provide a viable efficiency benchmark for tourism and hospitality operations. In their article, Wöber and Fesenmaier introduce DEA for evaluating efficiency in tourism advertising programs and identify optimal comparison partners for benchmarking. Evaluating state tourism advertising programs in the United States, they demonstrate how DEA can be implemented for benchmarking tourism destinations. Using data from sample restaurants, Reynolds' study reveals that DEA offers considerable potential for managers attempting to accurately assess productivity. As the study shows, the potential of the DEA model to include multiple output and input factors underlines the technique's versatility and portability. In this special volume, two articles explore DEA applications in the hotel industry. In their empirical illustration using California hotels data, Hu and Cai propose DEA as an effective method to measure hotel labor productivity and further recommend a relational model to identify determinants of labor productivity variance. On the other hand, utilizing data of UK hotels, Sigala demonstrates the value of stepwise DEA for measuring and benchmarking hotel productivity.

Another focus of this special volume is forecasting methodology. In their paper, Law, Goh, and Pine apply the rough sets theory to establish a forecasting model for tourism demand. Utilizing Japanese arrivals data in Hong Kong, they show that the induced decision rules could forecast arrivals with reasonably high accuracy. Another study by Law proposes an improved extrapolative time series technique for forecasting hotel occupancy. His empirical results based on Hong Kong hotels indicate the new technique's potential in raising forecasting accuracy. Hu, Chen and McCain compare eight forecasting models using the data of an on-premises buffet restaurant in a Las Vegas casino. They show that the double moving average model is the best forecaster. Finally, in their article on a separate subject, Dolnicar and Grabler propose a city perception analysis model, a destination marketing decision-making approach designed to avoid sub-optimal decisions.

It would be impossible to publish this special volume without the assistance of many people, especially the reviewers. Therefore, I would like to express my sincere thanks to them for their critiques and constructive comments that have helped enhance the quality of the articles.

Zheng Gu
University of Nevada, Las Vegas

[Haworth co-indexing entry note]: "Preface." Gu, Zheng. Co-published simultaneously in *Journal of Travel & Tourism Marketing* (The Haworth Hospitality Press, an imprint of The Haworth Press, Inc.) Vol. 16, No. 2/3, 2004, pp. xvii; and: *Management Science Applications in Tourism and Hospitality* (ed: Zheng Gu) The Haworth Hospitality Press, an imprint of The Haworth Press, Inc., 2004, pp. xi. Single or multiple copies of this article are available for a fee from The Haworth Document Delivery Service [1-800-HAWORTH, 9:00 a.m. - 5:00 p.m. (EST). E-mail address: docdelivery@haworthpress.com].

http://www.haworthpress.com/web/JTTM
© 2004 by The Haworth Press, Inc. All rights reserved.

A Multi-Criteria Approach to Destination Benchmarking: A Case Study of State Tourism Advertising Programs in the United States

Karl W. Wöber
Daniel R. Fesenmaier

SUMMARY. This paper introduces Data Envelopment Analysis (DEA) for the evaluation of inefficiencies in tourism advertising programs and the identification of optimal comparison partners for benchmarking. The implementation of DEA for benchmarking tourism destinations is demonstrated by assessing state tourism advertising programs in the United States. This evaluation includes information on the advertising budgets of state tourism offices, the allocation of market effort in international and domestic segments, and the number of visitors and expenditures generated in the various destinations. A proximity measure was used as an exogenously fixed input variable in order to reflect differences in domestic market size. Findings include efficiency scores for state tourism offices offering several possibilities for managerial implications. Furthermore, the concept of a virtual reference destination assisting managers to analyze their individual strength and weaknesses is introduced. Finally, a discussion of the potential and limitations of DEA for benchmarking of tourism destinations is provided. *[Article copies available for a fee from The Haworth Document Delivery Service: 1-800-HAWORTH. E-mail address: <docdelivery@haworthpress.com> Website: <http://www.HaworthPress.com> © 2004 by The Haworth Press, Inc. All rights reserved.]*

KEYWORDS. Destination benchmarking, Data Envelopment Analysis, efficiency analysis, tourism advertising

INTRODUCTION

Benchmarking has experienced increased popularity, both in the hospitality as well as in the tourism industry. The increased interest in benchmarking has been stimulated with the publication of Xerox's manager Robert Camp's book on benchmarking (Camp, 1989). Since then, the phenomenon of benchmarking has been discussed by many authors primarily in the form of management guidebooks (e.g., Spendolini, 1992; Watson, 1992; Cook, 1995;

Karl W. Wöber is Associate Professor, Department for Tourism and Leisure Studies, Vienna University of Economics and Business Administration, Augasse 2-6, 1090 Vienna, Austria (E-mail: karl.woeber@wu-wien.ac.at). He is also free consultant for the Austrian Society of Applied Research in Tourism, and Technical Advisor of European Cities Tourism and the European Travel Commission. Daniel R. Fesenmaier is Professor and Director, National Laboratory for Tourism and eCommerce, School of Tourism and Hospitality Management, Temple University, 201-C Vivacqua Hall, 1700 N. Broad Street, Philadelphia, PA 19122 (E-mail: drfez@temple.edu).

[Haworth co-indexing entry note]: "A Multi-Criteria Approach to Destination Benchmarking: A Case Study of State Tourism Advertising Programs in the United States." Wöber, Karl W. and Daniel R. Fesenmaier. Co-published simultaneously in *Journal of Travel & Tourism Marketing* (The Haworth Hospitality Press, an imprint of The Haworth Press, Inc.) Vol. 16, No. 2/3, 2004, pp. 1-18; and: *Management Science Applications in Tourism and Hospitality* (ed: Zheng Gu) The Haworth Hospitality Press, an imprint of The Haworth Press, Inc., 2004, pp. 1-18. Single or multiple copies of this article are available for a fee from The Haworth Document Delivery Service [1-800-HAWORTH, 9:00 a.m. - 5:00 p.m. (EST). E-mail address: docdelivery@haworthpress.com].

http://www.haworthpress.com/web/JTTM
© 2004 by The Haworth Press, Inc. All rights reserved.
Digital Object Identifier: 10.1300/J073v16n02_01

Zairi, 1996; Cross, 1998). The practice of benchmarking as detailed by Camp and widely followed by practitioners has focused attention on the search for specific practices which will enhance performance with a controlled allocation of resources. This improved efficiency is achieved by the discovery of specific practices relying on simple engineering ratios.

In tourism the focus and methodologies used in benchmarking studies can be very different and can be classified into three approaches: (1) benchmarking of profit-oriented tourism businesses (e.g., accommodation suppliers, restaurants, tour operators and travel agencies, airlines); (2) benchmarking of non-profit oriented tourism businesses/organizations (e.g., tourist boards/organizations, attractions operated by public authorities or other forms of non-profit oriented businesses); and (3) destination benchmarking (national, regional or local benchmarking). The majority of benchmarking initiatives can be found among profit-oriented tourism businesses, particularly in the hospitality sector. Benchmarking in all other tourism areas has been very limited in terms of number and their technical quality. Few attempts have been made to apply benchmarking methodologies for measuring the efficiency of regional tourism management or to assess the competitiveness of tourism destinations.

The evaluation of destination marketing performance involves multiple objectives and resources. A large literature exists describing the operational requirements and managerial implications of benchmarking (e.g., McNair & Leibfried, 1992; Watson, 1992; Karlof & Ostblom, 1994; Cross, 1998); however, very little attention has focused on methodological aspects in conjunction with situations where managers are facing multiple objectives and resources. Data Envelopment Analysis (DEA) has been identified as an appropriate technique for the evaluation of efficiencies and the identification of benchmarking partners in situations where multiple inputs and outputs occur. DEA is a linear programming model which was first introduced by Charnes, Cooper and Rhodes (1978) to measure the relative efficiency of operating units (for this study state tourism offices) with the same goals and objectives. DEA can be used to separate efficient units from inefficient ones on the basis of whether or not they lie on the "efficient frontier," which is defined by the best units in the data set. More specifically, the efficiency measure employed in DEA is established mathematically as the ratio of the weighted sum of outputs to the weighted sum of inputs.

DEA has been successfully applied for the selection of benchmarking partners in the hospitality industry (Morey & Dittman, 1995; Morey & Morey, 1999; Wöber, 2002). However, several important issues remain to be addressed when it comes to implementing this methodology within the context of tourism destination management. This paper introduces this tool for evaluating the performance of tourism management in 48 state tourism offices in the United States. The evaluation was based upon their advertising budgets, the allocation of market effort in international and domestic segments, and the number of visitors and expenditures generated in the various destinations. Furthermore, the concept of a virtual reference destination assisting managers is introduced as means for state tourism offices to analyze their individual strength and weaknesses. Finally, the article ends with a discussion of the strengths and weaknesses of DEA for benchmarking tourism destinations.

TOURISM DESTINATION BENCHMARKING

Studies on tourism destination benchmarking are rare (Kozak, 2002). Probably one of the most comprehensive examples of regional benchmarking was first presented by Wöber (1997). In this study Wöber described a Web-based decision support system that enables European tourism organizations to compare the market segment performance of one city with other cities in Europe. More recently, Kozak and Rimmington (1999) reviewed the literature on tourism destination competitiveness, stressing the requirement to establish which destinations are in direct competition. They noted the importance of systematically evaluating such competitiveness both quantitatively through measurement of hard data (such as arrivals and tourism receipts) and qualitatively through soft data. To demonstrate the applicability of their proposal, the authors sought to benchmark Turkey as a destination against its competitors, which they identified by means of a guest survey among British visitors. Destination performance was evaluated in various attributes (such as availability and quality of facilities, friendliness and natural environment) in comparison with other destinations, and complaints with regard to all destinations, in order to discover the relative performance of destinations. The importance of benchmarking for the development of a systematic approach to tourism policy was also stressed by Alavi and Yasin (2000). They presented a benchmarking model based upon "shift-share" analysis whereby each country's growth in tourist arrivals from different parts of the world was compared against that of the region. Finally, the German Institute for Future Studies and Technology Assessment (IZT) has sought to develop and evaluate destination benchmarks (quantitative criteria) which enables one to assess the strengths and weaknesses of tourism related IT investments (e.g., online information and reservation systems) in European destinations (Oertel et al., 2002). The project provides information on best practices in Website-presentations and suggestions on how tourism managers can improve their use of new media.

What becomes clear from the literature is that a comprehensive theory does not yet exist for performance benchmarking of tourism destinations. An exception might be the proposal made by Ritchie and his colleagues who developed operational measures for evaluating competitiveness and sustainability of a tourism destination (Crouch & Ritchie, 1999; Ritchie & Crouch, 2000; Ritchie et al., 2001). Although their framework provides a detailed set of measures and guidelines, their concept has not been empirically tested. The main problems associated with benchmarking tourism destinations result from the lack of availability and comparability of quantitative and qualitative data which need to be considered when measuring the performance of tourism destinations. This is particularly true for international benchmarking endeavors where different economic and legal systems exist. Further problems are associated with methodological questions regarding how to identify "who is best" in environments with multiple resource and success measures.

The definition of productivity is extremely complex and therefore cannot be assessed using a single output measure. This is especially true in the tourism destination management, where predominantly non-profit organizations often provide a range services including cooperative marketing, visitor information services, and the management of public attractions, etc. In general, the efficiency of a tourism destination can be considered the result of the interaction between two important factors. The first factor determines management's ability to use its resources to adapt to, and to take advantage of, the constantly changing environment and is referred to as "controllable inputs" (Anderson et al., 1997). These "inputs" are determined by the manager and define the manager's decision alternatives and thus, are also referred to as the decision variables or discretionary variables. Controllable variables in tourism destination management can be further categorized into financial and non-financial indicators. In any realistic situation, however, there will exist exogenously fixed or nondiscretionary inputs that are beyond the control of an organization's management. These uncontrollable variables are either factors determined by aspects related to a destination's market area (e.g., the proximity to the main generating markets) or by physical characteristics of the destination (e.g., climate conditions).

Success in tourism destination management is frequently measured using a variety of indicators including: (1) the number of visitors and expenditures generated (e.g., Van der Borg et al., 1996; Archer & Fletcher, 1996), (2) the degree to which the negative effects of seasonality are successfully opposed by management (e.g., Butler, 1994; Baum, 1999), (3) if existing capacities are used efficiently (e.g., McElroy & De Albuquerque, 1998; Ritchie et al., 2001), (4) the extent to which natural and cultural resources are preserved (e.g., Inskeep, 1987; Ritchie et al., 2001; Lee & Han, 2002), (5) visitor satisfaction with the tourism product provided (e.g., Kozak, 2002), and/or (6) the degree to which local residents accept the existing tourism policy (e.g., Bachleitner & Zins, 1999; Williams & Lawson, 2001).

DATA ENVELOPMENT ANALYSIS

Data Envelopment Analysis (DEA) is a non-parametric technique that can be used to measure the relative efficiency of operating units with the same general goals and objectives (Charnes, Cooper & Rhodes, 1978). DEA can separate the efficient operating units (firms, organizations, managers, etc.) from the inefficient on the basis of whether they lie on the efficient frontier which is spanned by the best units in the data set. The efficiency measure employed in DEA is established mathematically by the ratio of the weighted sum of outputs to the weighted sum of inputs. They defined an operating unit as 100 percent efficient when and only when:

1. None of its outputs can be increased without either
   i. increasing one or more of its inputs, or
   ii. decreasing some of its other outputs; and
2. None of its inputs can be decreased without either
   i. decreasing some of its outputs, or
   ii. increasing some of its other inputs.

This definition is based upon the concept of Pareto optimality and is free of the arbitrariness of any weighting imputation used in other approaches. Hence, by definition, DEA seeks to identify, either for a given level of output the operating units which achieved the lowest observed costs, or for a given level of costs the operating units which achieved the highest observed output.

A simple DEA computational program is formulated as a fractional programming problem and is then reduced to a linear programming problem. DEA starts by building a relative ratio consisting of total weighted outputs to total weighted inputs for each institution in a given data set. The best organizations in the data set form an "efficient frontier" and the degree of the inefficiencies of the other units relative to the efficient frontier are then determined using a linear programming algorithm. An advantage of DEA is that it needs no *a priori* information regarding which inputs and outputs are most important in the evaluation procedure.

Charnes, Cooper and Rhodes (1978) have demonstrated that DEA can simultaneously handle multiple cost drivers and multiple types of costs. In their original paper they formulated their DEA program as a fractional programming problem and then reduced it to a linear programming problem which is easy to compute. Later, they demonstrated that DEA can also handle the effect of non-discretionary input variables (Charnes & Cooper, 1985; Banker & Morey, 1986b). The linear programming formulation of the basic input-oriented DEA model is:

$$\min e_k$$

subject to

$$\sum_{m=1}^{n} \lambda_{km} y_{um} \geq y_{uk} \quad u = 1, \ldots, r$$

$$\sum_{m=1}^{n} \lambda_{km} x_{vm}^{D} \leq e_k x_{vk}^{D} \quad v = 1, \ldots, s^{D}$$

$$\sum_{m=1}^{n} \lambda_{km} x_{wm}^{N} \leq x_{wk}^{N} \quad w = 1, \ldots, s^{N}$$

For a particular operating unit k, a linear programming algorithm can easily find the minimum proportion, e_k, which allows a weighted combination of the performance of all operating units, λ_{km}, such that for each controllable input, $x_{vk}{}^{D}$, the weighted combination of input does not exceed the proportion e_k of the input of operating unit k, for each uncontrollable input, $x_{wk}{}^{N}$, the weighted combination of input does not exceed that of operating unit k, and for each output, $y_{uk}{}^{D}$, the weighted combination of output is at least as great as that of operating unit k.

Variable Returns to Scale (BCC Model)

The Charnes, Cooper, and Rhodes (CCR) model described before is only appropriate when all units are operating at an optimal scale. Imperfect competition, constraints on finance, etc., however, may cause a tourism organization to not be operating at optimal scale. Returns to scale are technical properties of the production function. If the quantity of all factors employed by the same (proportional) amount increases, output will increase. The question of interest is whether the resulting output will increase by the same proportion, more than proportionally, or less than proportionally. There are three basic outcomes that can be identified respectively as increasing returns to scale, constant returns to scale, and decreasing returns to scale. Figure 1 which is a one-input one-output example illustrates this (Coelli, 1996). It shows DEA results under (a) constant returns to scale, (b) non-increasing returns to scale, and (c) variable returns to scale assumptions applied on the same data set. For example, under the constant returns to scale assumption the input-oriented technical inefficiency of point P_1 is the distance $\overline{P_1P_{c1}}$, while under the variable returns to scale model the technical inefficiency would only be $\overline{P_1P_{v1}}$. The difference between these two, $\overline{P_{c1}P_{v1}}$, is put down to scale inefficiency.

Tourism destination management experience, according to their different environmental conditions they are exposed, result in different returns to scale situations. Banker et al. (1984) suggest an extension of the CCR-DEA model to account for variable returns to scale. They modified the CCR model to account for variable returns to scale by adding the convexity constraint $\sum_{m=1}^{n} \lambda_{om} = 1$ to the original formula and is referred to as the BCC-DEA model. This approach forms a convex hull of intersecting planes which envelops the data points more tightly than the constant returns to scale conical hull and thus provides technical efficiency scores which are greater than or equal to those obtained using the CCR model (see Figure 1c). The variable returns to scale model provided by Banker et al. (1984) has been the most commonly used DEA model in the 1990s.

Within DEA the overall efficiency of a destination is measured by its "total factor productivity output-to-input ratio" which takes into account of all outputs and all inputs. However, an attempt to measure total factor productivity encounters difficulties such as choosing the inputs and outputs to be considered and the weights to be used in order to obtain a composite overall measure. Other problems and limitations which occur in traditional attempts to evaluate productivity refer to the need for prescribing the functional form of the input-output relationship (e.g., in regression analysis).

FIGURE 1. Various Returns to Scale Specifications in DEA

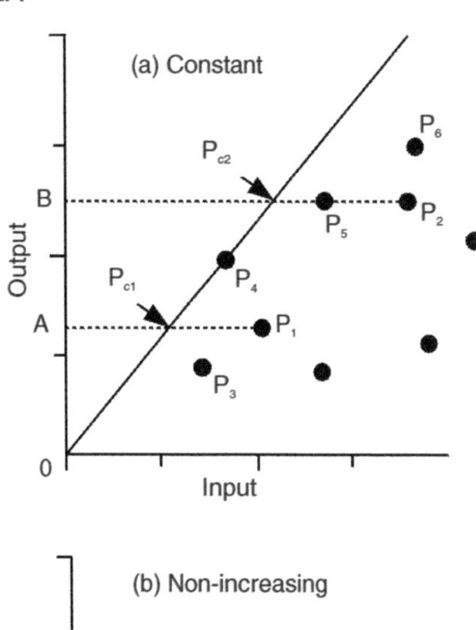

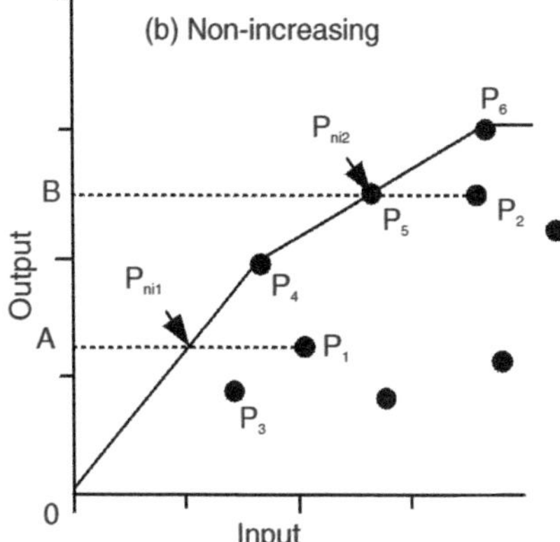

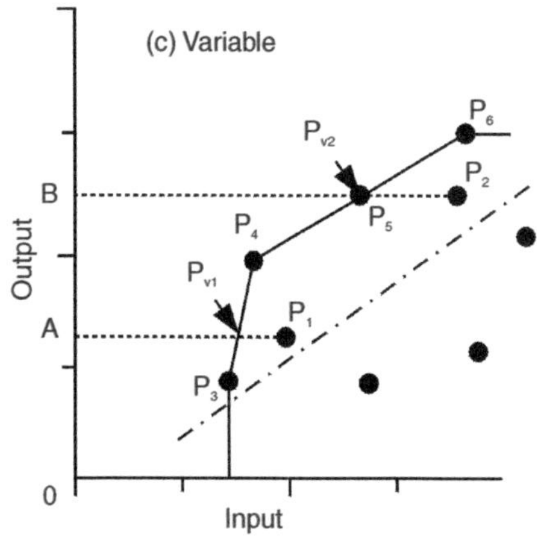

The Measurement of Inefficiency by DEA

Methodologically, the DEA algorithm can be best described through the original model developed by Charnes, Cooper and Rhodes (1978), which is also comprehensively discussed in Norman and Stoker (1991), Charnes, Cooper, Lewin and Seiford (1994), and Cooper, Seiford and Tone (2000). For instance, consider the simple single input/single output situation illustrated in Figure 2c where the plotted black dots indicate operating units with varying cost/output combinations. DEA labels operating units such as P_3, P_4, P_5, and P_6 as efficient or "best practice" units since no other operating units with the same output and lower costs can be identified. This line connecting all the efficient operating units is the fitted DEA frontier, which envelops the data (and which gave the procedure its name).

Note that operating units P_1 and P_2 are located above the regression line and therefore, are often classified as efficient units by many benchmarking studies which use ordinary mean values or regression analysis for the identification of "best-practicing" partners. DEA, however, labels units such as P_2 as inefficient since compared with its counterpart operating unit P_5 it has the same level of output but higher costs. The distance P_2P_5 measures the inefficiency of operating unit P_2. What about operating unit P_1? Operating unit P_1 has a different level of output from all the other units, and therefore cannot be directly compared. DEA compares it with an artificially constructed operating unit (P_{c1}, P_{ni1}, P_{v1}), which exists at the intercept between the dashed line and the frontier. In the variable returns to scale situation whereby P_{v1} which is a linear combination of units P_3 and P_4, the operating units P_3 and P_4 are said to be the "benchmarking partners" of P_1. Thus, as compared with its benchmark P_{v1}, operating unit P_1 is inefficient as it produces the same level of output but at higher cost.

Several computer programs can be used to solve the bulk of linear programming in one step. Commercial software packages are available from Banxia Frontier Analyst (www.banxia.co.uk), OnFront (www.emq.se/onfront1.htm), Warwick-DEA (www.warwick.ac.uk/~bsrlu/dea/deas/deas1.htm), IDEAS (www.ideas2000.com), and DEA-Solver (www.saitech-inc.com). Free DEA software products which can be downloaded from the Web for academic use include DEAP (www.une.edu.au/econometrics/deap.htm) developed by Tim Coelli (University of New England) and EMS (www.wiso.uni-dortmund.de/lsfg/or/scheel/ems/) developed by Holger Scheel (University of Dortmund), which was employed in the present study.

CASE STUDY: ASSESSING STATE TOURISM ADVERTISING PROGRAMS IN THE UNITED STATES

The tourism industry in the United States has grown to be approximately $584 billion (in 2000) including international and domestic travel expenditures, generating 7.8 million jobs and $100 billion in tax revenue (TIA, 2001b). Competition for these expenditures among state tourism offices has increased substantially over the years to reach $685.1 million (an average of $13.7 million/state) for 2000-2001. Of this amount, $178.2 million was spent for domestic advertising and $49.7 for international advertising. Concomitant with this growth in investments in tourism, many state tourism offices face the need to evaluate the efficacy of these programs. A variety of approaches have been taken including advertising tracking studies, conversion studies and other forms of program evaluation (Burke & Gitelson, 1990; Ritchie & Crouch, 2000; Wöber, 1997; Woodside, 1990; 1996; Woodside & Sakai, 2001). For example, conversion studies have been used widely by state, regional and local tourism organizations in the United States for advertising evaluation (Burke & Gitelson, 1990; McWilliams & Crompton, 1997; Woodside, 1990; 1996). This approach has generally focused on evaluating individuals' responses to advertising campaigns including awareness and image of the particular destination, as well as levels of visitation and visitor expenditure. A number of conversion-based efficiency measures have been proposed including return on investment (ROI) which is calculated using the ratio of estimates of total visitor expenditures and total campaign costs.

Conversion studies have been criticized because they often fail to reflect the underlying behavioral process of information search and decision making as well as the specific goals of an advertising campaign such as creating awareness and/or branding a destination that might not translate into an immediate decision to visit a destination (Siegel & Ziff- Levine, 1990). Woodside (1990; 1996) and others have advocated the use of experimental approaches where attention focuses on assessing the degree to which a state's advertising program actually influences/changes individuals' attitudes and behavior towards the particular destination. Still others have proposed a more aggregate buyer-purchase approach to advertising evaluation, suggesting that attention should focus on estimating the marginal number of visits and the economic impact of these visits resulting from the promotional effort (Butterfield, Deal & Kubursi, 1998; Silberman & Klock, 1986). This approach adopts a general econometric perspective whereby travel from an "origin" (i.e., city or state) to the destination state is a function of the size and nature of the visitor market, distance as well as the size/nature/effectiveness of advertising expenditures (Butterfield, Deal & Kubursi, 1998; Fotheringham, 1983; Wilson, 1971). It is argued that if the model can be correctly specified, the effectiveness of the campaign can be assessed by holding all other factors constant. The advantages of this aggregate approach include the relative high level of "explanation," ease of data collection and the ability to control for exogenous factors while the disadvantages stem from the inability to incorporate actual traveler decision making processes. This study adopts the latter approach and seeks to contribute to this literature by incorporating a DEA-based benchmarking methodology to examine the "efficiency" of state tourism advertising programs in the United States.

The DEA Model

The data set consisted of 48 state tourism offices (Alaska and Hawaii were excluded) measuring 4 input factors of which 3 were defined as controllable and 6 outputs. More specifically, the 3 advertising related inputs were: (1) total state tourism office domestic advertising budget (TIA, 2001a); (2) total state tourism office international advertising budget (TIA, 2001a); (3) other budget sources invested by the state tourism offices (TIA, 2001a). These three measures were used to reflect the amount of direct investment state tourism offices have made in attracting tourists to their respective states; it is important to note these measures do not reflect private sector investments which may substantially exceed those by the state tourist office (Woodside & Sakai, 2001). A fourth input factor, Market Size, was defined as a non-controllable input factor and measured by summing the state population and those of adjacent states (for the year 2000) weighted inversely by the travel distance to major population center(s) of adjacent states (U.S. Census Bureau, 2001).

Market size was incorporated into the analysis in order to measure the relative proximity/distance of each state to domestic markets. Specifically, market size was measured based upon a simple gravity model assumption where the number of trips taken by a given population from an origin to a particular destination is a function of both the total population and the distance (Ewing, 1983; Fotheringham, 1983; Freund & Wilson, 1974; Van Doren, 1967; Wilson, 1971). The proposed model for market size, m_i, consisted of two components and was calculated using the following formula:

$$m_i = \left(\frac{\sqrt{s_i}}{2}\right)^{-1} * p_i + \sum_{j=1}^{48} d_{ij}^{-1} * p_j \quad j = 1, \ldots, 48;\ j \neq i$$

where:

m_i = market size of destination i.
s_i = square miles of destination i.
p_j = population of state j.
d_{ij} = distance in miles between state i and state j.

The first component measures the "density" of the population within the state and used as a surrogate for the attractiveness of the "domestic" market due to the absence of information regarding travel attractions in the respective US states. The second component, "reachability," was measured in terms of the average distance a visitor has to travel during a domestic trip assuming a uniform topological shape of the US states and an evenly distributed population density. The principle idea is that a US state located close to other states with high populations has a competitive advantage as compared to more spatially "exposed" states with lesser populated neighboring states. For example, one would expect the markets of California, Illinois, New York, as well as Maryland and Virginia, to be much larger than those of North Dakota or Montana simply because they are much nearer to population centers. Adopting this approach resulted in estimates of the total (domestic) market size ranging from 196,000 (Oregon) to over 2.1 million (New Jersey) with a mean of 492,000. Note that using market size as a uncontrollable input variable in the analysis will increase the efficiency of some state tourism offices since its reference groups are more restrictive (i.e., the reference group evaluated by the DEA consists only of states with the same or lower volume of market size).

The outputs used in this study measure visitor impacts that are often reported by national and state tourism offices and used to describe the nature and size of the industry (Van der Borg et al., 1996; Archer & Fletcher, 1996; TIA, 2001b). Specifically, the outputs included were: (1) the estimated annual number of business trips in the year 2000 (TIA, 2001b; BTS, 1996a; BTS, 1996b); (2) the estimated annual number of leisure trips in the year 2000 (TIA, 2001b; BTS, 1996a; BTS, 1996b); (3) domestic expenditures of visitors in 1999 (TIA, 2001b); (4) international expenditures of visitors in 1999 (TIA, 2001b); (5) total accommodation sales generated in 1997 (U.S. Census Bureau, 1997); and (6) total revenues by taxable and non-taxable arts and entertainment enterprises in 1997 (U.S. Census Bureau, 1997).

It is important to note that there is considerable debate concerning the potential impact of an advertising campaign and the linkage between advertising expenditures and overall visitation and resulting visitor expenditures (Woodside & Sakai, 2001). It is posited here, however, that these relationships are relatively consistent for all states and therefore controlled with the DEA benchmarking process. Also, output missing values cannot be handled by DEA and therefore must be replaced by meaningful substitutes (or the state is excluded from the analysis). For this study the missing international advertising budgets for Arkansas and Connecticut and the domestic advertising budget for Vermont was replaced by the respective average advertising budget ratio of the other states. The data on business trips included the following categories: convention, seminar/training, other group meetings, sales/consulting, repair/services, government/military, and other business trips; leisure travel included getaway weekends, general vacation, visiting friends and relatives, special events, and other personal reasons.

Findings

The DEA model employed here is an input-oriented model which seeks to identify technical efficiency as a proportional reduction in input usage. The linear programming formulation shown above was applied for each of the 48 US states. The values of the 4 input and the 6 output factors for the 48 US states are presented in the appendix. For the 48 state tourism offices, the total annual budget ranged from $2.2 million to over $61 million with a mean of approximately $13 million. Analysis of the distribution of the respective budgets in relation to the various input factors showed that the tourism offices, on average, spent 31.4 percent of their budget for advertising (domestic 26.7% and international 4.7%) and 68.6 percent for other purposes. The majority of states appear to be heavily dependent on their domestic tourism markets. Consider, in detail, the results for one of the states. Table 1 presents the results for Wisconsin as well as for one of the three benchmarking partners identified from the analysis (Colorado; Michigan; Ohio); the characteristics of the "best practices" composite US state on the frontier surface to which Wisconsin is eventually compared are also given. First, the values presented in Table 1 seem to indicate that the advertising program in Wisconsin is somewhat inefficient as measured by its average return on invested dollar (i.e., $404); the corresponding average number for all 48 states is $814. This value was estimated by calculating the ratio of tourism revenue to advertising expenditures (i.e., $6,254 million for domestic and international visitor expenditures and $15.5 million spent for domestic advertising, international advertising and other costs). However, it also is clear that Wisconsin has a slightly more difficult situation than the average state in terms of access to the domestic market (i.e., its relative market size is 482,182 as compared to a nationwide average of 492,024). Thus, the conclusion that Wisconsin's advertising program is "inefficient" must be tempered by its lower than average market size indicator and its higher than average number of business and leisure trips.

Next, consider column 2 of Table 1 where the values for one of Wisconsin's three "best practices" tourism offices (Colorado) are presented. One can observe that Colorado substantially exceeds Wisconsin in outputs (i.e., visitor expenditures, etc.) with less of every input (i.e., advertising investments). Indeed, its average return on invested dollar is about $1,500 as compared to $404 for Wisconsin. In addition, Colorado's access to the domestic market appears to be more difficult than for Wisconsin (262,910 compared to 482,182). An important problem with using Colorado as a benchmark for Wisconsin, however, is that Colorado generates significantly less business and leisure trips. One strategy adopted in DEA to address problems of incomparability and to satisfy the output envelopment constraint of the linear programming model is to merge potential benchmark tourism offices into a "composite" tourism office. This is achieved by taking *a given fraction* of all of one state tourism offices' inputs, outputs and environment and adding them to a fraction of another state's inputs, outputs and environment (where the sum of the weights equals one). This procedure assumes that the resulting composite state tourism office represents a feasible solution for the state under evaluation.

Consider, for example, the final results of the evaluation process for the Wisconsin tourism office. The characteristics of the composite state tourism office is estimated by taking a linear combination of all of the inputs, outputs and environment for Colorado, Michigan, and Ohio; the respective weightings are 0.39, 0.39, and 0.21. The budget resources of this hypothetical efficient composite tourism office are: (1) $4.1 million for domestic advertising; (2) $66,172 for international advertising; and (3) $5.9 million for other costs. The domestic advertising budget

TABLE 1. Representative Analysis (for Wisconsin)

Factor	State under evaluation (Wisconsin)	Typical benchmarking group member (Colorado)	Composite state[1]
Domestic advertising budget	$6,500,000 (above average)	$4,400,000	$4,119,785 (−36.6%)
International advertising budget	$100,000 (below average)	$25,000	$66,172 (−33.9%)
Other CVB budget	$8,900,000 (above average)	$1,816,554	$5,889,091 (−33.9%)
Market size	482,182 (below average)	262,910	413,605
Business trips	15,631,925 (above average)	10,982,956	18,356,611
Leisure trips	46,842,248 (above average)	30,695,956	46,842,645
Domestic visitor expenditures	$5,987 mn (below average)	$8,624 mn	$10,263 mn
International visitor expenditures	$267 mn (below average)	$731 mn	$662 mn
Accommodation sales	$5,649,870 (below average)	$6,710,540	$9,278,442
Arts and entertainment revenues	$1,704,255 (below average)	$2,203,907	$2,620,735

[1]The composite state consists of a linear combination of U.S. states Colorado, Michigan, Ohio, the respective weightings being 0.3933, 0.3954, and 0.2113.

is 36.6 percent less as compared to the actual $6.5 million and the other two budgets represent a reduction of 33.9 percent as compared to the actual figures for Wisconsin. The characteristics of the composite state tourism office are shown in column 3 of Table 1. Note that by the construction of this composite benchmark the uncontrollable input factor market size remains below the market size of Wisconsin and at the same time the composite state's numbers of business and leisure trips must be the same or larger than that which actually occurred for Wisconsin. With this composite tourism office as the benchmark, the final efficiency score for Wisconsin was estimated at 66.1%; that is, the percentage of Wisconsin's actual tourism budget needed if the "best-practices" strategy were to be met. This target-setting capability of DEA can be used to develop policy making scenarios that would enable managers to identify the operating response to different managerial priorities (Athanassopoulos et al., 1999).

This analysis was conducted for each of the state tourism offices (where the constraints are altered to focus on the characteristics of each individual state) and the efficiency score, corresponding benchmarking partners and their associated weights are summarized in Table 2. As can be seen, the efficiency scores range from a low of 20.0 percent to unity with 15 of the 48 states being rated as perfectly efficient. Those tourism offices rated "efficient" include large population states such as California, Florida, and New York, major tourism states such as Colorado and Nevada, as well as smaller, lesser known as tourism states such as Iowa, Indiana, Oregon, and North Dakota. Three state tourism offices rated marginally inefficient (90% and higher) included Rhode Island (93.5%), Kentucky (92.5%) and New Jersey (90.0%) and nine state tourism offices rated moderately inefficient (60% to 89%) included a number of traditional tourism states such as New Hampshire (74.6%), Wisconsin (66.1%), and Maine (60.8%). Interestingly, 21 state tourism offices were rated moderately to very inefficient using the DEA model. These included Wyoming (55.5%) and New Mexico (53.3%) on the high end, and Illinois (20.0%) and Pennsylvania (22.1%) on the low end.

The interpretation of these efficiency scores is clear. For example, the value 66.1 percent for Wisconsin indicates that it is 33.9 percent inefficient. That is, as compared to members of the efficient reference set, it is possible to reduce all input factors (frequently referred to as technical inefficiency in the DEA literature) by at least 33.9 percent while at the same time maintaining the same level in all output factors. The shortfall in Wisconsin's input can be repaired by decreasing all inputs without changing their proportions. It is important to note that this improvement in efficiency does not remove all of its inefficiencies. Another type of inefficiency remains when only some (but not all) inputs are identified as exhibiting inefficient behavior. This kind of inefficiency is referred to as "input mix inefficiency" because its elimination will alter the proportions in which inputs are utilized (for a detailed explanation see Cooper et al., 2000:10).

Table 2 identifies the top benchmarking partners for each of the states and the relative contribution of each state towards a composite "best practices" tourism program. The analysis identified Delaware, North Dakota and Oregon as benchmarking partners for Rhode Island whereas Minnesota's partners are California, Delaware, Kansas, Ohio and Oregon. As can be seen, the benchmarks for each state are not bound by geography or population size and therefore, are uniquely defined for each of the respective state advertising programs.

One criticism often cited of DEA is that it focuses attention on inefficient organizations (Ganley & Cubbin, 1992); the concern is that very little, or even nothing can be said about the efficient units included in the study. However, Andersen and Petersen (1993) proposed a modified version of DEA which allows the ranking of efficient organizations. Their basic idea was to compare the organization under evaluation with a linear combination of all other organizations in the sample where the organization itself is excluded. Under this approach it is possible for an efficient organization to increase its input vector proportionally while preserving efficiency and therefore obtains an efficiency score above one. The score reflects the radial distance from the operating unit under evaluation to the production frontier estimated with that operating unit excluded from the sample. The approach provides an efficiency rating of efficient or-

TABLE 2. Summary of DEA Findings for 48 U.S. States

State	Score in %	Benchmarking Partners
California	100	
Florida	100	
Oregon	100	
Washington	100	
Delaware	100	
Colorado	100	
Kansas	100	
New York	100	
Ohio	100	
Michigan	100	
North Dakota	100	
Nebraska	100	
Iowa	100	
Indiana	100	
Nevada	100	
Rhode Island	93.5	DE (.3938) ND (.5253) OR (.0393) WA (.0416)
Kentucky	92.5	CO (.1720) DE (.2734) IA (.4067) MI (.1479)
New Jersey	90.0	CA (.1186) CO (.7156) NY (.1658)
Montana	76.7	CO (.0241) OR (.9759)
New Hampshire	74.6	DE (.0427) ND (.6747) OR (.2826)
Utah	68.1	CA (.0110) CO (.0106) ND (.5345) OR (.4439)
Wisconsin	66.1	CO (.3933) MI (.3954) OH (.2113)
Idaho	65.4	CO (.0012) OR (.9988)
Connecticut	64.0	CA (.1530) DE (.3595) ND (.4874)
North Carolina	63.3	CA (.1748) CO (.1806) OR (.6446)
Georgia	61.3	CA (.1708) CO (.0504) OH (.0878) OR (.6910)
Maine	60.8	CA (.0108) DE (.1342) KS (.1080) NE (.0444) ND (.5911) OR (.1116)
Wyoming	55.5	CO (.0434) ND (.9566)
New Mexico	53.3	CO (.2478) NE (.1257) ND (.2493) OR (.3772)
Tennesee	46.7	CO (.1538) KS (.1148) OH (.5622) OR (.1692)
South Dakota	46.2	CO (.1464) DE (.0699) ND (.7732) OR (.0105)
Arizona	42.1	CA (.0982) CO (.2828) ND (.5423) OR (.0767)
West Virginia	40.8	DE (.1042) NE (.5623) ND (.0280) OR (.3055)
Texas	38.0	CA (.7373) CO (.1446) OR (.1181)
Oklahoma	37.8	CO (.0686) NE (.4077) OH (.1054) OR (.4182)
Vermont	37.6	CA (.0054) DE (.1927) ND (.8019)
Arkansas	37.3	CA (.0024) CO (.1526) ND (.5363) OR (.3087)
Alabama	36.4	DE (.1157) KS (.0254) NE (.2968) OH (.2377) OR (.3245)
Minnesota	34.7	CA (.0133) DE (.0039) KS (.0491) OH (.3213) OR (.6125)
Virginia	34.7	CA (.1532) DE (.0876) KS (.6468) OH (.1125)
South Carolina	30.9	CA (.0415) IN (.1943) OR (.7641)
Massachusetts	30.0	CA (.0858) DE (.3201) KS (.2987) NV (.2954)
Mississippi	29.4	DE (.0683) KS (.0196) NE (.1107) OH (.2459) OR (.5556)
Maryland	29.1	CA (.0916) DE (.4996) IN (.0069) KS (.0840) OR (.3179)
Missouri	26.4	CA (.0880) CO (.0620) OR (.8500)
Louisiana	25.1	CA (.0713) CO (.1646) ND (.4052) OR (.3589)
Pennsylvania	22.1	CA (.3448) KS (.6552)
Illinois	20.0	CA (.3274) DE (.2453) KS (.4274)

ganizations similar to the rating of inefficient organizations.

An illustration of Andersen and Petersen's idea is given by Figure 2. Consider the evaluation of the efficient operating unit P_3 in Figure 2. According to the definition of the DEA efficiency measure, the reference point in the evaluation of P_3 is the observation itself, and P_3 is assigned the index one. Elimination of P_3 in the spanning of the reference set implies that P_3 is compared to that (inefficient) point in the input possibility set spanned by the remaining set of observations with the minimal distance of P_3. The reference point, thus, becomes P_3'. In analogy to the inefficiency index, the efficiency index is calculated by $0P_3'/0P_3$ and has the same interpretation as the Farrell measure; P_3 may increase its input vector proportionally up to the efficiency index and still remain efficient, but it will be dominated by a combination of P_2 and P_4 if the proportional increase in the input vector exceeds the efficiency score.

Although the approach proposed by Andersen and Petersen is an important extension and can enhance existing DEA models, it has been rarely applied outside of research applications. In the present study the Andersen and Petersen procedure was used to rank efficient tourism offices based upon the results of the DEA model. A summary of the findings including information on the frequency of how many times an efficient state appeared as a benchmark is summarized in Table 3 and identifies the most robustly efficient state tourism advertising program (i.e., those state programs that appear as benchmarking partners most often). Oregon, for instance, is the most frequently referenced tourism office (i.e., considered a benchmarking partner for 23 state tourism programs). The table also provides insights into the geometric properties of the empirical production function. That is, state tourism offices with high counts tend to be located near the center of the production frontier while others with lower counts are located near the edges. Last, the analyses provide scores even for efficient state tourism offices and are referred to as "superefficiency scores." According to this analysis Delaware, Colorado and Kansas are leading the list of efficient tourism offices, whereas tourism offices in Indiana and Nevada are at the margin of being classified as "efficient."

Repeating the DEA analyses with the Andersen and Petersen modifications for efficient states tourism offices resulted in a number of infeasible solutions (4 out of 15). This is in line with results by others who have found estimates for operating units undefined because of the unfeasibility of the set of constraints of the modified DEA model (Pastor et al., 1999; Boljunčić, 1999). Boljunčić indicated that infeasible solutions are caused either by zero values in the variable set or by cases where operating units show extremely high efficiency values (Boljučić, 1999:243).

FIGURE 2. Ranking Efficient Organizations

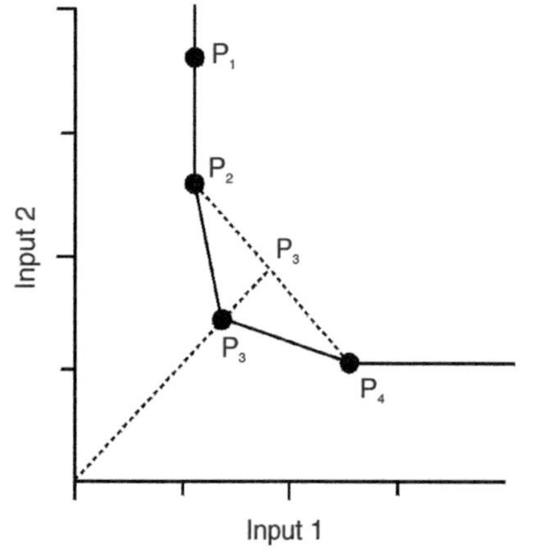

TABLE 3. Superefficiency Scores and Number of Times a State Appeared as a Benchmark

State		Score in %	Benchmark Appearance
CA	California	infeasible	19
FL	Florida	infeasible	0
OR	Oregon	infeasible	23
WA	Washington	infeasible	1
DE	Delaware	832.9	15
CO	Colorado	614.3	18
KS	Kansas	188.6	10
NY	New York	177.5	1
OH	Ohio	171.4	8
MI	Michigan	162.0	2
ND	North Dakota	148.3	13
NE	Nebraska	139.6	6
IA	Iowa	124.2	1
IN	Indiana	109.2	2
NV	Nevada	108.8	1

In general, infeasible solutions occur in attempts to solve large linear programming problems where the constraints specified cannot be simultaneously satisfied (Schrage, 1997:7). There is nothing much that can be done with infeasible linear programming solutions; hence, the cases impacted (California, Florida, Oregon, Washington) cannot be evaluated any further.

SUMMARY AND CONCLUSIONS

The tremendous growth in tourism and its importance as a vehicle for economic development combined with calls for more efficient allocation of investment dollars has focused attention on various strategies for programmatic evaluation. Benchmarking has been proposed as one approach that can be used to effectively measure the efficiency of tourism management programs. DEA has been developed to address some of the limitations of more traditional benchmarking approaches. The results of the application of DEA within the context of tourism advertising programs in the United States provide a useful illustration of the power of this approach. The results demonstrate a wide range in efficiency among the state tourism advertising programs. A number of states (15) appear to be extremely efficient in their advertising efforts but many of the remaining 33 states appear to face substantial challenges to building defensible programs. Those state tourism advertising programs rated below 50 percent efficient, in particular, seem to be largely inefficient in attracting visitor expenditures and therefore, creating tourism-related employment. Importantly, DEA identifies existing and composite benchmark state tourism advertising programs that are "optimal" within specific constraints such as market size and therefore, enable policy makers to further assess the effectiveness of a specific promotional program.

It is important to note that the results obtained in this study depend to a large extent upon the definition of inputs and outputs and that the results of the DEA analyses do not provide detailed recommendations concerning a particular marketing program. However, these limitations reflect more on the availability of information regarding specific state marketing efforts than the methodology itself. In this study various measures of expenditures on state tourism advertising programs were used to reflect the "inputs" into the advertising programs where it was assumed that these inputs determine to a large extent the level of visitation and resulting economic impact. However, a number of alternative input and output measures are possible (and more realistic) thereby mitigating or modifying the specific findings of this particular study. The input measures might include levels of advertising expenditures by the private sector and/or not-for-profit organizations, the extent to which the state tourism programs conduct co-operative marketing programs with the private sector and/or not-for-profit organizations, and/or the extent to which the state tourism agencies are involved in long term product development programs. In addition, uncontrollable input measures for such factors as the potential for visitors to "pass through" on the way to another destination (i.e., residents of northeastern states driving through a number of states on their way to Florida), the existence of unique attractions such as the Grand Canyon or Washington D.C., and the system of airline hubs may be important when identifying appropriate benchmarks. Alternative output measures include the results of specific marketing programs within target markets, the changes in consideration of a state as a potential destination or other measurable factors resulting from a promotional campaign (McWilliams & Crompton, 1997). Thus, it may be argued that for any state deemed inefficient (or efficient, for that matter) there may exist a number of special circumstances that make the findings of a specific DEA result misleading. The ability to test alternative model specifications, in fact, is a very important *strength* of the DEA approach. That is, one can systematically evaluate the impact of alternative factors (for both inputs and outputs) on alternative model designs. These analyses should provide a strong indication of the adequacy of model specification as well as appropriate benchmarks.

The DEA model selected here was an input-oriented model, which seeks to identify technical inefficiency as a proportional reduction in input usage. It is also possible to measure technical efficiency as a proportional increase in output production; however, the former appears to be a more adequate model for managers of tourism related organizations. This is because tourism destination managers usually have objectives to fulfill, either set by stakeholder defined management goals or by self-defined business plans, and hence the input quantities appear to be the primary decision variables. Nevertheless, the analyses conducted for the present study was repeated using an output-oriented model in order to capture situations where tourism officials have to achieve a maximum of output with a given fixed quantity of resources. The findings of this endeavor were very similar to the input-oriented model and therefore, were not presented for clarity reasons.

Today, there exist approximately 2,000 publications on DEA in the management science and operation research literature (see for instance the DEA bibliography compiled at Warwick University at http://www.csv.warwick.ac.uk/~bsrlu/dea/deab/bib-s.htm). Many authors have been working on DEA extensions in order to make this methodology even more usable. For instance, authors have extended the original DEA models for use with categorical as well as for ordinal data (Banker & Morey, 1986a; Cook, Kress & Seiford, 1993). The technique is almost never affected by the number of variables in the model and, certainly, this is one of the reasons why DEA gained much popularity in the last twenty years. An additional advantage of DEA is that it needs no *a priori* information regarding which inputs and outputs are most important in the evaluation procedure. Finally, DEA is not based upon any formal system of hypothesis testing as it makes no explicit assumptions on the distributions of the residuals (Seiford & Thrall, 1990).

A number of studies have documented with DEA. Ganley and Cubbin (1992:128), for example, reported that a data error on one variable at one operating unit reduced the average efficiency of the whole cross section by 12 percent. They argued that noise in outcomes might be identified in unexpected or abrupt change in the efficiency ranking of utilities year-by-year. They suggest using Spearman's rank correlation coefficients to test whether the efficiency rankings change significantly when excluding individual units from the data set. More recently, Brockett and Golany (1996) recommended another approach where analysis is conducted using groups level rather than individual units, arguing that analysis on aggregated data leads to a stochastic extension of DEA where random deviations from the group's behavior can be studied. A similar form of data pooling was suggested by Charnes et al. (1985) as part of their "window-analysis." The resulting composite frontier derived by the window-analysis gives less weight to unusual observations and is therefore, more robust to stochastic events.

The wide acceptance of DEA as means for benchmarking is based upon a number of important attributes. First, it focuses on observed operating practice, and circumvents specifying the complete functional form of the production function. Second, it has greater practical appeal and higher perceived fairness than normative industrial engineering standards. Last, recent extensions to DEA have offered substantive flexibility to incorporate realistic assumptions such as variable returns-to-scale properties and non-discretionary input variables. Although DEA has fewer limitations than other econometric approaches in the choice of input and output variables, it nonetheless suffers from a variety of weaknesses which should be subject for future research. Wöber (2002), for example, has proposed incorporating an interactive environment so that the user can go back and forth thereby learning the impact of various inputs and outputs on the efficiency of the overall system and specific units. Hence, the user will soon realize that the results may vary significantly, sometimes even through minor changes in the variables selected. It is argued that this system will enable the user to gain a better understanding of how to interpret benchmarking results.

REFERENCES

Alavi, J. & Yasin, M.M. (2000). A systematic approach to tourism policy. Journal of Business Research, 48 (2): 147-157.

Andersen, P. & Petersen, N.C. (1993). A procedure for ranking efficient units in data envelopment analysis. Management Science, 39 (10): 1261-1264.

Anderson, D.R., Sweeney, D.J. & Williams, T.A. (1997). An introduction to management science:

Quantitative approaches to decision making. 8th edition. St. Paul, MN: West Publishing.
Archer, B. & Fletcher, J. (1996). The economic impact of tourism in the Seychelles. Annals of Tourism Research, 23 (1): 32-47.
Athanassopoulos, A.D., Lambroukos, N. & Seiford, L. (1999). Data envelopment scenario analysis for setting targets to electricity generating plants. European Journal of Operational Research, 115 (3): 413-428.
Bachleitner, R. & Zins, A.H. (1999). Cultural tourism in rural communities: The residents' perspective. Journal of Business Research, 44 (2): 199-209.
Banker, R.D., Charnes, A.C. & Cooper, W.W. (1984). Some models for estimating technical and scale inefficiencies in data envelopment analysis. Management Science, 30 (9): 1078-1092.
Banker, R.D. & Morey, R.C. (1986a). The use of categorical variables in data envelopment analysis. Management Science, 32 (12): 1613-1627.
Banker, R.D. & Morey, R.C. (1986b). Efficiency analysis for exogenously fixed inputs and outputs. Operations Research, 34 (4): 513-521.
Baum, T. (1999). Special issue: Seasonality in tourism–understanding the challenges. Tourism Economics, 5 (1). London: IP Publishing.
Boljunčić, V. (1999). A note on robustness of the efficient DMUs in data envelopment analysis. European Journal of Operational Research, 112 (1): 240-244.
Brockett, P.L. & Golany, B. (1996). Using rank statistics for determining programmatic efficiency differences in data envelopment analysis. Management Science, 42 (3): 466-472.
Bureau of Transportation Statistics (1996a). 1995 American Travel Survey: Profile. U.S. Department of Transportation, Washington D.C.
Bureau of Transportation Statistics (1996b). 1995 American travel survey: Technical documentation. U.S. Department of Transportation, Washington D.C.
Burke, J. F. & Gitelson, R. (1990). Conversion studies: Assumptions, accuracy, and abuse. Journal of Travel Research, 28 (3): 42-44.
Butler, R.W. (1994). Seasonality in tourism: Issues and problems. In Seaton, A.V. (ed.), Tourism: State of the Art (pp. 332-339). West Sussex: J. Wiley & Sons.
Butterfield, D.W., Deal, K.R. & Kubursi, A.A. (1998). Measuring the returns to tourism advertising. Journal of Travel Research 37 (1): 12-20.
Camp, R.C. (1989). Benchmarking: The search for industry best practices that lead to superior performance. Milwaukee, WI: American Society for Quality Control Quality Press.
Charnes, A.C. & Cooper, W.W. (1985). Preface to topics in data envelopment analysis. Annals of Operations Research, 2 (1): 59-94.
Charnes, A.C., Clark, T., Cooper, W.W. & Golany, B. (1985). A developmental study of data envelopment analysis in measuring the efficiency of maintenance units in the U.S. Air Force. Annals of Operations Research, 2 (1): 95-112.
Charnes, A.C., Cooper, W.W., Lewin, A.Y. & Seiford, L.M. (1994). Data envelopment analysis: Theory, methodology and applications. Boston, MA: Kluwer Academic Press.
Charnes, A.C., Cooper, W.W. & Rhodes, E. (1978). Measuring the efficiency of decision making units. European Journal of Operational Research, 2 (6): 429-444.
Coelli, T.J. (1996). A Guide to DEAP Version 2.1: A Data Envelopment Analysis (Computer) Program. CEPA Working Papers No. 8/96. Armidale, Australia: University of New England.
Cook, S. (1995). Practical benchmarking: A manager's guide to creating a competitive advantage. London: Kogan Page.
Cook, W.D., Kress, M. & Seiford, L.M. (1993). On the use of ordinal data in envelopment analysis. Journal of the Operational Research Society, 44 (2): 133-140.
Cooper, W.W., Seiford, L.M. & Tone, K. (2000). Data envelopment analysis. A comprehensive test with models, applications, references and DEA-Solver software. Boston, MA: Kluwer Academic Publishers.
Cross, M. (1998). The benchmarking sourcebook. London: Batsford Ltd.
Crouch, G.I. & Ritchie, J.R.B. (1999). Tourism, competitiveness, and societal prosperity. Journal of Business Research, 44 (2): 137-152.
Ewing, G. (1983). Forecasting recreation trip distribution behavior, in Recreation Planning and Management (eds. S.R. Lieber and D.R. Fesenmaier), State College, Venture Publications.
Fortheringham, S. (1983). A new set of spatial interaction models: The theory of competing destinations. Environment and Planning A 15: 15-36.
Freund, J.R. & Wilson, R.R. (1974). An example of a gravity model to estimate recreation travel. Journal of Leisure Research, 6 (Summer): 241-256.
Ganley, J.A. & Cubbin, J.S. (1992). Public sector efficiency measurement. Applications of data envelopment analysis. Amsterdam: Elsevier.
Haag, S., Jaska, P. & Semple, J. (1992). Assessing the relative efficiency of agricultural production units in the Blackland Prairie, Texas. Applied Economics, 24 (5): 559-565.
Inskeep, E. (1987). Environmental planning for tourism. Annals of Tourism Research, 14 (1): 118-135.
Karlof, B. & Ostblom, S. (1994). Benchmarking: A signpost of excellence in quality and productivity. West Sussex: John Wiley & Sons.
Kozak, M. (2002). Destination benchmarking. Annals of Tourism Research, 29 (2): 497-519.
Kozak, M. & Rimmington, M. (1999). Measuring tourist destination competitiveness: conceptual considerations and empirical findings. International Journal of Hospitality Management, 18 (3): 273-284.

Lee, C.-K. & Han, S.-Y. (2002). Estimating the use and preservation values of national parks' tourism resources using a contingent valuation method. Tourism Management, 23 (4): 531-540.

McElroy, J.L. & de Albuquerque, K. (1998). Tourism penetration index in small Caribbean islands. Annals of Tourism Research, 25 (1): 145-168.

McNair, C.J. & Leibfried, K.H. (1992). Benchmarking: A tool for continuous improvement. New York, NY: Harper Business.

McWilliams, E. & Crompton, J.L. (1997). An expanded framework for measuring the effectiveness of destination advertising. Tourism Management, 18 (3): 127-137.

Morey, R.C. & Dittman, D.A. (1995). Evaluating a hotel GM's performance. A case study in benchmarking. Cornell Hotel and Restaurant Administration Quarterly, 36 (5): 30-35.

Morey, M.R. & Morey, R.C. (1999). Mutual fund performance appraisals: A multi-horizon perspective with endogenous benchmarking. Omega, International Journal of Management Science, 27 (2): 241-258.

Norman, M. & Stoker, B. (1991). Data envelopment analysis. The assessment of performance. West Sussex: John Wiley & Sons.

Oertel, J.R.B., Feil, T. & Thio, S.L. (2002). Benchmarking information and communication applications for the purpose of marketing and sales in the tourism sector. In: Wöber, K.W., Frew, A.J. & Hitz, M. (eds.) Information and Communication Technologies in Tourism (pp. 387-396). Wien-New York: Springer.

Pastor, J.T., Ruiz, J.L. & Sirvent, I. (1999). A statistical test for detecting influential observations in DEA. European Journal of Operational Research, 115 (3): 542-554.

Ritchie, J.R.B. & Crouch, G.I. (2000). The competitive destination: A sustainability perspective. Tourism Management, 21 (1): 1-7.

Ritchie, J.R.B., Crouch, G.I. & Hudson, S. (2001). Developing operational measures for the components of a destination competitiveness/sustainability model: Consumer versus managerial perspectives. In: Mazanec, J.A., Crouch, G.I., Ritchie, J.R.B. & Woodside, A.G. (eds.) Consumer Psychology of Tourism, Hospitality and Leisure (pp. 1-17). Wallingford: CABI Publishing.

Schrage, L. (1997). Optimisation Modeling with LINDO. 5th edition. Pacific Grove, CA: Duxbury Press.

Seiford, L.M. & Thrall, R.M. (1990). Recent developments in DEA. The mathematical programming approach to frontier analysis. Journal of Econometrics 46 (1/2): 7-38.

Siegel, W. & Ziff-Levine, W. (1990). Evaluating tourism advertising campaigns: Conversion vs. advertising tracking studies. Journal of Travel Research, 28 (3): 51-55.

Silberman, J. and Klock, M. (1986). An alternative to conversion studies for measuring the impact of travel ads. Journal of Travel Research 24 (Spring): 12-16.

Spendolini, M.J. (1992). The benchmarking book. 2nd edition. New York, NY: Amacom.

Tourism Industry Association of America (2001a). 2002-2002 survey of U. S. State & Territory tourism offices, Washington D.C.

Tourism Industry Association of America (2001b). The economic review of travel in America: 2000 Edition, Washington D.C.

U.S. Census Bureau (1997). Economic Census. Selected industry statistics by state, Washington D.C.

U.S. Census Bureau (2001). Population estimates program: 2000 Population Estimates, Washington D.C.

Van der Borg, J., Costa, P., & Gotti, G. (1996). Tourism in European heritage cities. Annals of Tourism Research, 23 (2): 306-321.

Van Doren, C.S. (1967). An Interaction travel model for projecting attendance of campers at Michigan state parks: A study in recreational geography, Ph.D. thesis, Michigan State University, Department of Geography.

Williams, J. & Lawson, R. (2001). Community issues and resident opinions of tourism. Annals of Tourism Research, 28 (2): 269-290.

Wilson, A.G. (1971). A family of spatial interaction models and associated developments, Environment and Planning A 3: 1-32.

Watson, G.H. (1992). The benchmarking workbook: Adapting best practices for performance improvement. Portland, OR: Productivity Press.

Wöber, K.W. (1997). International city tourism flows. In: Mazanec J. (ed.) International City Tourism. Analysis and Strategy (pp. 39-53). London: Cassell.

Wöber, K.W. (2002). Benchmarking in tourism and hospitality industries: The selection of benchmarking partners. Wallingford: CABI Publishing.

Woodside, A.G. (1990). Measuring advertising effectiveness in destination marketing strategies. Journal of Travel Research, 29 (2): 3-8.

Woodside, A.G. (1996). Measuring the effectiveness of image and linkage advertising. Westport, CT: Quorum Books.

Woodside, A.G. & Sakai, M.Y. (2001). Meta-Evaluation: Achieving effective tourism marketing programs. Champaign: Sagamore Press.

Zairi, M. (1996). Benchmarking for best practice: Continuous learning through sustainable innovation. Oxford: Butterworth-Heinemann.

APPENDIX

Data Set

State	Domestic advertising budget ($)	International advertising budget ($)	Other budget sources ($)	Market size	Business trips	Leisure trips	Domestic visitor expenditures (in mn $)	International visitor expenditures (in mn $)	Accommodation sales ($)	Arts and entertainment revenues ($)
Alabama	3200000	250000	7537897	441081	12579806	25630845	5002	108	3881782	584403
Arizona	5111309	830000	5600411	263813	13630665	29699740	7868	1620	6634744	2294422
Arkansas	3500000	658635	4716565	402251	7041004	14291643	3612	47	2179696	315286
California	4650000	830000	9120000	308497	80593339	199708878	57542	13828	42312641	17946053
Colorado	4400000	25000	1816554	262910	10982956	30695956	8624	731	6710540	2203907
Connect	1756400	499648	4476775	993400	6114741	17043724	4960	282	3746560	2970088
Delaware	160000	6000	2142400	1124935	1320726	5780397	1002	86	1008954	359684
Florida	10175221	4119857	45499632	415260	38927949	120442075	39137	16648	24165336	8931977
Georgia	2737492	408500	5856211	478935	24546462	43137309	13655	883	9689927	1962411
Idaho	1657000	210000	3670958	196471	4957947	10015459	2001	101	1233215	211127
Illinois	8534000	5400000	47125000	522278	28512104	51580278	20500	1648	14826805	4774139
Indiana	921710	180000	3434290	547404	16982934	39213683	5814	244	6646318	2331655
Iowa	2340000	30000	3799216	385515	10364218	24843483	4038	134	2762766	1072882
Kansas	350000	100000	4171987	340111	6374886	18540450	3314	98	2685732	503697
Kentucky	2719000	30000	4508700	591673	9417171	22877535	4945	123	4056107	772563
Louisiana	6437943	1090000	9266294	370157	12852913	26699025	7631	459	5259921	2098222
Maine	1150000	150000	3322711	381260	4084093	14074856	1828	246	1510182	326508
Maryland	2679414	491604	10263324	685057	12224677	23529350	7701	343	5972467	1784050
Massach	3455958	1365000	19676416	573091	13110823	29510219	10268	1939	9282541	2304401
Michigan	5160900	65000	10636900	485546	19958842	53369443	10868	644	10158693	2717089
Minnesot	3077000	422000	9129922	325236	14571455	34877938	6535	384	5934155	1942951
Mississip	3496200	400000	9557370	369539	10504012	23180479	4299	48	3064753	1450975
Missouri	5000000	800000	10649060	376676	17214695	47958478	9089	258	6780812	2173678
Montana	2336900	175655	4560226	197993	4606170	10829752	1813	91	1199251	346024
Nebraska	1698243	30000	1961757	355891	5889461	13067242	2533	59	1726647	362854
Nevada	1631332	524937	9101127	287578	14072844	44816963	18373	2661	15323751	1688257
NewHam	952902	163690	2266860	584339	2847176	14592463	2218	129	1544942	417003
NewJers	5702500	187500	4886855	2159706	12664510	44734047	14164	890	13416088	2491917
NewMex	3315417	158600	9914370	248311	8461072	16302512	3418	127	2146558	586092
NewYork	7462400	316000	12160700	1263413	33497652	82750149	26868	9448	21680529	9761298
NCarolina	3302120	1000000	5306149	508400	23233782	53028171	11452	416	8624993	2049546
NDakota	729790	91500	1438433	258130	3243986	8072531	1100	48	684930	193237
Ohio	1650000	145000	4585000	559478	29083238	64683614	12181	567	12410978	3216286
Oklahom	3919188	229275	6189801	340159	10866740	19491855	3653	81	3151332	656795
Oregon	751665	137500	2232918	196389	11108335	33975478	5072	389	4388304	1053695
Pennsylv	8265000	1895000	35744180	767094	31040804	80998866	13733	1031	12227177	3654928
RIsland	553000	97000	1918000	711551	2218270	4713446	1312	113	1220865	306031
SCarolina	3062972	729740	8906399	515378	15134208	32393713	6602	445	4835839	1251733
SDakota	2655000	165000	3356000	356589	3286897	11496205	1149	41	888148	334744
Tennes	3791000	257000	8362800	427245	18434179	47167317	9414	338	6790159	1526553
Texas	10921000	2186590	19065160	312624	62323203	112360269	29889	3242	22698848	4763771
Utah	2264500	610300	2760500	231332	6716605	20676139	3566	359	2313309	490905
Vermont	1704747	500000	4295253	609116	2030425	7192084	1312	130	910188	268662

APPENDIX (continued)

State	Domestic advertising budget ($)	International advertising budget ($)	Other budget sources ($)	Market size	Business trips	Leisure trips	Domestic visitor expenditures (in mn $)	International visitor expenditures (in mn $)	Accommodation sales ($)	Arts and entertainment revenues ($)
Virginia	3273105	600000	19069295	428664	15593931	43478134	12415	448	8281218	1983048
Washingt	996000	250000	2579020	198969	13601723	35761291	7568	931	7001716	2034775
WVirginia	2992000	152000	5017792	504589	6933728	16212445	1610	32	1633164	324534
Wiscons	6500000	100000	8900000	482182	15631925	46842248	5987	267	5649870	1704255
Wyoming	1632413	234591	2618042	270923	2781917	7011838	1427	70	808887	119574
Averages	3431932	610378	8816151	492024	15253567	37069792	9147	1318	7126299	2158723
Minimum	160000	6000	1438433	196389	1320726	4713446	1002	32	684930	119574
Maximum	10921000	5400000	47125000	2159706	80593339	199708878	57542	16648	42312641	17946053

An Exploratory Investigation of Multiunit Restaurant Productivity Assessment Using Data Envelopment Analysis

Dennis Reynolds

SUMMARY. Conventional approaches to assessing unit-level productivity, such as labor-cost percentages or basic ratio analysis including sales per labor hour, are limited in utility because they integrate too few operational characteristics to portend true operational efficiency. Moreover, current parametric approaches impose a functional form relating independent variables uniformly to dependent variable(s) and provide only an average by which other operations are compared. Data envelopment analysis (DEA), a linear-programming-based benchmarking technique that explicitly considers weighted outputs and inputs, is introduced as an alternative. DEA does not require any assumptions about functional form and calculates a maximal performance measure for all units in the population. As an exploratory investigation, data from 38 same-brand midscale restaurants were analyzed. Results, which include relative-to-best efficiency valuations, suggest that data envelopment analysis offers considerable potential for managers looking to accurately assess productivity. The viability of key variables as part of the DEA application is also discussed. *[Article copies available for a fee from The Haworth Document Delivery Service: 1-800-HAWORTH. E-mail address: <docdelivery@haworthpress.com> Website: <http://www.HaworthPress.com> © 2004 by The Haworth Press, Inc. All rights reserved.]*

KEYWORDS. Productivity, efficiency, management, multiunit restaurants, data envelopment analysis

In the last few decades, academicians have encouraged the practice and widespread adoption of productivity assessment (Bloom, 1972; Doutt, 1984; Reynolds, 1998). Specific to the hospitality industry, Avkiran (2002, p. 51) notes, "There is a pressing need to address productivity if [hospitality operations] are to exist as sustainable business entities in rapidly maturing markets." While easily said, the actual mechanisms for calculating and analyzing productivity in the service sector have remained less-than-ideal, as articulated well by Andersson (1996).

Even with narrowly and, too often, inaccurately deduced measures, foodservice operators have long understood the linkage between

Dennis Reynolds is the Ivar Haglund Distinguished Professor of Hospitality Management, School of Hospitality Business Management, College of Business and Economics, Washington State University, Pullman, WA 99164-4742.

Address correspondence to: Dennis Reynolds, School of Hospitality Business Management, College of Business and Economics, Washington State University, Todd 470–Box 644742, Pullman, WA 99164-4742 (E-mail: dennis.reynolds@wsu.edu).

[Haworth co-indexing entry note]: "An Exploratory Investigation of Multiunit Restaurant Productivity Assessment Using Data Envelopment Analysis." Reynolds, Dennis. Co-published simultaneously in *Journal of Travel & Tourism Marketing* (The Haworth Hospitality Press, an imprint of The Haworth Press, Inc.) Vol. 16, No. 2/3, 2004, pp. 19-26; and: *Management Science Applications in Tourism and Hospitality* (ed: Zheng Gu) The Haworth Hospitality Press, an imprint of The Haworth Press, Inc., 2004, pp. 19-26. Single or multiple copies of this article are available for a fee from The Haworth Document Delivery Service [1-800-HAWORTH, 9:00 a.m. - 5:00 p.m. (EST). E-mail address: docdelivery@haworthpress.com].

http://www.haworthpress.com/web/JTTM
© 2004 by The Haworth Press, Inc. All rights reserved.
Digital Object Identifier: 10.1300/J073v16n02_02

productivity and desirable business outcomes. During economically challenging times, restaurateurs look to increase productivity by attempting to maintain sales while minimizing costs, especially those associated with labor and food; in economic booms, operators strive to leverage inputs to attain disproportionately greater increases in outputs such as overall sales volume (Brown & Dev, 1999). In either case, productivity measurement, monitoring, and improvement lead to overall gains in profitability (Eccles, 1991).

Restaurant operators have traditionally relied on two key indicators of productivity. The first, labor-cost percentages, is useful to monitor since labor is typically the largest expense category. However, such a metric provides cost information alone and presents an incomplete picture of labor utilization (Burritt, 1967).

The second evolved from the manufacturing sector and is more directly linked to Bloom's (1972) definition of productivity: a ratio of output measured in specific units and any input factor also measured in specific units. Such measures are usually operationalized as partial-factor statistics including sales per labor hour (Jablonsky, 1994), revenue per available seat hour (Kimes, Chase, Choi, Lee, & Ngonzi, 1998), or transactions per hour (Filley, 1983). While useful for specific intertemporal or intrafirm analyses, these measures have limited utility and frequently do not adequately correlate to true efficiency, reflecting only specific operational attributes.

Specifically, most partial-factor ratios fail to account for potentially meaningful differences among foodservice operations. For example, sales per labor hour may be subject to differing wage levels. Even total-factor productivity models, as recommended by Brown and Hoover (1990), are not adequate for comparing multiple units with considerably different operating characteristics. Furthermore, both partial- and total-factor ratios statistically generate only an average measure. While useful for comparison purposes, related averages reveal little regarding the best operations–those that might better serve as benchmarks.

While still residing in the output-to-input ratio measurement domain, data envelopment analysis (DEA) solves many of the problems associated with the aforementioned measures by integrating multiple outputs and inputs simultaneously. The operations-research-based approach allows for both controllable and uncontrollable variables, producing a single relative-to-best productivity index that relates all units under comparison. Thus, DEA allows for assessment of contingent productivity, which takes into account the performance of each restaurant despite differing environmental or situational factors. This also allows operators, as recommended by Farrell (1957), to use the best performing units as the bases for evaluation.

This notion of benchmarking by using performance-related indices such as productivity measures that focus on the best performers and that integrate exogenously fixed variables is principally important for operators. As noted by Wöber (2002), benchmarking is useful particularly when indicators span operations that are dissimilar but compete for similar target-market constituents. Using DEA-generated productivity indices facilitates such comparison.

The objective of this study, then, is to establish and demonstrate the utility of DEA as a productivity-assessment method for the restaurant industry that extends the traditional ratio approach. Specifically, the purpose is to (1) empirically formulate a new productivity measure using data envelopment analysis, one that integrates several operation-specific variables, and (2) establish a preliminary productivity model appropriate for the segment of the industry under investigation.

DATA ENVELOPMENT ANALYSIS

DEA is a linear-programming-based benchmarking technique that explicitly considers multiple outputs and inputs, producing a single measure of performance. In contrast to parametric approaches whose purpose is to optimize a single regression plane through the data, DEA optimizes on each individual observation with an objective of calculating a discrete piecewise frontier occupied by the most efficient units. This frontier–and the associated measure for each unit, which is generally referred to as relative efficiency or productivity–has particular managerial relevance in that it allows for comparison of disparate operating units.

Charnes, Cooper, and Rhodes (1978) first proposed DEA methodology as an evaluation tool for decision units. Since then, DEA has been applied successfully to evaluate performance in diverse fields including banking (Jemric & Vujcic, 2002), nursing (Nunamaker, 1983), insurance (Mahajan, 1991), sales (Boles, Donthu, & Lohtia, 1995), farming (Thompson, Langemeier, Lee, Lee, & Thrall, 1990), marketing (Charnes, Cooper, Learner, & Philips, 1985), public services (Hammond, 2002), and telecommunications (Uri, 2001). Of topical importance, Donthu and Yoo (1998) demonstrated DEA's applicability in foodservice, although their study focused on quick-service restaurants only as an example of a general retailing environment.

As fully described by Charnes, Cooper, Lewin, and Seiford (2001), DEA extends the basic output-to-input calculation of productivity by integrating the weighted sum of outputs to the weighted sum of inputs. For example, if restaurant 1 is evaluated using two output variables, Y_1 and Y_2, and three input variables, X_1, X_2, and X_3, its efficiency (P_1) is calculated as:

$$P_1 = \frac{U_1Y_1 + U_2Y_2}{V_1X_1 + V_2X_2 + V_3X_3}$$

In applying DEA, the weights (U_s and V_s) are estimated separately for each restaurant such that the efficiency is the maximum attainable. Moreover, the weights estimated for restaurant 1 are such that when they are applied to corresponding outputs and inputs from other units in the analysis, the ratio of weighted outputs to weighted inputs is less than or equal to 1. On a more general basis, assuming the number of outputs and inputs is infinite, the maximum efficiency of restaurant o as compared with n other restaurants is calculated as follows:

$$\text{Maximum } P_o = \frac{\sum_{r=1}^{s} U_r Y_{ro}}{\sum_{i=1}^{s} V_r X_{io}}$$

$$\text{subject to } \frac{\sum_{r=1}^{s} U_r Y_{rj}}{\sum_{i=1}^{s} V_r X_{ij}} \leq 1 \text{ for all } j = 1, \ldots n$$

$$U_r, V_i > 0;\ r = 1, \ldots, s;\ i = 1, \ldots m$$

where:

Y_{rj} is the rth output for the jth restaurant.

X_{ij} is the ith input for the jth restaurant.

U_r and V_i are the variable weights estimated and used to determine the relative efficiency of o.

s is the number of outputs.

m is the number of inputs.

Since DEA seeks optimization contingent on each individual restaurant's performance in relation to the performance of all other units, those with the greatest productivity have a productivity score (P) of 1, suggesting 100 percent efficiency. These optimal units lie on a multidimensional frontier; the efficiency frontier "envelops" the inefficient units within and quantifies the inefficiency by a relative score of less than 100 percent and a relational measure on each output and input.

The application of DEA to the foodservice industry is particularly advantageous because the method accommodates controllable and uncontrollable factors. Controllable factors include those within management's purview, such as labor hours, number of servers during a given shift, or wage paid to employees. Uncontrollable factors, which are potentially critical to efficiency analysis as noted by Banker and Morey (1986), might include a restaurant's maximum seating capacity, location, and number of nearby competitors; these are typically ignored in other methods of productivity assessment owing to the difficulty in making comparisons across units, particularly when units possess dissimilar uncontrollable characteristics.

Given the earlier discussion of the differing measures of productivity, using DEA effectively is predicated first on the accurate identification of pertinent output variables. The literature suggests that some are essential while others offer provocative possibilities. For example, revenue is cited frequently as an indicator of organizational performance across industries (e.g., Sarkis, 2000). Specific to the restaurant industry, Lusch and Serpkenci (1990) made a persuasive case for not only including sales but also segregating sales by daypart. Profit, too, may be a good output indicator of productivity. Yet, as Zeithaml (2000) notes, in the service industry the link between service delivery and profitability "is neither straightforward nor simple" (p. 67). Additional problems are encountered when using profit as an output variable, for example factors that transcend operational prowess such as disproportionate levels of debt service (Solovy & Serb, 2000).

The relationship between customer satisfaction and productivity in the restaurant industry is less ambiguous. As noted by Parasuraman, Zeithaml, and Berry (1994), customer satisfaction in many ways embodies the ultimate outcome associated with productivity. This is underscored by the correlation between customer satisfaction and organizational profitability reported in numerous studies (e.g., Anderson, 1996; Ittner & Larcker, 1996; Nelson et al., 1992).

A related variable—although beyond the scope of this paper–involves what Rust, Zeithaml, and Lemon (2000) call *customer equity*. The construct is comprised of three determinants: brand equity, value equity, and retention equity. Because of the construct's multifaceted nature, however, operationalizing it for the purposes of productivity analysis is more problematic than using more-readily available data. Nonetheless, such an output measure might prove interesting.

Similar to the case of output variables, the number of potential input variables that affect productivity–both controllable and uncontrollable–while numerous, must be selected with deference to the industry segment, economic conditions, and availability of reliable data. Previous research, such as a study conducted by Yoo, Donthu, and Pilling (1997), suggests front-of-the-house labor is a decisive variable. Similarly, Powers (1974) indicated that the number of servers is influential in predicting unit-level productivity. Information relative to environmental characteristics such as location and competitive conditions (Goldman, 1992; Ortiz-Buonafina, 1992), and wage rate (Bucklin, 1978; Zolber & Donaldson, 1970) also appear important. Finally, Doutt (1984) demonstrated that service capacity is fundamental to any measure of productivity.

METHODOLOGY

Given the research objective to identify a robust productivity measure using DEA, data were collected from 38 same-brand units located throughout the northeastern United States. The period of time included 31 consecutive days during the summer of 2001. All of the units are operated by the same franchisee and all share the same menu; thus, the resulting analyses are best described as internal benchmarking.

The primary data source was point-of-sale (POS) reports generated by the corporate office. The information was augmented through data gathered from sources such as interviews with regional managers (regarding seating capacity and average wage). Public-domain records detailing the number of similarly positioned restaurants within a two-mile radius of each unit were also used.

Using the above mentioned literature as the basis for selecting likely variables, the *a priori* model for a new productivity measure included four output variables and five input variables (three controllable and two uncontrollable). Specifically, the output variables and their associated measures included lunch sales, dinner sales, charged tips for lunch as a percentage of charged lunch sales (as a surrogate for customer satisfaction during lunch), charged tips for dinner as a percentage of charged dinner sales (as a surrogate for customer satisfaction during dinner). Input variables included front-of-the-house hours worked during lunch, front-of-the-house hours worked during dinner, average wage, number of competitors within a two-mile radius, and seating capacity.

A number of assumptions were made. First, gratuities serve as an indicator of customer satisfaction. While such an assumption is supported by some (e.g., Bodvarsson & Gibson, 1997), others argue that gratuity variability is not consistently associated with service (e.g., Lynn, 2001). Hence, given the exploratory nature of the inquiry and bolstered by the secondary objective of using data available from all stores, we included gratuities as a surrogate for customer satisfaction. Furthermore, since a calculation of total gratuities would require self-reports of all servers, only charged gratuities as a percentage of charged sales were used, operating under the assumption that patrons using a credit card tip similarly to those paying cash. In addition, while some guests use a credit card for the meal but tip in cash, it was assumed that such practices would be proportionately similar across units.

Second, it was assumed that back-of-the-house labor hours were relatively constant among stores; this assumption was based on information supplied by the company. Officials of the organizations also noted that while most front-of-the-house employees are part-time, the majority of back-of-the-house employees are full-time employees and work according to structured staffing schedules that are very similar throughout the chain.

Next, it was assumed that since all restaurants included in the study were in suburban settings and all sites were selected according to a well-defined set of site-selection criteria, differences in traffic patterns and related environmental factors were negligible. Another assumption pertains to competitors. While it is arguable that any restaurant is a competitor of another, we identified only those within the same segment (with correspondingly similar positioning strategies). Finally, while the cost of capital and indeed the investment-related strategies might certainly affect financial outcomes (and therefore result in differences among units), the company takes the position that these factors are very similar for stores throughout the chain given its investment strategies; hence, we, too, treat such factors as similar across units.

FINDINGS

In applying the DEA methodology, the outputs and inputs in the *a priori* model were first assessed using Frontier Analyst, an efficiency-analysis software package capable of executing a number of DEA-related analyses. Furthermore, the analyses were completed using a CCR model as introduced by Charnes, Cooper, and Rhodes (1978); differing constraints were not made owing to the exploratory nature of the investigation.

Despite the foundation provided by Lusch and Serpkenci (1990), separating sales by daypart did not appear important; using total sales by day offered the same level of sensitivity. The gratuity percentages separated by daypart, however, did serve to delineate differences among units. Regarding the input variables, wage proved to be immaterial because the organization under study has a policy of paying all foodservers the same wage regardless of experience or tenure. In much the same way that separating sales by daypart did not improve the model, separating hours worked by daypart did not appear important. For both sales and hours worked, the delineation by daypart is likely sublated by the absence of lunch-versus-dinner serving times and a menu that is constant for all serving times. The uncontrollable inputs, nearby competitors and seating capacity, did aid in defining the productivity model.

As shown in Table 1, 7 of the 38 stores proved to be 100 percent efficient according to the data and the selected model, with productivity of one unit falling below 57 percent. (The unit numbers were randomly assigned to the restaurants; further delineation is not possible given the proprietary nature of the data and the associated restrictions posed by the organization.)

These results also offer a number of surprises. First, the more efficient restaurants were not those with the greatest sales. This is surprising from the perspective that the organization cites sales as the leading function in their internal analyses of productivity. Second, it appears that service, even when using charge tips as a surrogate measure of customer satisfaction and understanding the implications of such an assumption as noted earlier, is important in the determination of operational productivity.

In comparing the results with productivity statistics provided by the organization, a number of discrepancies appear. For example, unit number 18, which is 88.15 percent efficient, is considered the most productive of the organization's restaurants using the traditional mea-

TABLE 1. Efficiency Scores Report

Unit Number	Efficiency Score
1	77%
2	87%
3	100%
4	69%
5	100%
6	75%
7	84%
8	89%
9	92%
10	93%
11	65%
12	81%
13	79%
14	57%
15	75%
16	100%
17	100%
18	88%
19	95%
20	91%
21	81%
22	97%
23	73%
24	100%
25	61%
26	92%
27	100%
28	71%
29	70%
30	84%
31	81%
32	89%
33	100%
34	68%
35	93%
36	91%
37	87%
38	73%

sure of sales per labor hour. Closer inspection of the data reveals that the partial-factor productivity statistic used by the company erroneously indicates maximum productivity since it fails to account for the smaller number of competitors and less-than-optimal customer satisfaction.

Another way to look at restaurant number 18, using it as a discussion point, is to examine the specific areas deserving improvement. Relational-improvement information–that is, indicators of which variable impacted the productivity determination more than others for the specific unit–suggests that the principal areas of potential productivity enhancement are customer satisfaction during dinner, which needs to improve, and hours worked, which need to be reduced. DEA analysis does not integrate relational-improvement information regarding uncontrollable variables because, by definition, management cannot manipulate them.

The implications, using only the data from this pilot study, indicate that DEA analysis does have utility for foodservice operators. DEA overcomes most of the constraints of traditional productivity techniques, both implicit and explicit, including cost functions and partial- and total-factor ratios. Most notably, DEA does not impose any particular functional form on the data, achieved through more flexible piecewise linear functions, and can include any number of output and input variables. Furthermore, unlike total-factor productivity indices, DEA assigns each individual restaurant its own set of weights, thereby allowing for comparison of operations with dissimilar compositions.

For the chain of restaurants examined here, which is best described as midscale, it appears that a preliminary model appropriate for assessing productivity integrates sales, customer satisfaction by daypart, labor hours, competitive conditions, and seating capacity. Practically speaking, however, these variables need considerably more empirical attention, in terms of both definition and measurement. For example, it is possible that a certain restaurant simply may not ever achieve 100 percent efficiency using the proposed model. It may be that number of seats precludes optimizing sales while concurrently reducing staffing levels. Nonetheless, if such an operation at least nears the efficiency frontier as depicted by DEA, then management can act on the supposition that the restaurant is operating proficiently.

While the potential for DEA in foodservice management is evident, there are a number of limitations, both with the empirical illustration provided and the method of analysis. Regarding the pilot study presented here, the number of restaurants was relatively small. While this was the result of the limited size of the organization, which is comprised of only the 38 units involved in the study, a larger number of operations would likely add more depth to the findings. In addition, such similarities as a constant wage paid to foodservers regardless of restaurant or tenure and similarities in site selection likely belie the absence of these variables in the final model.

Other related limitations pertain to the assumptions described earlier. Are charged gratuities a viable surrogate for satisfaction? While earlier studies suggest the validity of such an assumption, a better, more aptly defined measure of customer satisfaction would be desirable. Finally, are there other variables that may hold greater importance in assessing productivity? The number and experience of managers in the restaurant is one possibility; another is training that takes place at the unit level. Finally, how does employee turnover affect productivity? Anecdotal evidence suggests that turnover can serve as a crucial detriment to restaurant productivity. Inclusion of such information would likely provide more provocative results.

While DEA may address many of the problems of conventional productivity measures, it also has limitations. For example, DEA is extremely sensitive to outliers, as these serve to influence the optimal frontier. Thus, it is possible that one restaurant could anomalously create a benchmark–potentially resulting from a variable not included in the analysis–that no other operation can match. Finally, DEA is not stochastic in nature, which means it does not allow for an error structure. Hence, there is no goodness-of-fit information as is found in more traditional statistical techniques such as regression analysis.

The empirical illustration of assessing multi-unit restaurant productivity provides evidence of DEA's utility for foodservice management. The potential to include multiple output and input variables underscores the technique's versatility and portability. The next step is to create a more inclusive model with a substantially larger data set. The findings of such research will likely provide the necessary impetus for managers to more accurately focus on maximizing the requisite assets–including human capital–ultimately leading to more profitable operations.

REFERENCES

Andersson, T. D. (1996). Traditional key ratio analysis versus data envelopment analysis: A comparison of various measurements of productivity and efficiency in restaurants. In: Johns, N. (ed.), *Productivity management in hospitality and tourism* (pp. 209-226). London: Cassell.

Avkiran, N. K. (2002). Monitoring hotel performance. *Journal of Asia-Pacific Business, 4*(1), 51-66.

Banker, R. D., & Morey, R. C. (1986). Efficiency analysis for exogenously fixed inputs and outputs. *Operations Research 34*(4), 513-521.

Bloom, G. F. (1972). *Productivity in the food industry: Problems and potential.* Cambridge, MA: MIT Press.

Bodvarsson, O. B., & Gibson, W. A. (1997). Economics and restaurant gratuities: Determining tip rates. *American Journal of Economics and Sociology, 56*(2), 187-203.

Boles, J., Donthu, N., & Lohtia, R. (1995). Salesperson evaluation using relative performance efficiency: The application of data envelopment analysis. *Journal of Personnel Selling and Sales Management, 15*(3), 31-49.

Brown, J. R., & Dev, C. S. (1999). Looking beyond RevPAR: Productivity consequences of hotel strategies. *Cornell Hotel and Restaurant Administration Quarterly, 40*(2), 23-33.

Brown, M. D. M., & Hoover, L. W. (1990). Productivity measurement in foodservice: Past accomplishments–a future alternative. *Journal of the American Dietetic Association, 90*, 973-981.

Bucklin, L. P. (1978). *Productivity in marketing.* Chicago: American Marketing Association.

Burritt, M. B. (1967). Projected labor costs in future food systems. *Cornell Hotel and Restaurant Administration Quarterly, 8*, 55-63.

Charnes, A. C., Cooper, W. W., Learner, D. B., & Philips, F. Y. (1985). Management science and marketing management. *Journal of Marketing, 49*, 93-105.

Charnes, A. C., Cooper, W. W., Lewin, A. Y., & Seiford, L. M. (Eds.). (2001). *Data envelopment analysis: Theory, methodology, and application.* Norwell, MA: Kluwer Academic Publishers.

Charnes, A. C., Cooper, W. W., & Rhodes, E. (1978). Measuring efficiency of decision making units. *European Journal of Operations Research, 2*, 429-449.

Donthu, N., & Yoo, B. (1998). Retail productivity assessment: Using data envelopment analysis. *Journal of Retailing, 74*(1), 89-105.

Doutt, J. T. (1984). Comparative productivity performance in fast-food retail distribution. *Journal of Retailing, 60*, 98-106.

Eccles, R. G. (1991). The performance measurement manifesto. *Harvard Business Review, 69*, 131-137.

Farrell, M. (1957). The measurement of productive efficiency. *Journal of the Royal Statistical Society*, Series A, General, 120, Part 3, 253-281.

Filley, R. D. (1983). Putting the 'fast' in fast foods: Burger King. *Industrial Engineering*, *15*(1), 44-47.

Goldman, A. (1992). Evaluating the performance of the Japanese distribution system. *Journal of Retailing*, *68*, 11-39.

Hammond, C. J. (2002). A data envelopment analysis of UK public library systems. *Applied Economics*, *34*(5), 649-657.

Ittner, C., & Larcker, D. F. (1996). Measuring the impact of quality initiatives on firm financial performance. In S. Ghosh & D. Fedor (Eds.), *Advances in the Management of Organizational Quality–Vol. 1* (pp. 1-37). Greenwich, CG: JAI, 1-37.

Jablonsky, M. (1994). Productivity in industry and government. *Monthly Labor Review*, *117*(8), 49-57.

Jemric, I., & Vujcic, B. (2002). Efficiency of banks in Croatia: A DEA approach. *Comparative Economic Studies*, *44*(2/3), 169-193.

Kimes, S. E., Chase, R. B., Choi, S., Lee, P. Y., and Ngonzi, E. N. (1998). Restaurant revenue management: Applying yield management to the restaurant industry. *Cornell Hotel and Restaurant Administration Quarterly*, *39*(3), 32-39.

Lynn, M. (2001). Restaurant tipping and service quality: A tenuous relationship. *Cornell Hotel and Restaurant Administration Quarterly*, *42*(1), 14-20.

Lusch, R. F., & Serpkenci, R. R. (1990). Personal differences, job tension, job outcomes, and store performance: A study of retail store managers. *Journal of Marketing*, *54*, 85-101.

Mahajan, J. (1991). Data envelopment analytic model for assessing the relative efficiency of the selling function. *European Journal of Operational Research*, *53*, 189-205.

Nelson, E., Rust, R. T., Zahorik, A., Rose, R. L., Batalden, P., & Siemanski, B. (1992). Do patient perceptions of quality relate to hospital financial performance? *Journal of Healthcare Marketing*, (December), 1-13.

Nunamaker, T. R. (1983). Measuring routine nursing service efficiency: A comparison of cost per patient day and data envelopment analysis models. *Health Services Research*, *18*(2, Part 1), 183-205.

Ortiz-Buonafina, M. (1992). The evolution of retail institutions: A case study of the Guatemalan retail sector. *Journal of Macromarketing*, *12*, 16-27.

Parasuraman, A., Zeithaml, V. A., & Berry, L. L. (1994). Alternative scales for measuring service quality: A comparative assessment based on psychometric and diagnostic criteria. *Journal of Retailing*, *70*, 193-199.

Powers, T. F. (1974). Productivity in the service restaurant. *Cornell Hotel and Restaurant Administration Quarterly*, *15*, 49-57.

Reynolds, D. (1998). Productivity analysis in the on-site food-service segment. *Cornell Hotel and Restaurant Administration Quarterly*, *39*(3), 22-31.

Rust, R. T., Zeithaml, V. A., & Lemon, K. N. (2000). *Driving customer equity: How customer lifetime value is reshaping corporate strategy*. New York: The Free Press.

Sarkis, J. (2000). An analysis of the operational efficiency of major airports in the United States. *Journal of Operations Management*, *18*(3), 335-351.

Solovy, A., & Serb, C. (2000). Financial performance. *Hospitals & Health Networks*, *74*(2), 50-58.

Thompson, R. G., Langemeier, L., Lee, C., Lee, E., & Thrall, R. (1990). The role of multiplier bounds in efficiency analysis with application to Kansas farming. *Journal of Econometrics*, *46*, 93-108.

Uri, N. D. (2001). Changing productive efficiency in telecommunications in the United States. *International Journal of Production Economics*, *72*(2), 121-137.

Wöber, K. W. (2002). *Benchmarking in tourism and hospitality industries*. London: CABI.

Yoo, B., Donthu, N., & Pilling, B. K. (1997). Channel efficiency: Franchise versus non-franchise systems. *Journal of Marketing Channels*, *4*(1), 211-223.

Zeithaml, V. A. (2000). Service quality, profitability, and economic worth of customers: What we know and what we need to learn. *Journal of the Academy of Marketing Science*, *28*(winter), 67-85.

Zolber, K. K., & Donaldson, B. (1970). Distribution of work functions in hospital food systems. *Journal of the American Dietetic Association*, *56*, 39-46.

Hotel Labor Productivity Assessment: A Data Envelopment Analysis

Bo A. Hu
Liping A. Cai

SUMMARY. The purpose of this study is to propose Data Envelopment Analysis (DEA) as an effective tool to measure labor productivity of hotels. Using the data collected from the hotels in the State of California, the study applies DEA to calculate the labor productivity score of each sampled hotel. The internal and external determinants of labor productivity are examined. Implications of the study's results are also discussed. *[Article copies available for a fee from The Haworth Document Delivery Service: 1-800-HAWORTH. E-mail address: <docdelivery@haworthpress.com> Website: <http://www.HaworthPress.com> © 2004 by The Haworth Press, Inc. All rights reserved.]*

KEYWORDS. Hotel, labor productivity, Data Envelopment Analysis

INTRODUCTION

The purpose of this study is to propose Data Envelopment Analysis (DEA), a linear programming technique, to assess hotel labor productivity and examine its determinants. As a service industry, hotels are labor intensive. The importance of labor productivity in the lodging industry can be readily illustrated by the dominance of labor costs in the profit and loss accounts of hotel companies. A recent study revealed that costs associated with labor, including salaries, wages and benefits, comprised approximately 33 percent of total revenue, and 43 percent of all operating expenses in a hotel (Quek, 2000). Therefore, measuring the labor portion of productivity–the ratio of labor inputs and service outputs–is and should be a priority consideration of hotel operations in both economic upsurge and

---

Bo A. Hu is Assistant Professor, School of Hotel and Restaurant Administration, College of Human Environmental Sciences, Oklahoma State University, 210L HES West, Stillwater, OK 74078-6173 (E-mail: boh@okstate.edu). Liping A. Cai is Associate Professor and Director, Purdue Tourism & Hospitality Research Center, Department of Hospitality and Tourism Management, Purdue University, 700 W. State Street, West Lafayette, IN 47907-2059 (E-mail: liping@purdue.edu).

The authors would like to acknowledge the generosity of California Hotel and Motel Association (CHMA) for providing the data set. However, CHMA bears no responsibility for the analysis or interpretations presented in this study. The authors are also grateful to three anonymous reviewers whose constructive comments and suggestions made valuable contributions to the improvement of this manuscript.

An earlier version of the paper was presented at the Seventh Annual Graduate Education and Graduate Student Research Conference in Hospitality and Tourism, Houston, Texas, January 2002.

[Haworth co-indexing entry note]: "Hotel Labor Productivity Assessment: A Data Envelopment Analysis." Hu, Bo A. and Liping A. Cai. Co-published simultaneously in *Journal of Travel & Tourism Marketing* (The Haworth Hospitality Press, an imprint of The Haworth Press, Inc.) Vol. 16, No. 2/3, 2004, pp. 27-38; and: *Management Science Applications in Tourism and Hospitality* (ed: Zheng Gu) The Haworth Hospitality Press, an imprint of The Haworth Press, Inc., 2004, pp. 27-38. Single or multiple copies of this article are available for a fee from The Haworth Document Delivery Service [1-800-HAWORTH, 9:00 a.m. - 5:00 p.m. (EST). E-mail address: docdelivery@haworthpress.com].

http://www.haworthpress.com/web/JTTM
© 2004 by The Haworth Press, Inc. All rights reserved.
Digital Object Identifier: 10.1300/J073v16n02_03

downturn periods. When the hotel industry experiences periodic financial downturns, hotel companies would hesitate to raise room rates to achieve profitability. The logical alternative is to reduce labor cost by keeping the most efficient employees and leveraging labor productivity. When the industry enjoys a positive economic outlook, hotel companies emphasize labor productivity as a means of enhancing their prosperity. Understanding how to measure and improve a hotel's labor productivity contributes directly to its bottom line.

However, management sciences, which have been successfully applied in other service sectors, have not been as actively adopted in the hotel industry to improve labor productivity and other operation activities. Most hotel operators seldom use or have never heard such useful techniques as linear programming and Pareto analysis (Witt & Witt, 1993), which is evident in the scarcity of existing literature on the measurement methods of labor productivity in the hotel industry. While a hotel's performance was measured in some previous studies, only a few works, such as Ball, Johnson, and Slattery (1987), Brown and Dev (1999), have specifically investigated methodological issues on how to effectively measure labor productivity of a hotel. Furthermore, there has yet to be an agreed-upon definition of what a hotel's labor productivity is.

This study proposes a linear programming technique called Data Envelopment Analysis (DEA) as a tool to measure hotel labor productivity. DEA can measure labor productivity at the individual hotel level by simultaneously incorporating multiple inputs and outputs. With DEA, those hotels with the most productive labor are identified and can be used as a benchmark. A productivity index is calculated for each hotel relative to the best performers. Furthermore, the study develops a relational model to investigate factors that determine labor productivity. Both methods are empirically applied to the hotels in the State of California.

LABOR PRODUCTIVITY

In its most general application, as a construct of the "manufacturing paradigm" (Jones & Hall, 1996), productivity is defined as the effective use of resources to achieve operational goals (Reynolds, 1998), which is usually expressed by a ratio of the outputs to the inputs. The measurement of productivity varies from precise quantitative to broad qualitative ones (Donthu & Yoo, 1998), from aggregate to disaggregate levels (Reynolds, 1998), from single-factor to multi-factor (Bucklin, 1978), and its interpretations are also different (Lee, 1991; Dean & Kunze, 1992; Pickworth, 1987). In measuring the productivity of the service firms, two single-factor measures are most often used: (1) labor productivity output per unit of labor, and (2) capital productivity output per capital (Brown & Dev, 1999). This study focuses on the measurement and determinants of labor productivity in the lodging industry. In such context, labor productivity is defined as a hotel's ability to obtain maximum outputs from a given set of labor inputs or minimize its labor inputs to reach an expected level of output. The important aspect of the definition of labor productivity concerns the establishment of a relationship between the number of employees or labor hours and the amount of service provided (Clark & Kirk, 1997; Ball, Johnson & Slattery, 1986).

Existing labor productivity measurements have been developed mostly as macro tools, such as those created by the Bureau of Labor Statistics (Dean & Kunze, 1992). The labor productivity is computed by dividing an index of output by hours of labor input. These measures have been developed to show how effectively an industry, or economy, is growing, absorbing technology, or offsetting rising wages. However, they cannot assess the individual unit level as micro tools. Research on hotel labor productivity at the micro level of individual hotel units is scarce, and there is no consensus on its measurement either. By using the food and beverage department as an example, Ball, Johnson and Slattery (1986) illustrated how to measure a hotel's labor productivity by utilizing two single ratios–Revenue/Full-Time Equivalent Employee (FTEE) and Covers/FTEE. The empirical study results of nine hotels demonstrated the two ratios were useful to identify hotel, departmental, and temporal ranges in labor performance through comparative analysis. Clark and Kirk (1997) investigated the relationship between labor productivity and three factors of production: the use of ready prepared vegetables, the amount of equipment available, and the use of cook-chill technology in the foodservice departments of up-scale hotels and large hospitals within the UK. A positive correlation was found between labor productivity and both the use of ready prepared vegetables and the use of cook-chill. In contrast, there was a negative correlation between labor productivity and the use of large amount of equipment.

Brown and Dev (1999) measured labor productivity by using three single-factor measures: total annual sales per number of full-time equivalent employees (FTEs) (SalesEmp), gross operating profit per FTEs (GOPEmp), and income before fixed charges per FTEs (ProfitEmp). The ANOVA results of their study indicated that SalesEmp varied according to the hotel's size, its service orientation, and ownership and management arrangements. Only the factor of ownership and management arrangements associated with higher GOPEmp and the two factors of size and ownership structure were significantly associated with ProfitEmp. Baker and Riley (1994) argued for a holistic model of labor productivity and did a comparative analysis of 20 hotels in each of Germany, France, and the UK. Labor productivity was measured by three single- factor elements: added value per full-time employee, sales per full-time employee and food and beverage sales per full-time employee. The linear regression results showed a positive correlation between added value per full-time employee and number of employees per available rooms against room rate in all three countries. The study also regressed the number of full-time employees on sales of food and beverage and the multiplicity of the number of available rooms and average occupancy. The results suggested that the higher numbers of employees in the UK hotels was largely due to lower productivity in food and beverage departments.

DATA ENVELOPMENT ANALYSIS

Existing research on hotel labor productivity resolves to calculate various single output-input ratios. Such ratios aim at either assessing the overall productivity of the hotel or applying to a section or a function of the hotel. There are at least two drawbacks using single ratios. First, they tend to be crude measures of labor productivity. For example, a hotel may show a reduction in its total annual sales per number of full-time equivalent employees from one year to another, but neither does the measure reveal why the decline has come about, nor does it indicate options for improvement. Second, looking at many individual ratios gives the analyst a fragmented picture (Anderson & Hartman, 1995).

Aggregate and multiple-factor measures of labor productivity have been proven to be more robust and meaningful for analyzing the labor productivity on an operational level (Reynolds, 1998). The measurement method proposed in this study is DEA, a linear programming technique. DEA is characterized by converting multiple inputs and outputs of a decision unit, such as a hotel, into a single measure of performance, generally referred as relative efficiency. This enables the development of an output-to-input ratio system that can handle multiple labor inputs and outputs and go beyond basic single ratio labor productivity measurements. DEA was initially used as an evaluation tool for "not-for-profit" organizations (Farrell, 1957; Charnes, Cooper & Rhodes, 1978). It has also been applied successfully as a performance evaluation tool for retailing (Donthu & Yoo, 1998), nursing homes (Nyman & Bricker, 1989; Fizel & Nunnikhoven, 1993), ferry services (Forsund & Hernaes, 1990), fast food (Banker & Morey, 1986), restaurants (Anderson & Hartman, 1995), and banking (Barr, Seiford & Siems, 1992; Hartman & Storbeck, 1994).

Labor productivity in the context of DEA deals with producing the maximum quantity of outputs for any given amount of labor inputs or the minimum use of labor inputs for any given amount of outputs. Input minimization approach was used in this study. DEA first identifies the most productive units, which comprise a frontier isoquant as the "reference set." The frontier is a series of points, a line, or a surface connecting the most productive units, which are determined from the comparison of inputs and outputs of all units under consideration. DEA then calculates a productivity score for all other units producing similar outputs that are not on the isoquant. The identification of the reference set distinguishes the DEA's key feature of comparability. For example, when used to measure the labor productivity for a specific segment of the hotel industry, the best performing hotels can be identified to be the reference set. The set in turn can be used as the benchmarks, with which the labor productivity score of each of all other hotels is computed and compared. Hotels can use internal standards, such as hotels within the same chain company, or external standards, such as other hotels in the same segment, as their benchmarks. Although parametric techniques, such as regression analysis and some traditional production functions, can be used to measure hotel labor productivity, the DEA method is advantageous in being based on a description of the best unit's performance rather than of the expected performance of a "normally good" unit (Andersson, 1996).

In using DEA, the productivity score of any unit is computed as the maximum of a ratio of weighted outputs to weighted inputs, subject to the condition that for all other units under consideration, similar ratios are less than or equal to one (Donthu & Yoo, 1998). The productivity of a hotel can be obtained by solving the following model (M1) (Charnes, Cooper & Rhodes, 1978):

$$\text{Max } h_o = \frac{\sum_{r=1}^{t} U_r Y_{rj_0}}{\sum_{i=1}^{m} V_i X_{ij_0}} \qquad \text{(M1)}$$

subject to

$$\frac{\sum_{r=1}^{t} U_r Y_{rj}}{\sum_{i=1}^{m} V_i X_{ij}} \le 1 \quad \text{for all } j = 1, \ldots n.$$

$$U_r, V_i > 0; r = 1, \ldots s; i = 1, \ldots m.$$

Y_{rj} and X_{ij} are the amount of the *r*th output and the *i*th input for the *j*th hotel, and U_r and V_i are the weights to be estimated by the data of all comparable hotels that are being used to arrive at the relative productivity for the *o*th hotel. The model has *t* output variables, *m* input variables and *n* hotels. In practice, the DEA model M1 is first linearized and then solved by using the methods of linear programming. The linear programming version of the model known as the multiplier form is shown in model M2 (Boussofiane, Dyson & Thanassoulis, 1991; Coelli, Rao & Battese, 1998; Dyson, Thanassoulis & Boussofiane, 1995):

$$\text{Max } h_o = \sum_{r=1}^{t} U_r Y_{rj_0} \qquad \text{(M2)}$$

subject to

$$\sum_{i=1}^{m} V_i X_{ij_0} = 1\,(say).$$

$$\sum_{r=1}^{t} U_r Y_{rj} - \sum_{i=1}^{m} V_i X_{ij} \le 0 \quad \text{for all } j = 1, \ldots n.$$

$$U_r, V_i > 0; r = 1, \ldots s; i = 1, \ldots m.$$

If a hotel is on the frontier isoquant, i.e., among the reference set, the solution will be $h_o = 1$ and the productivity score is 1, which can be described as being 100% productive as compared with other hotels under consideration. Other hotels, using these inputs less efficiently, will locate above the frontier isoquant and their productivity score will be smaller than 1. For example, a hotel having the productivity score of 0.75 can be interpreted as being 75% as productive as a hotel on the frontier isoquant. Thus, the productivity score allows a relative ranking of hotels by levels of labor productivity.

EMPIRICAL ANALYSIS

Data for the empirical illustration were drawn from the 1999 California Lodging Industry Employee Compensation Survey, which was conducted by California Hotel and Motel Association (CHMA) in the year of 2000. The target population was all the hotels in the State of California. The survey randomly selected 3,000 hotels. To increase the response rate, postcard reminders were sent to the non-respondents in three weeks after mailing out the questionnaires. Respondents returned 257 questionnaires with a response rate of 8.5%, consistent with response levels found in studies of the lodging industry (e.g., Reid & Sandler, 1992; David, Grabski, & Kasavana, 1996). Five cases were detected to have participant errors,[1] and 10 cases did not provide enough data to be included. As a result, the study's sample size was 242.

The sample was divided into three pre-determined segments to account for the disparity in total revenues and operational differences among bed & breakfast (B&B), limited-service, and full-service hotels. The three segments were analyzed separately. Inputs in a hotel are traditionally defined as the firm's labor costs and capital investment (Acabal, Heineke & McIntyre, 1984). However, this study measures labor inputs by using the number of employees, which is consistent with input measurements in other hotel productivity studies (Brown & Dev, 1999; McMahon, 1994; Prais, Jarvis & Wagner, 1989) and also with DEA applications in other service industries (Fizel & Nunnikhoven, 1993; Nyman & Bricker, 1989; Soteriou & Zenios, 1998). The financial measurement of labor cost is not included, because "if the production technology is broadly separable in capital and labor inputs, the omission of capital would not distort labor use efficiency" (Fizel & Nunnikhoven, 1993, p. 53). There are several well-accepted outputs to measure a hotel's performance, such as total revenue and number of rooms sold (McMahon, 1994; Brown & Dev, 1999). These measures were also used in this study. The data were analyzed by using the Efficiency Measurement System to compute the efficiency scores (see Seiford, 1996, for citations on DEA-related computer programs).

The study first examined labor productivity in the three hotel segments by using two inputs and one output, allowing the DEA process to be visualized graphically in two-dimensional settings. The two inputs were full-time equivalent managers and workers, counting both full- and part-time. It was assumed that each part-time employee represents one-half of a full-time employee, which was an acceptable method to address the problem of the nonequivalence of full- and part-time employees (Brown & Dev, 1999). Total room revenue, a well-accepted performance indicator used in the lodging industry, was used as the single output.

Figures 1, 2 and 3 illustrate DEA analysis results of labor productivity in each of the three Californian hotel segments within a two-dimensional context. About seven hotels form the isoquant of the limited service segment, acting as labor productive benchmarks in this segment. The number of full-time equivalent managers and workers per total revenue unit in the seven best performers is the smallest when compared with other peer hotels. The seven hotels were connected to form the productivity isoquant of 1. For the hotels scattered above the isoquant, the farther away they are from the isoquant, the less labor productive they tend to be. For the full service segment, eight hotels compose the isoquant, and other hotels evenly spread above the isoquant. While six benchmarking hotels in the B&B segment lie on the isoquant, the labor productivity differences among the others are more distinctive. The one in the upper-right corner with the lowest score seems to be an outlier; however, due to the diversified nature of the B&B sector, a case-by-case explanation might be more appropriate in explaining their labor productivity differences.

Since DEA accommodates multiple inputs and outputs, it allows a precise analysis of labor productivity by using individual inputs and outputs instead of their aggregates. For example, four inputs–the number of full-time managers, part-time managers, full-time workers, and part-time workers–are more precise measurements of labor than that of the total number of employees. Multiple outputs should be more desirable in empirical analysis because most hotels have several goals or objectives to be assessed, although the multiple input-output DEA analysis is difficult to be visualized graphically.

A further DEA analysis of the labor productivity in the three segments is conducted by using two outputs–total revenue and number of rooms sold, and four inputs–the number of

FIGURE 1. Labor Productivity of California Limited Service Hotels

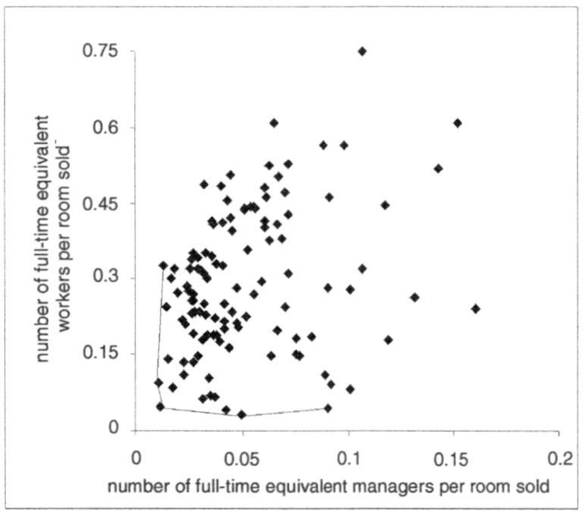

FIGURE 2. Labor Productivity of California Full Service Hotels

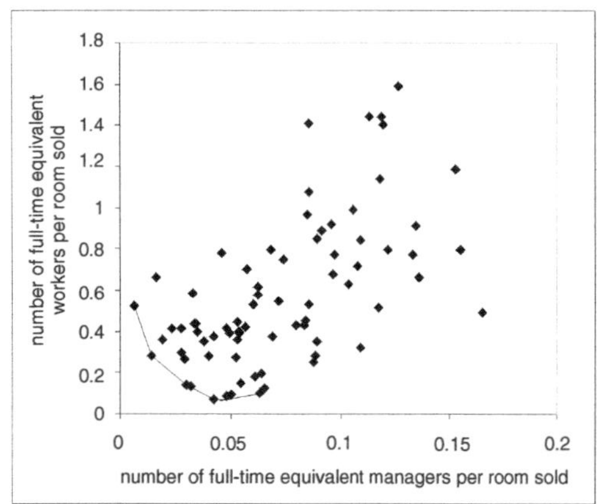

FIGURE 3. Labor Productivity of California B&Bs

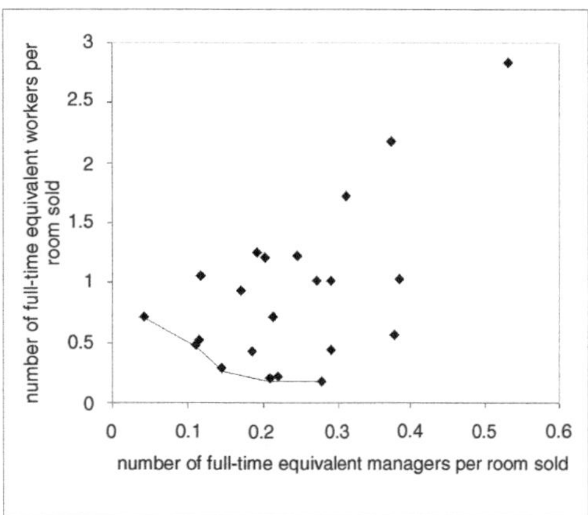

full-time managers, part-time managers, and full-time workers, and part-time workers. The distributions of DEA productivity scores in each segment are reported in Table 1.

The average labor productive scores in the three segments were different: B&B having the highest and limited service having the lowest. The isoquant frontiers of the three segments were formed by different numbers of benchmarking hotels, ranging from 8 in B&B to 15 in full service. In each segment the hotels have a wide range of labor productivity compared with their corresponding best practices–the reference set. The distributions of labor productivity scores in the limited service and full service hotels skew to the lower end. Eight out of 125 properties in the limited service segment were identified as benchmarking hotels. There was a significant variation of labor productivity in this segment. Nearly 80 percent of the hotels scored less than 0.5. They were 50% (or less) as productive as the reference set. Within the full-service segment of 86 hotels, the frontier isoquant consisted of 15 properties. Close to 60% of the 86 hotels scored below 0.5. They were 50% (or less) as productive as the reference set. The B&B segment fared the best. Of the 31 responding properties, more than a third (11) were located on the frontier isoquant. Compared with the other two segments, labor productivity scores

TABLE 1. Frequencies and Summary Statistics of DEA Scores with Four Inputs*

Range	Limited Service (n = 125)	Full Service (n = 86)	B&B (n = 31)
1	8	15	11
0.90-0.999	1	4	0
0.80-0.899	2	4	1
0.70-0.799	3	5	3
0.60-0.699	5	2	3
0.50-0.599	7	6	1
0.40-0.499	10	9	2
0.30-0.399	26	17	6
0.20-0.299	36	16	0
0.10-0.199	22	7	4
0-0.099	5	1	0
Mean	0.375	0.533	0.649
Standard deviation	0.240	0.304	0.319
Range	0.02-1.00	0.03-1.00	0.12-100

*Four inputs are full-time managers, part-time managers, full-time workers and part-time workers.

of B&B were more evenly distributed, with approximately a third in scoring less than 0.5 and another third between 0.5 and 0.99.

DETERMINANTS OF LABOR PRODUCTIVITY–BEYOND DEA

DEA effectively delineated the labor productivity level of each hotel in the sample, and identified a set of benchmarking hotels with the productivity score of 100%. These benchmarking hotels formed the frontier isoquant. A hotel that was less productive was placed above the frontier. Further, the productivity score indicated the extent to which the hotel was less productive relative to those on the frontier isoquant. Yet, DEA revealed nothing about the underlying factors that contributed to the differential productivity scores. Indeed, DEA goes as far as telling symptoms but does not provide diagnosis for the underlying causes of, or factors contributing to, the symptoms. Practically, DEA results only allow the ranking of sampled hotels in their labor productivity, but fail to provide directions for the hotels to account for their different productivity levels. A relational model such as regression analysis can be utilized to augment for this deficiency. In this study, the development of the relational model began with the identification of factors that could help account for the variation of the model's dependent variable–the productivity score. Literature review on labor productivity in hospitality and other service industries (e.g., Witt & Witt, 1989; Nyman & Bricker, 1989; Fizel & Nummikhoven, 1993) resulted in a number of factors, which could be categorized into three groups for reference convenience: (1) service quality, (2) physical properties, and (3) employees' expertise levels. In the relational model, these factors were the independent variables or determinants of the productivity score.

Service Quality. A negative relationship between service quality and hotel labor productivity was suggested by Lee-Ross (1994) and Witt and Witt (1989). Higher quality requires more intensive service, which usually leads to an increase in labor hours or staffing. While "quality" is a crucial element of productivity, it poses problems of measurement (Fletcher & Snee, 1985; Schroeder, 1985; Lee-Ross, 1994). Following the recommendations in Fizel and Nunnikhoven (1993) and Elsworth (2000), the current study chose three proxies to measure hotel service quality: room rate, occupancy rate, and hotel category. An analysis of the data compiled by the National Economic Development Office showed that there was a significant negative correlation between room rate and labor productivity (Baker & Riley, 1994). Fizel and Nunnikhoven (1993) and Nyman (1988) found that decreased occupancy rate might be an indication of poor service quality. Baker and Riley (1994) also found that the number of employees increased with occupancy. The productivity of employees is an important condition to deliver higher quality service, and higher occupancy rate would tend to be associated with higher labor productivity scores. In this study, the proxy of occupancy rate was represented by average number of rooms sold–available rooms multiplied by average room occupancy, which takes into account the size of the hotel. Hotel category was chosen as another proxy for service quality in the study. Room rates were used as classification criteria to categorize hotels into budget/economy, commercial, and luxury hotels, as it was assumed that the higher the room rate was, the better service a hotel tended to provide. Hotels with an average rate below $55 are categorized in budget/economy category, while those between $55 and $125 are in commercial hotels category, and those above $125 in luxury category. B&Bs, an alternative lodging property to the normal hotel or motel, has many different styles with prices ranging from about $30 to $300 or more. It was defined as an accommodation with the owner, who lives on the premises or nearby, providing lodging and breakfast (Walker, 1999).

Physical Properties. As an "upstream" factor, Rimmington and Clark (1996) suggested the inclusion of hotel size to measure labor productivity. Brown and Dev (1999) indicated the size of a hotel, service orientation, and ownership and management arrangements exerted significant impact on the productivity of its employees. In their DEA study, Anderson and Hartman (1995) found distinctive differences in the labor productivity among five different types of restaurants. As an important physical feature of a hotel, the number of rooms was used as the sole proxy for its physical properties. In their study of labor productivity of nursing homes, Nyman and Briker (1989) found a positive correlation between number of rooms and productivity. Such finding is consistent with the theory of economy of scales, which is often invoked in a cost function to determine the optimal firm size. The positive relationship between firm size and labor productivity has been well documented in the studies of both hospitality and other service industries (Baker & Riley, 1994; Lee-Ross, 1994; Brown & Dev, 1999; Elsworth, 2000).

Employee Expertise. Witt and Witt (1989) posited that factors influencing hotel labor productivity should include management expertise. Alpert (1986) further identified the significance of the differences between skilled and unskilled labor and concluded that low skill levels had a major negative impact on labor productivity. When the service is essentially the labor input itself, such as in the lodging industry, firms are likely to hire more skillful workers by offering a higher wage or salary and better benefits to increase their labor productivity. Particularly with the low national unemployment rate since 1993 (Quek, 2000), hotel operators are more willing to pay higher wages and offer better benefit packages to attract or retain a skilled employee (Alpert, 1986; Baker & Riley, 1994). This study used average wage rates of managers and staff to represent employee expertise.

Relational Model. The proxies and representations of Service Quality, Physical Properties, and Employee Expertise form the independent variables in a relationship model. Descriptive statistics were reported in Table 2. The dependent variable was the productivity score of each hotel from the earlier DEA. With luxury hotels being the reference group, budget/economy and commercial hotels were dummy variables. The function of the model can be specified as follows:

$$y = \beta_0 + \beta_1(\textit{Service Quality}) + \beta_2(\textit{Physical Properties}) + \beta_3(\textit{Employee Skills}) + \varepsilon$$

where y is dependent variable of hotel labor productivity; β_0 represents the intercept; β_1, β_2, and β_3 are coefficients of the variable vectors; ε is the error term.

Ordinary least square (OLS) was used to estimate the model's coefficients for each of the three segments. The assumptions of regression analysis were checked and the three samples were found normally distributed. Diagnostic statistics revealed the presence of heteroskedasticity in the residuals of each model. The problem was corrected by taking the log form of the labor productivity scores, following the suggestion of Neter, Hutner, Nachtsheim, and Wasserman (1996). Variance inflation factor (VIF) for each variable was below 10, showing the absence of multicollinearity. The model was found to be significant with R-square of 32.06%, 24.79%, and 38.69%, respectively for limited service hotels, full service hotels and B&B (see Table 3).

Average daily rate (ADR) was found to be a significant factor contributing to the variation of labor productivity in the segment of limited service hotels, but not in the segments of full service hotels and B&B. An analysis of sum of squares showed that ADR explains most variation in the limited service model. Higher hotel room rates were associated with lower labor productivity, indicating a higher ratio of

TABLE 2. Descriptive Statistics

Variable	Limited Service Hotels (n = 125)		Full Service Hotels (n = 86)		B & B (n = 31)	
Productivity scores (%)	35.63*	(23.76)**	28.63	(19.87)	35.46	(33.40)
ADR	90.83	(39.97)	125.58	(71.62)	160.56	(60.02)
Occupancy rate (%)	72.71	(31.72)	75.53	(9.25)	60.85	(18.34)
Budget/economy hotel dummy	0.38	(0.49)	0.30	(0.46)	-	
Commercial hotel dummy	0.34	(0.48)	0.33	(0.47)	0.32	(0.48)
Number of rooms	95.78	(78.39)	233.80	(153.91)	11.42	(9.11)
Average manager wages ($)	30.06	(10.65)	37.15	(9.66)	28.75	(11.75)
Average staff wages ($)	15.01	(2.75)	18.16	(3.44)	14.20	(33.30)

Note: *Mean. **Standard deviation.

TABLE 3. Determinants of Labor Productivity

Independent Variables	Limited Service Hotels		Full Service Hotels		B&B	
	Coefficient	VIF	Coefficient	VIF	Coefficient	VIF
Constant	2.0716	-	2.2073	-	3.06255	-
ADR	−0.0036*	2.06	−0.0011	1.54	−0.0012	3.38
Occupancy rate	0.0056	1.25	0.0079	1.05	0.0018	1.59
Budget/economy hotel dummy	0.0178	2.09	0.1776	1.6	-	-
Commercial hotel dummy	0.2436**	1.83	0.1673	1.61	0.5589**	1.73
Number of rooms	0.0015*	1.3	0.0011*	1.25	0.0147	2.41
Average manager wages ($)	0.000229*	1.3	0.000155*	1.33	0.000270*	2.27
Average staff wages ($)	0.000186	1.62	0.000153	1.55	0.000201	3.33
F value	7.89		3.67		2.55	
R-Square	0.3206		0.2479		0.3869	
Adjusted R-Square	0.2800		0.1804		0.2369	

Note: *Significant at p = 0.05 level. **Significant at p = 0.10 level.

employees per room in more expensive hotels. This was suggested in the positive coefficients of the hotel category variable. The results showed that on average commercial hotels in both the limited service and B&B segments were more labor productive than those in the reference group of luxury hotels. However, no significant difference was observed between the two categories in the full service segment. The results also indicated the average difference in labor productivity between budget/economy hotels and luxury hotels were not significant in limited and full service hotel categories. The occupancy rate, as another service quality proxy, was not significant in explaining the variations. This might suggest that in contrast to the belief that occupancy rate is a reflection of service quality; it is more of a function of quantity and an indicator of room rates or seasonality impacts.

Representing the physical properties of a hotel, the number of rooms was found to be significant in the limited and full service segments. Consistent with the theory of economy of scales, the larger size of a hotel was associated with higher labor productivity. The sum of square analysis revealed that the number of rooms explains a significant proportion of the variation in the full service model. Of the two variables representing employee expertise, the average manager wages were found to be a significant factor in contributing to the variation of labor productivity in all three segments. Assuming the compensation paid to a manager was consummate with his or her skill level, a hotel operated by highly paid managers tends to be more labor productive. The incomplete measurement of staff wages might explain the insignificance of average staff wages in the model. Although the data showed tips were an important income source for some hotel staffs, tips were not included in calculating their wages. As a result, average staff wages seemed inappropriate as an indicator of the skill levels of hotel staffs.

CONCLUSIONS AND IMPLICATIONS

Due to the labor-intensive nature of hotel operations, the labor portion of productivity is a primary consideration for hoteliers. However, its measurement remains *ad hoc* at individual property or company levels; and methods employed vary. Few have adopted advanced yet pragmatic techniques. Moreover, labor productivity is a relative concept. The true performance of a hotel cannot be appreciated unless performance of their counterparts is also taken into consideration. These attributes make the measurement of hotel labor productivity a crucial and challenging task. This study acknowledged hotel labor productivity as the relative labor performance of a hotel characterized by multiple inputs and outputs. It proposed Data Envelopment Analysis as an effective method to measure hotel labor productivity, and further recommended a relational model to identify determinants of labor productivity variance among hotels of different lodging segments.

Data Envelopment Analysis (DEA), which has been proven to be a valid linear programming technique to measure productivity in other service industries, appeals to the lodging industry in two-fold: (1) it can convert multiple inputs and outputs of a hotel into a single measure of performance; (2) it allows one hotel to compare its inputs and outputs with those of all other comparable hotels within a specific segment through benchmarking. As illustrated by the empirical example of California, DEA can set the benchmarks, and allow relative comparisons among the hotels in a specific segment within a region. The results are useful for hotel associations and operators to determine the most productive players and detect the discrepancies between the best and themselves. The comparative labor productivity is also of strategic importance when assessing the labor performance of hotels in a chain or franchise system.

The relational model further identified the determinants that explain the different levels of labor productivity among hotels. The review of previous work both in and outside the hospitality literature resulted in the identification of three types of possible independent variables–service quality, physical properties, and employees' expertise levels. They were represented by a total of nine proxy variables, including ADR, occupancy rate, and hotel category, number of rooms, average wage rate of managers, and average wage rate of workers. The OLS results indicated managerial capability tends to be an important underlying factor that affects a hotel's productivity, while a hotel's size, category, and service quality can explain the variation in some segments. The results not only provide the less productive hotel's directions to pinpoint the causes, but can also be used for fair performance evaluation by compensating for market situations, such as room rate, and scale of a hotel.

The contributions of this study are constrained by three major limitations, which are inherent with the use of secondary data in an empirical investigation. The first and foremost limitation lies with the use of hotel category as a proxy variable in developing the construct of service quality. Underlying the construct was the assumption that budget and economy hotels offer low service quality and that the opposite is true for luxury hotels. When a hotel's service quality is expressed only in tangible terms, such as grades of facilities, room size, and amenities, the assumption might be valid from the demand perspective. Guests staying in budget and economy hotels have a lower expectation of service quality than those staying in luxury hotels. However, this assumption ignored the intangible aspects of service quality. Therefore, caution should be in order in generalizing the service quality construct beyond the contexts similar to this study. Caution should also be taken in interpreting the finding that service quality was inversely related to labor productivity. Within the same category of hotels, the positive relationship is likely to be true. This limitation would be lessened if the service quality is measured by such well-developed scales as SERVQUAL and LODGESERV. The second limitation was the measurement of the hotel workers' compensation would have been more desirable. A complete measurement of the employees' compensation or other methods of measuring the employees' skills should be used to further assess its relationship to hotel labor productivity. Third, compared to full and limited hotels, the sample size of B&Bs are relatively small (31 cases). The diversification nature of the B&B segment might not be captured fully in this study.

Despite the growing attention to hotel labor productivity issue, there is still great scope for further research contributions. Ownership arrangements (company-owned versus franchised) and management arrangement (branded management company, independent management company, independent management) might play an important role in determining a hotel's productivity, which deserves further examination. In addition, although empirical studies have demonstrated a clear positive correlation between labor productivity and technology in some service sectors (Clark & Kirk, 1997), the role of technology in hotel labor productivity is considered the weakest area of productivity literature (Baker & Riley, 1994). Future studies should explore the impact of labor substitution of using automation and technology to increase labor productivity in the lodging industry.

NOTE

1. According to CHMA, Hilton San Francisco & Towers with 1,891 rooms is the largest hotel in California. The room numbers responded by the five hotels are over this number, which may be caused by the misunderstanding of the participants. (Reference: "How to find and reserve a lodging property?" http://www.chma.com/cgi-bin/chma/default.asp)

REFERENCES

Acabal, D. D., Heineke, J. M. and McIntyre, S. H. (1984). Issues and perspectives on retail productivity. Journal of Retailing, 60(3): 107-127.

Alpert, W. T. (1986). The Minimum Wage in the Restaurant Industry. Westpoint, Connecticut: Praeger.

Andersson, T. D. (1996). Traditional key ratio analysis versus data envelopment analysis: A comparison of various measurements of productivity and efficiency in restaurants. Productivity Management in Hospitality and Tourism (pp. 209-226). London: Cassell.

Andersson, T. D. and Hartman, T. E. (1995). Productivity and efficiency in restaurants: A data envelopment approach. The Journal of Hospitality Financial Management, 4(1): 1-20.

Baker, M. and Riley, M. (1994). New perspectives on productivity in hotels: Some advances and new directions. International Journal of Hospitality Management, 13(4): 297-311.

Ball, S. D., Johnson, K. and Slattery, P. (1986). Labor productivity in hotels: An empirical study. International Journal of Hospitality Management, 5(3): 141-147.

Banker, R. D. and Morey, R. C. (1986). Efficiency analysis for exogenously fixed inputs and outputs. Operations Research, 34: 513-521.

Barr, R., Seiford, L. and Siems, T. (1992). An envelopment analysis approach to measuring the managerial quality of banks. Technical report 91 CSE-22, Department of Computer Science and Engineering, Southern Methodist University. Annals of Operations Research, 32: 21-34.

Boussofiane, A., Dyson, R. G. and Thanassoulis, E. (1991). Applied data envelopment analysis. European Journal of Operational Research, 52: 1-15.

Brown, J. R. and Dev, C. S. (1999). Looking beyond RevPAR. Cornell Hotel and Restaurant Quarterly, 40(2): 23-33.

Bucklin, L. P. (1978). Productivity in Marketing. Chicago: American Marketing Association.

Coelli, T., Rao, D. S. P. and Battese, G. E. (1997). An Introduction to Efficiency and Productivity Analysis. Boston: Kluwer Academic Publishers Group.

Charnes, A., Cooper, W. W. and Rhodes, E. (1978). Measuring the efficiency of decision making units. European Journal of Operational Research, 2: 429-444.

Clark, J. and Kirk, D. (1997). Relationship between labor productivity and factors of production in hospital and hotel foodservice departments–empirical evidence of a typology of food production systems. Journal of Foodservice System, 10: 23-39.

David, J. S., Grabski, S. and Kasavana, M. (1996). The productivity paradox of hotel-industry technology. Cornell Hotel and Restaurant Administration Quarterly, 37(2): 64-70.

Dean, E. R. and Kunze, K. (1992). Productivity measurement in service industries. In Z. Griliches (Ed.), Output Measurement in the Service Sectors (pp. 73-108). Chicago: The University of Chicago Press.

Donthu, N. and Yoo, B. (1998). Retail productivity assessment using data envelopment analysis. Journal of Retailing, 74(1): 89-105.

Dyson, R. G., Thanassoulis, E. and Boussofiane, A. (1995). A DEA (Data Envelopment Analysis) Tutorial [On-line]. Available: www.warwick.ac.uk/~bsrlu/dea/deat/deat1.htm

Elsworth, J. D. (2000). Determinants of wages in the food service industry. In D. F. Cannon (Ed.), Advances in Hospitality and Tourism Research: Vol. 6. Proceedings of the Sixth Annual Graduate Education and Graduate Student Research Conference in Hospitality and Tourism (pp. 142-149). Atlanta, Georgia: Georgia State University.

Farrell, M. J. (1957). The measurement of productive efficiency. Journal of Royal Statistical Society, Series A 120: 253-290.

Fizel, J. L. and Nunnikhoven T. S. (1993). The efficiency of nursing home chains. Applied Economics, 25: 49-55.

Fletcher, J. and Snee, H. (1985). The need for output measurements in service industries: A comment. Service Industries Journal, 5(1): 73-78.

Forsund, F. R. and Hernaes, A. (1990). Ferry in Norway: An application of DEA analysis. W. P. SAF Oslo, 15.

Jones, P. and Hall, M. (1996). Productivity and the new service paradigm, or servicity and the "neo-service paradigm. In N. Johns, (Ed.), Managing Productivity in Hospitality and Tourism (pp. 227-240). London: Cassell.

Hartman, T. and Storbeck, J. E. (1994). Efficiency in Swedish banking: An analysis of loan operations. Paper presented at the Eighth International Seminar on Production Economics in Igls, Austria. In Pre-prints, Linkoping University of Technology, Sweden.

Lee, J. Y. (1991). Measuring productivity for service firms: It's tricky, but it can be done. Business Forum, 16(2): 11-14.

Lee-Ross, D. (1994). Increasing productivity in small hotels: Are academic proposals realistic? International Journal of Hospitality Management, 13(3): 201-207.

McMahon, F. (1994). Productivity in the hotel industry. In A. V. Seaton (Ed.), Tourism: The State of the Art (pp. 616-625). Chichester, England: Wiley.

Neter, J., Hutner, M. H., Nachtsheim, C. J. and Wasserman, W. (1996). Applied Linear Statistical Models (4th Edition). Chicago: The McGraw-Hill Companies, Inc.

Nyman, J. (1988). Excess demand, the percentage of medicaid patients and the quality of nursing home care. Journal of Human Resources, 23: 76-92.

Nyman, J. A. and Bricker, D. L. (1989). Profit incentives and technical efficiency in the production of nursing home care. The Review of Economics and Statistics, 71: 586-594.

Pickworth, J. R. (1987). Minding the P's and Q's: Linking quality and productivity. Cornell Hotel and Restaurant Quarterly, 28(1): 40-47.

Prais, S. J., Jarvis, V. and Wagner, K. (1989). Productivity and vocational skills in services in Britain and Germany: Hotels. National Institute Economic Review, 11: 52-74.

Quek, P. (2000). Controlling labor costs [On-line]. Available: http://www.hotel-online.com/Neo/Trends/PKF/Special/LaborCosts_Feb00.html

Reid, R. and Sandler, M. (1992). The use of technology to improve service quality. Cornell Hotel and Restaurant Administration Quarterly, 33(3): 68-73.

Reynolds, D. (1998). Productivity analysis: In the on-site food-service segment. Cornell Hotel and Restaurant Administration Quarterly, 39(3): 22-31.

Rimmington, M. and Clark G. (1996). Productivity measurement in food service systems. In N. Johns (Ed.), Productivity Management in Hospitality and Tourism (pp. 194-208). London: Cassell.

Schroeder, R. G. (1985). Operations Management: Decision Making in Operation Function, 2nd ed., New York: McGraw-Hill.

Seiford, L. M. (1996). Data envelopment analysis: The evolution of the state of the art (1978-1995). Journal of Productivity Analysis, 7: 99-137.

Soteriou, A. C. and Zenios, S. A. (1998). Data envelopment analysis: An introduction and an application to bank branch performance assessment. Modern Methods in Business Research. Mahwah, NJ: Lawrence Erlbaum Associates.

Walker, J. R. (1999). Introduction to Hospitality. Upper Saddle River, NJ: Prentice Hall.

Witt, C. A. and Witt, S. F. (1989). Why productivity in the hotel sector is low. International Journal of Contemporary Hospitality Management, 1(2): 28-34.

Using Data Envelopment Analysis for Measuring and Benchmarking Productivity in the Hotel Sector

Marianna Sigala

SUMMARY. Low productivity within the hospitality industry has been a major concern, but this situation is unlikely to improve without a general change in the way productivity is measured and managed. This paper aims to illustrate the value of stepwise Data Envelopment Analysis (DEA) for measuring and benchmarking hotel productivity. The issues regarding productivity measurement as well as the advantages of using DEA for measuring productivity are analysed. However, the paper extends current DEA applications by developing a stepwise approach to DEA. The latter technique combines correlation and DEA analysis for developing robust DEA models and its advantages are illustrated by applying it in a dataset of three star hotels in the UK. *[Article copies available for a fee from The Haworth Document Delivery Service: 1-800-HAWORTH. E-mail address: <docdelivery@haworthpress.com> Website: <http://www.HaworthPress.com> © 2004 by The Haworth Press, Inc. All rights reserved.]*

KEYWORDS. Productivity, measurement, benchmarking, stepwise Data Envelopment Analysis

INTRODUCTION

Comparatively low productivity within the hospitality industry has been identified as a source of concern by a number of authors (McKinsey Global Institute, 1998; Witt & Witt, 1989; Johns & Wheeler, 1991). However, this situation is unlikely to improve without a general change in the way productivity is managed within the industry (Johns, Howcroft & Drake, 1997), but productivity management requires regular monitoring, measurement and benchmarking. Although there have been some attempts to identify satisfactory productivity monitoring procedures (e.g., Ball, Johnson & Slattery, 1986), these have been heavily criticised and no generally accepted means of productivity measurement exists in the hotel sector (Brown & Dev, 1999).

This paper aims to develop and illustrate the value of stepwise Data Envelopment Analysis (DEA) for measuring and benchmarking hotel productivity. To that end, after reviewing the issues regarding productivity measurement both in general terms and specifically within the hospitality industry, the paper debates the advantages of DEA relative to other frequently used productivity measurement methods. However, the paper extends current applications of DEA on productivity measurement and benchmarking by developing a stepwise model of DEA. The latter combines correla-

Marianna Sigala is affiliated with The Business Administration Department, University of Aegean, Chios, Greece (E-mail: m.sigala@aegean.gr).

[Haworth co-indexing entry note]: "Using Data Envelopment Analysis for Measuring and Benchmarking Productivity in the Hotel Sector." Sigala, Marianna. Co-published simultaneously in *Journal of Travel & Tourism Marketing* (The Haworth Hospitality Press, an imprint of The Haworth Press, Inc.) Vol. 16, No. 2/3, 2004, pp. 39-60; and: *Management Science Applications in Tourism and Hospitality* (ed: Zheng Gu) The Haworth Hospitality Press, an imprint of The Haworth Press, Inc., 2004, pp. 39-60. Single or multiple copies of this article are available for a fee from The Haworth Document Delivery Service [1-800-HAWORTH, 9:00 a.m. - 5:00 p.m. (EST). E-mail address: docdelivery@haworthpress.com].

http://www.haworthpress.com/web/JTTM
© 2004 by The Haworth Press, Inc. All rights reserved.
Digital Object Identifier: 10.1300/J073v16n02_04

tion and DEA analysis and its advantages for measuring productivity in the hotel industry are illustrated by applying it in a dataset from the three star hotel sector in the UK.

DEFINING AND MEASURING PRODUCTIVITY

The concept of productivity has been extensively researched in the manufacturing sector. For example, Schroeder (1985) defined productivity as the relationship between inputs and outputs of a productive system. Considering productivity in the hospitality industry, several authors based their approach on this original concept. Ritzer's (in Jones & Hall, 1996) concept of McDonaldization highlighted efficiency and predictability, Levitt (1972) talked about the "industrialisation" or "production-lining" of service, Dilworth (1989) defined productivity as the ratio of all outputs over all inputs, while Jones and Hall (1996) argued that the current thinking of productivity stems from and is a construct of the "manufacturing paradigm" developed during the Fordist period. However, Sigala (2002) questioned whether productivity should be approached differently in services and manufacturing, because in the knowledge era the distinction between products and services is blurred; services are increasingly being industrialised while products informalised.

Although the concept of productivity seems to receive approval from everyone, it is still rare that productivity has been defined satisfactorily and in fact, a widely accepted productivity definition cannot be found in the literature (Brown & Dev, 1999). Productivity means different things to different people, which is reflected in the different or even conflicting definitions and perceptions of productivity (Pickworth, 1987). Indeed, people have varying backgrounds, positions of responsibility, and goals, and so the way they conceive productivity and set about improving it is largely a reflection of their disciplinary predispositions, e.g., management, behavioural science or economics. In reviewing the productivity concept, Sigala (2002) argued that productivity has been approached both as an umbrella concept including efficiency, effectiveness, quality, predictability and other performance dimensions as well as a concept reflecting only production efficiency.

Confusion and disagreement over the concept and definition of productivity create difficulties in productivity measurement and vice versa, the numerous productivity measurements also lead to disagreement and confusion over the concept of productivity (Mahoney, 1988). Thus, some measurements relate to efficiency of performance (e.g., cost per unit, output per employee), other measurements relate to outcomes (e.g., sales, customer satisfaction) reflecting effectiveness. While efficiency measures show whether an organization is doing things in the right way, they do not indicate effectiveness and so, whether the organization is doing the right things.

Andersson (1996) identified three difficulties in measuring productivity, namely identification of the appropriate: inputs and outputs; measures of those inputs and outputs; ways of measuring the relationship between inputs and outputs. Productivity measurement in hospitality in particular faces additional difficulties due to the specific characteristics of its service nature that in turn create problems such as labour and process scheduling, consistency and demand (Witt & Witt, 1989). Indeed, several authors (Sasser, Olsen & Wyckoff, 1978; Jones & Lockwood, 1989; Witt & Witt, 1989; Jones, 1988) argued that productivity management and measurement has been limited in the hospitality sector by the features and characteristics of services. Specifically, the intangible nature of hospitality services suggests that it is difficult to objectively define and measure the service outputs being provided (e.g., number of guest-nights versus number of satisfied guests). The measurement and management of hospitality inputs and outputs is also complicated because of the simultaneous production and consumption of the hospitality services as well as their perishability and heterogeneity, as service encounters are experienced differently by different people or even by the same people at different circumstances. For example, in a hotel stay, only the physical items can be easily measured and controlled, while many of the other features of the hotel experience, such as service and atmosphere, are intangible. Moreover, because each transaction with each customer can be regarded as unique, a quality challenge is created.

In summary, Jones and Lockwood (1989) explained that productivity measurement and management in services is extremely difficult because: inputs and outputs are difficult to standardise (mainly due to the unique nature of service transactions); input/output relationships are not constant (not standardised between units or departments); inputs and outputs may be difficult to measure (due to their variability and intangibility). In this vein, Witt and Witt (1989) identified three problems regarding productivity measurement in hospitality which are compatible to those identified by Andersson (1996): the "definition problem"; the "measurement problem"; and the "ceteris paribus" problem.

The definition problem refers to those difficulties encountered when attempting to define precisely what are the outputs and inputs of a given industry, which is particularly difficult when the outputs/inputs are intangible or are highly heterogeneous. Thus, the definition problem is similar to the problem of identifying the right inputs and outputs. The measurement problem was described as the problem encountered when outputs/inputs can be defined but cannot be measured. However, even if outputs/inputs can be measured in some way, there may be problems in terms of using suitable units of measurement. The "ceteris paribus" problem involves holding the other influences constant when examining the impact of a particular factor on productivity. Productivity in hotels may be said to be a function of several factors both internal/controllable (e.g., type and classification of hotel) and external/uncontrollable (e.g., demand levels) to the hotel. Thus, comparisons of productivity metrics can be misleading unless "other factors" are held constant. Sigala (2002) illustrated that the way of relating inputs and outputs can be used to address the "ceteris paribus" problem.

The following analysis reviews the theoretical debates regarding the three difficulties in productivity measurement in order to identify and clarify the issues that a robust productivity metric and method should address.

Selecting Outputs and Inputs

Sigala (2002) illustrated that the selection of inputs/outputs refers and needs to deal with two issues: the approach to productivity definition, namely partial or total approach; the identification of the level and/or unit of analysis. Partial productivity metrics focus on specific inputs that can be easily identified and measured. However, because of the synergy between all inputs as well as the fact that hospitality inputs/outputs are amalgams of tangible and intangible/qualitative elements, a multi-factor (Chew, 1986) or total factor view to productivity is proposed that takes into account all inputs as well as the structural complexity of hospitality outputs/inputs, owning to the typical intangibility, perishability, heterogeneity and simultaneity characteristics of services (Mahoney, 1988). Indeed, because in the long-term, customer satisfaction is perhaps the most important service output, intangible elements that are an intrinsic part of the service experience, such as management style, staff flair and expertise, should undoubtedly consist crucial components of both productivity inputs and outputs.

Productivity measurement becomes even more complex when one also examines the array of factors (e.g., aesthetics, ergonomics) that face managers attempting to enhance their companies' productivity. In summary, research revealed that productivity can be significantly impacted by the following major factors (Johns et al., 1997; National Economic Development Council, 1992; Van der Hoeven & Thurik, 1984; Brown & Dev, 1999; McKinsey Global Institute, 1998; Cizmar & Weber, 2000; Sigala, 2002): hotel size, location, service orientation, ownership and management arrangement; hotel age, design, type and number of facilities; demand patterns; staff flexibility (reflected in the use of part-time and full-time employees); marketing practices (e.g., distribution, promotion, frequent guest programs) effectiveness. It has been argued that such factors, acknowledged as "upstream" factors (Rimmington & Clark, 1996) or "top-line" factors (Heap, 1992) should be included in productivity definition and measurement.

Overall, there is no conclusive agreement to whether total factor productivity refers to: the inclusion of all inputs and outputs rather than the consideration of each input at a time (partial measures); the measurement of both tangible and intangible features of inputs/outputs regardless whether partial or total productivity ratios are calculated; the consideration of other factors that may be external to the control of management but can crucially affect productivity, e.g., level of competition, location; or to the consideration of all the previous factors or a combination of them. Nevertheless, such conflicting approaches clearly indicate and highlight the issues that should be taken into account when constructing and interpreting productivity measurement metrics. Although the importance of using a total approach to productivity has been highlighted, authors have simultaneously stressed the difficulty for one metric to encompass all different measured factors. In other words, the definition problem is closely interrelated to the other two measurement problems.

The selection of appropriate outputs/inputs is also related to the level and unit of analysis. Depending on what is the focus of analysis (e.g., hotel department, product, market segment) relevant inputs/outputs should be used (Johns & Wheeler, 1991). Aggregated input/output metrics can be disaggregated at any level in order to construct a whole "family"/"hierarchy" of partial productivity ratios. However, aggregated metrics tend to obscure information, whereas partial measures tend to hide information and trade-offs among other dimensions (e.g., departments, resources). The latter can be overcome by considering partial metrics simultaneously, but this is very laborious and sometimes may lead to conflicting results (Baker & Riley, 1994).

To overcome limitations of partial and aggregated metrics, Brown and Dev (1999) suggested that the unit of analysis should be modified from product-oriented measures to customer-oriented measures, e.g., productivity measurement at an even lower level of analysis and disaggregate inputs/outputs at the individual customer level. Sigala (2002) also advocated that revenue per available customer (RevPAC) is a crucial productivity measure for hotels in the information era, because as technological developments have enabled hotels to personally serve, satisfy and keep their most valuable customers, hotels should change the way they measure themselves. On the other hand, traditional ways in which hotels gauge performance (e.g., revenue per available room) reflect their historic roots and basic orientation to creating values, as the industry's fundamental structure and value proposition was long-based on physical assets (hotel rooms) as the driver of wealth.

Selecting Measurement Units of Inputs/Outputs

Ball et al. (1986) identified three main categories of measurement units, namely financial, physical and a combination of the previous two. Both financial and physical units have been used in previous studies. For example, in developing their DEA model, Johns et al. (1997) used simple inputs and outputs, no ratios or composite data were employed, and non-financial data was preferred. Specifically the following three outputs and five inputs were used: number of room nights sold, total covers served and total beverage revenue; and number of room nights available, total labour hours, total food costs, total beverage costs and total utilities cost. Anderson, Fish, Xia, and Michello (1999) used a stochastic frontier analysis in order to measure the performance of 48 hotels by using four outputs (total revenue generated from rooms, gaming, food and beverage and other revenues) and five inputs (number of full time equivalent employees, the number of rooms, total gaming related expenses, total food and beverage expenses and other expenses).

Sigala (2002) illustrated that the conceptualisation of productivity influence the use of units measuring productivity inputs/outputs. Specifically, it is generally agreed that quantitative physical measures reflect a quantitative approach to productivity that equates productivity with production efficiency only (Andersson, 1996), while a total factor approach would require more sophisticated and qualitative measures. However, there are arguments supporting the view that the truly quantitative, aggregate, "broad" measures (e.g., profit, sales) implicitly encapsulate intangible qualitative performance (Rimmington & Clark, 1996; Johns & Wheeler, 1991). This is for two reasons. First, only if the intangibles are as they should be will customer levels be sustained and income earned. Secondly, only if the tangibles are as they should be will income and costs be controlled in such a way that profit is produced at the required rate in relation to the capital employed.

Ways of Measuring the Relationship Between Inputs and Outputs

The complexity of the relationship between inputs and outputs is affected by both the number of inputs/outputs as well as their measurement units, because different combinations between number and types of units can result in a huge number of productivity metrics each one having its own information value and reflecting different things. In fact, there are several ways of comparing inputs and outputs. The most commonly used in the hospitality sector are ratio analysis, multi-factor ratios and regression analysis (Sigala, 2002), but their major limitations is their inefficiency in simultaneously handling multiple inputs and outputs. However, given the number of possible productivity measurements, there is a need to condense several measurements into a single productivity metric through multidimensional analysis that can combine two or more key ratios into one measurement. Moreover, the productivity metric that would take into consideration multiple inputs and outputs should be computed in a way that it does not directly relate certain inputs with outputs but it would rather highlight the interrelationships and trade-off between all of them.

To achieve that a technique called Data Envelopment Analysis (DEA) has been heavily applied, DEA is a powerful non-parametric, multivariate, multiple linear programming technique that benchmarks units by comparing their ratios of multiple inputs to produce multiple outputs at the same time (Charnes, Cooper & Rhodes, 1978; Charnes, Cooper, Lewin & Seiford, 1994). DEA constructs a frontier function in a piecewise linear approach by comparing like units (the decision-making units, DMU) with like taken from the observed dataset. Since DEA uses the production units that are "best in its class" as reference material, the method is very much in line with the basic ideas underlying the concept of benchmarking (Al-Faraj, Alidi & Bu-Bhsait, 1993). Overall, DEA's advantages relative to the previous techniques are summarised as follows (Cooper, Seiford & Tone, 2000; Sengupta, 1988; Banker & Thrall, 1992):

- It provides a comprehensive productivity evaluation as it generates a single aggregate score by comparing simultaneously multiple inputs and outputs of comparable units and using a benchmark of 100% efficiency;
- It is independent of the units of measurement allowing flexibility in specifying inputs/outputs to be studied;
- It objectively assesses the "importance" of the various performance attributes;
- It evaluates each entity in the best possible light–all alternative priorities will reduce performance;
- It calculates efficiency based on observed best practice–not against an "average" or "ideal" model;
- Best practices are identified;
- No functional relationship between inputs and outputs needs to be prespecified;
- Inefficient DMUs are identified as well as the sources and amounts of their inefficiency. Thus, DEA answers both questions: *"how well a unit is doing"*; *"which dimension and how much could the unit improve"*;
- DEA can identify economies of scale and take them into account.

DEA can also consider external factors that can affect productivity overcoming in some extent the "ceteris paribus" problem. Dyson, Thanassoulis and Boussofiane (1990) also argued that a key aspect of DEA is the incorporation of environmental factors into the model. Banker and Thrall (1992) distinguished between controllable and uncontrollable inputs (e.g., demand levels, competition) in order to measure and interpret performance in the context of uncontrollable environmental conditions. Avkiran (1999) highlighted that failure to account for environmental factors is likely to confound the DEA results and lead to unreliable analysis. Norman and Stoker (1991) argued that DEA models not including demand factors measure production efficiency only, while DEA models including demand factors also reflect market efficiency referring to the ability to control production efficiency given the demand factors.

However, the reliability and benefits of DEA are as good as the inputs/outputs that it uses. Sengupta (1988) introduced a useful way for selecting and using appropriate inputs/outputs in DEA analysis, which is called stepwise approach to DEA and is based on stepwise regression. The stepwise approach is an iterative procedure in which productivity is measured in terms of the important factors identified up to that step (Figure 1). Other important factors are identified by examining factors that correlate with the measure of efficiency and applying judgments in terms of cause and effect. Then, these factors are incorporated into the DEA model and the process is repeated until no further important factors emerge. At that stage, a metric accounting for all the identifiable factors that influence productivity is constructed.

In their study, Parkin and Hollingsworth (1997) also proposed and used a stepwise DEA approach by correlating potential variables with DEA efficiency scores in order to validate and get their DEA model specification. A stepwise approach also helps to interpret why particular units are efficient. A table of the efficiency scores of the units at each step can be produced whereby the efficient units introduced at each step can be separated. Basically, the units found to become efficient from one step to another are efficient because of the incorporation of the respective inputs/outputs in the step they were found to be efficient.

FIGURE 1. Stepwise Approach to DEA

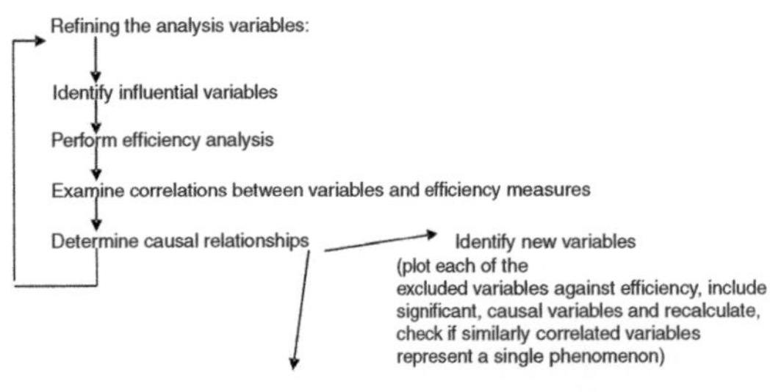

DEA has been extensively used for performance and productivity benchmarking (Al-Shammari & Salimi, 1998; Chatzoglou and Soteriou, 1999) in various industries (Avkiran, 1999), the hotel industry included (e.g., Morey & Dittman, 1995; Johns et al., 1997; Avkiran, 1999; Anderson, Fok & Scott, 2000; Tarim, Dener & Tarim, 2000; Wöber, 2000, 2002; Sigala & Christou, 2001). However, the present paper extends previous applications by proposing a stepwise approach to DEA for identifying the appropriate DEA inputs/outputs and developing robust DEA models.

RESEARCH AIMS AND METHODOLOGY

Research Aims, Instrument and Sample Design

The main purpose of this paper is to develop and illustrate the value of using the stepwise DEA approach for developing robust productivity models and then determining appropriate productivity improvement strategies. A productivity model is considered as robust when it constructs productivity frontiers by identifying and simultaneously considering the multiple factors that can significantly determine productivity. The advantages, validity and value of this technique for productivity measurement and management are tested and illustrated by gathering data from the three star hotel sector in the UK. By focusing on a specific sector, contextual factors and business operational characteristics that could also have an impact on productivity are eliminated.

A structured questionnaire gathering information regarding several inputs, outputs and factors that can affect productivity in the hotel sector was developed. For ensuring consistency amongst respondents, all data were asked to refer to the financial year ending 1999. The questionnaire was also piloted with six hotel managers for testing its reliability and validity. Specifically, the format, wording and variables of the questions were pre-tested in order to ensure a mutual understanding between the researcher and the respondent. As a result, some fine-tuning was conducted in order to enhance the quality and accuracy of the research instrument, e.g., the term independent and consortia management was replaced with independent management and consortia membership and annual hotel profit with annual profit before fixed charges to enhance clarity.

In developing the study's sample, initially, the Automobile Association's hotel directory was used for compiling a random sample of 300 full service three star hotels in the UK. Hotel managers were targeted by a mail survey in June 2000. However, despite the use of a pre-paid envelope, a covering letter assuring managers for data confidentiality and a follow-up, the mail survey achieved a very low response rate (12 responses), mainly due to the sensitivity of the data required. To increase responses, contacts with consultancy companies, individual hotels, chains and consortia were used in order to identify potential hotels willing to participate in the study and provide information. The names of the latter cannot be identified due to confidentiality reasons. Overall, 93 questionnaires were received out of 1,233 hotels contacted.

Stepwise DEA Methodology for Constructing Robust DEA Productivity Models

As previously mentioned, in developing a productivity metric the first steps involve the selection of inputs/outputs and their measurement units, which in turn requires the identification of the approach and the level/unit at which the productivity analysis is undertaken. Concerning the approach to productivity definition, given the limitations of partial productivity metrics, this study adopted a total factor approach meaning that the productivity concept incorporated both efficiency and effectiveness dimensions. To achieve that, the productivity metric included all factors of production as well as other factors that may affect productivity. Moreover, a great variety of inputs/outputs was used including both financial and physical measurement units in order to encapsulate both tangible and intangible aspects of productivity inputs and outputs.

The study aimed to measure productivity of hotel properties and so, productivity inputs/outputs were identified and measured at the organisational level. However, because hotels are made up of different departments, with different characteristics and so with different factors determining their productivity (Baker & Riley, 1994; Johns & Wheeler, 1991), an aggregate productivity metric and model may obscure and hide trade-offs among productivity variables. To overcome this, productivity metrics were calculated both at the organisational as well as at two departmental levels. Specifically, the stepwise DEA was first applied to rooms and F&B division separately in order to identify the specific disaggregated productivity inputs and outputs that determine productivity in these two divisions. Subsequently, the latter were compiled into a single DEA model that in turn represented the hotel property overall productivity metric. So in this way, hotel property productivity was not constructed by using inputs/outputs aggregated at an organisational level that can obscure and hide productivity effects.

Table 1 summarises the productivity inputs/outputs and factors that were considered in the stepwise DEA process. The selection and use of these measures are justifiable and compatible with previous studies, which are also identified in Table 1.

The final step of productivity measurement requires the selection of a way to relate the productivity inputs and outputs. To achieve that, DEA was adopted by using the *Frontier Analyst 2* software package. However, as DEA's validity and reliability depend on the selection of appropriate inputs and outputs, a stepwise DEA approach was followed for identifying those inputs/outputs that significantly determine productivity and developing a robust DEA productivity model. To that end, the first step involved the calculation of a DEA score for each hotel by using aggregated inputs and outputs. DEA scores were then correlated (Pearson correlations, $\alpha = 0.05$) with disaggregated inputs/outputs for distinguishing those determining productivity. When significant correlations were found and a cause and effect relation existed, disaggregated inputs/outputs were included into the DEA model and the relevant aggregated data were adjusted. Finally, a robust DEA model was concluded

TABLE 1. Productivity Inputs, Outputs and Factors Influencing Productivity

Hotel productivity inputs included: number of full time employees in front office, housekeeping, F&B, telephone/switchboard, administrative and general, minor operations, marketing, maintenance and other; the number of heads and/or managers of departments; the number of information technology technicians; total number of part time employees; annual expenditure regarding direct material expenses, payroll and related expenses and/or other expenses; annual expenditure was also broken down in the following: hotel divisions front office, housekeeping, F&B, telephone/switchboard, minor operations, administrative and general, marketing, maintenance and training on ICT; annual energy expenses; annual management fees.

Hotel productivity outputs included: average room occupancy; average room rate (ARR); roomnights achieved; restaurant covers; banquet covers; hotel profit before fixed charges; hotel revenue; percentage of hotel revenue corresponding to the following departments: rooms division; F&B; minor operations; and telephone/switchboard.

Factors and their metrics that previous studies found to influence productivity included:

- location: rural, city centre or suburban (TRI Hospitality Consulting, 2002; McKinsey Global Institute, 1998; National Economic Development Council, 1992; Johns et al., 1997).
- hotel design: old/traditional, redesigned/converted, purpose built (McKinsey Global Institute, 1998).
- ownership structure: independently or chain owned (Johns et al., 1997; Brown & Dev, 1999).
- management arrangement: independent management, chain management, independent management and consortia membership, franchise (NEDC, 1992; Van der Hoeven & Thurik, 1984; Brown & Dev, 1999; McKinsey Global Institute, 1998; Sigala, 2002).
- demand variability was calculated by asking respondents to characterize fluctuations in business both over the year as well as over the week as greatly, somewhat or not at all. Responses were scored (1 = greatly, 2 = somewhat and not at all = 3) and an overall score of business variability was calculated by multiplying the score of demand variability per year with the score of business variability per week. The higher score was chosen to correspond to little demand variability because of the following reason. Theoretically, the lower the variability the higher the productivity (outputs). DEA models treat demand variability as an uncontrollable input. However, because in DEA, higher values of inputs should relate to higher values of outputs, that meant that higher values of demand variability (i.e., lower demand fluctuations) should lead to higher outputs (National Economic Development Council, 1992; Sigala, 2002).
- a percentage of repeat guests (Cizmar & Weber, 2000).
- average length of stay: number of days (Sigala, 2002; National Economic Development Council, 1992; McKinsey Global Institute, 1998).
- market segments served: percentages of total roomnights referring to business, leisure, conference travelers and/or other (TRI Hospitality Consulting, 2002; Van der Hoeven & Thurik, 1984).
- distribution channels: percentages of total reservations received through a property owned system (e.g., telephone), third parties and Internet (Sigala, 2002; Sigala et al., 2001; O' Connor, 2002).
- part time staff: percentage of total payroll expenses referring to full time staff as well as the number of full time and part time staff employed in their property (McKinsey Global Institute, 1998; National Economic Development Council, 1992; Sigala, 2002).
- hotel size: number of rooms, bedspaces, banquet capacity and restaurant seats (Johns et al., 1997; National Economic Development Council, 1992; Van der Hoeven & Thurik, 1984; Brown & Dev, 1999; McKinsey Global Institute, 1998; TRI Hospitality Consulting, 2002).

Inputs/outputs used in previous studies:

Johns et al. (1997). Outputs: number of rooms sold, total covers served; total beverage revenue. Inputs: number of roomnights available, total labor hours, total F&B costs, total utilities costs.

Anderson et al. (1999). Outputs: total revenue generated from rooms, gaming, F&B and other revenues. Inputs: FTEE, number of rooms, total gaming related expenses, total F&B expenses other expenses.

Avkiran (1999). Outputs: revenue and cost of a double room. Inputs: number of full time, permanent part time and casual staff, total bed capacity and largest meeting capacity

Morey and Dittman (1995). Outputs: total room revenue, average level of guest satisfaction. Inputs: number of rooms, rooms division expenditure, average occupancy rate, average daily rate for a group of competitors (uncontrollable input)

Ball et al. (1986). Revenue/FTEE, covers/FTEE

Brown and Dev (1999). Total annual sales per number of FTEE, gross operating profit per FTEE, income before fixed charges per FTEE.

Baker and Riley (1994). Added value per full time employee, sales per full-time employee and F&B sales per full time employee.

when no other inputs/outputs were found to affect the DEA productivity score. At that stage, a robust productivity metric is constructed, as all potential factors that could have affected productivity had been taken into account and only those that had a significant impact were included in the DEA model. Moreover, because of that, productivity differences between hotels can be attributed to factors that the stepwise DEA analysis has not so far considered.

ANALYSIS OF THE FINDINGS

Profile of Respondents

Respondents consist a sample representing the diversity of the three star hotel sector in the UK (Table 2). Indeed, 51.6% of respondents were independently owned with the remaining being owned by a hotel chain. Concerning management arrangement, 47% of respondents were managed by a hotel chain, 28% were independently managed while 18% represent independents that were also members of a consortium. Moreover, 39.7% of respondents were located in the city center, fewer (34.4%) in rural and 25.8% in suburban places. Concerning hotel size and operation, respondents' room capacity varied from 18 to 283 rooms (average 90.4 rooms), number of restaurant seats ranged from 20 to 300 seats (average 109.4 seats) and banqueting capacity from 0 to 600 covers. Statistics regarding number of employees revealed a similar diversity of size of operations; minimum numbers of full time and part time employees were reported as 4 and 2 respectively, while maximum numbers were 143 to 155 respectively. Regarding the market segments served by respondents, on average 47.1% of the annual roomnights were from business guests, 36.8% from leisure guests, 11.3% from conference and only 4.3% from other guests, but the high standard deviations revealed that several re-

TABLE 2. Respondents' Profile

Ownership structure	**N**	**%**	**Management arrangement**	**N**	**%**
Independently owned	48	51.61	Independent management	28	30.11
Chain owned	45	48.39	Chain management	47	50.54
			Independent management and consortia membership	18	19.35
Location	**N**	**%**	**Design**	**N**	**%**
Rural	32	34.40	Old and/or traditional	31	33.33
City centre	37	39.78	Redesigned/converted	25	26.88
Suburban	24	25.81	Purpose built	37	39.79
Number of:	**Min**	**Max**	**Mean**	**Std. Deviation**	
Rooms	18	283	90.419	65.005	
Restaurant seats	20	300	109.408	48.316	
Banqueting covers	0	600	191.311	149.823	
Full time employees	4	143	50.817	38.012	
Part time employees	2	155	38.924	35.441	
Percentage of roomnights from:	**Min**	**Max**	**Mean**	**Std. Deviation**	
Business guests	0	90	47.153	21.349	
Leisure guests	2	90	36.841	23.810	
Conference guests	0	47	11.831	10.464	
Other guests	0	50	4.344	8.229	
% of reservations taken through:	**Min**	**Max**	**Mean**	**Std. Deviation**	
Property owned system	37	90	69.467	12.237	
Third parties	5	62.8	26.658	12.088	
Internet	0	20	3.411	4.215	
% of annual roomnights representing repeat customers	9	80	36.946	18.990	

spondents significantly differed from average values. Repeat customers represented on average 36.9% of annual roomnights, while respondents received a great majority of their annual reservations (69.4%) through property owned systems, fewer reservations (26.6%) from third parties and only 3.4% from the Internet. Great demand variations were also reported (average score 7.2).

Construction and Analysis of DEA Productivity Models

Productivity Measurement in Rooms Division

Table 3 illustrates the application of the stepwise DEA approach in rooms division, while Table 4 provides the DEA scores obtained for each hotel at the different steps. To ensure the validity of the DEA model specification, the following procedures were undertaken. Because inputs and outputs used in DEA should satisfy the condition that greater quantities of inputs provide increased output, the appropriateness of the inputs and outputs included at step 1 was tested by conducting an isotonicity test (Chen, 1997). An isotonicity test involves the calculations of all intercorrelations between inputs and outputs for identifying whether increasing amounts of inputs lead to greater outputs. Avkiran (1999, p. 50) also illustrated how intra-correlations among inputs and outputs can be used for identifying appropriate DEA variables. As positive intercorrelations were found (Pearson correlations, $\alpha = 0.05$), the isotonicity test was passed and the inclusion of the inputs and the outputs at step 1 was justified. DEA models assumed constant returns to scale, but their validity was tested by correlating the DEA scores obtained at all steps with a metric reflecting size of operation (number of rooms),

TABLE 3. Input and Output Metrics Included in the Stepwise DEA in Rooms Division

	Step 1 (input min)	Step 2 (input min)	Step 3 (input min)	Step 4 (output max)
Outputs				
Non-F&B total revenue	*			
ARR		*	*	***(48.2%)**
Roomnights		*	*	***(41%)**
Non-roomnights revenue		*	*	***(32.3%)**
Inputs				
Rooms	*	*	*	***(5.4%)**
Rooms division total payroll	*	*		
Rooms division total non-payroll expenses (material and other)	*	*		
Front office payroll			*	***(16.3%)**
Administration non-payroll expenses (material and other)			*	***(28.5%)**
Other rooms division payroll			*	***(12.1%)**
Other rooms division non-payroll (material and other)			*	***(8%)**
Total demand variability				***N.A.**
Other inputs/outputs and factors correlated with DEA scores in all steps				
DEA inputs: % of reservations from: property based reservation system, third parties and Internet; length of stay; number of: full time staff; part time staff; IT staff; managers; full time staff in: rooms division, front office, housekeeping, telephone, administration, marketing, minor operations; % of payroll for full time staff; payroll and material and other expenses in: front office, housekeeping, telephone, minor operations, marketing, administration. **DEA outputs:** % of roomnights from: repeat customers, business, leisure, conference and other; occupancy; ARR; total roomnights; non-FB revenue (revenue from minor operations + revenue from telephone); hotel profit; rooms division revenue; non-rooms division revenue.				

Non-F&B total revenue refers all hotel revenue except of revenue obtained from the FB division, i.e. it includes revenue from roomnights, telephone and minor operations.
Non-roomnights revenue refers to revenue obtained from telephone and minor operations.
Minor operations include activities such as laundry services, souvenirs' sales, that in three star hotel properties occupy staff from the rooms divisions department.
*Indicates that a variable is included in the DEA model.

TABLE 4. DEA Scores in Rooms Division

Hotel	Step 1	Step 2	Step 3	Step 4	Hotel	Step 1	Step 2	Step 3	Step 4
1	32.47	47.99	53.14	100	50	51.73	68.39	68.39	85.9
2	16.22	30.69	37.91	44.97	51	100	100	100	100
3	37.73	53.99	54.08	72.08	52	21.37	47.57	47.57	50.92
4	32.59	44.41	44.53	100	53	48.09	59.98	91.93	92.23
5	44.48	68.03	87.37	87.39	54	47.59	58.73	90.59	90.39
6	53.56	50.06	50.06	51.06	55	48.74	64.88	64.88	65.25
7	54.34	67.61	99.94	100	56	48.07	58.42	57.92	62.17
8	82.7	96.34	100	100	57	29.04	52.22	53.01	54.21
9	45.69	86.9	100	100	58	39.77	58.79	58.06	59.06
10	28.08	57.9	70.58	70.72	59	58.56	72.67	72.67	73.67
11	25.94	55.3	55.39	55.70	60	29.9	53.83	53.95	54.95
12	63.41	93.74	87.2	87.76	61	45.07	88.67	80.06	95.41
13	41.93	77.01	89.35	89.76	62	64.92	88.7	85.1	97.34
14	37.88	65.18	65.33	65.63	63	43.72	78.34	79.31	81.69
15	100	100	100	100	64	54.02	72.12	72.95	74.62
16	29.4	55.64	67.91	100	65	59.48	100	100	100
17	29.56	100	100	100	66	53.1	100	98.58	100
18	33.74	63.77	63.77	67.77	67	55.85	65.83	66.24	71.79
19	32.4	73.82	60.67	66.04	68	57.41	62.02	62.22	65.62
20	28.72	63.08	63.19	63.65	69	63.27	81.06	82.28	90.9
21	29.89	58.89	58.96	58.16	70	99.15	83.87	85.42	100
22	35.72	66.2	66.38	66.58	71	59.5	74.82	87.39	100
23	41.29	100	100	100	72	38	60.9	61.34	93.02
24	56.64	92.57	82.82	85.12	73	100	100	100	100
25	24.23	66.59	66.7	70.32	74	98.47	100	100	100
26	36.75	65.76	74.11	74.11	75	33.11	51.89	54.42	83.22
27	62.59	100	100	100	76	79.18	80.3	100	100
28	70.44	100	92.87	92.87	77	23.82	40.73	40.73	43.73
29	41.6	90.49	95.86	100	78	36.2	44.89	86.53	100
30	22.02	56.91	57.01	59.11	79	65.07	65.27	67.76	100
31	33.63	67.19	67.19	68.59	80	60.42	75.25	75.25	77.25
32	25.22	39.49	39.49	90.33	81	51.15	73.76	75.33	100
33	39.97	36.4	60.61	100	82	38.85	62.12	62.9	74.9
34	49.95	60.79	60.79	100	83	42.61	61.03	71.6	100
35	27.77	35.16	35.16	85.11	84	77	76.76	86.54	100
36	59.75	68.13	68.82	72.9	85	45.02	81.38	82.14	100
37	64.84	71.34	74.21	80.66	86	47.12	56.37	53.54	69.59
38	32.79	44.66	44.66	62.06	87	46.07	59.89	55.21	57.21
39	71.14	80.29	100	100	88	47.24	100	100	100
40	43.91	64.29	64.29	70.6	89	52.94	94.72	100	97.28
41	33.06	40.43	81.43	96.87	90	100	100	100	100
42	34.03	61.53	61.54	61.54	91	51.5	74.38	100	87.06
43	46.34	59.3	94.56	96.56	92	69.55	40.88	40.86	95.05
44	34.11	47.27	49.13	74.63	93	53.85	50.26	51.23	100
45	35.83	53.7	54.07	69.82					
46	57.12	68.46	73.84	75.81					
47	49.69	50.61	65.95	100					
48	70.17	74.86	88.36	100					
49	45.59	46.64	51.39	53.39					

as advocated by Avkiran (1999). As no significant correlations were identified, the assumption of constant returns to scale was maintained. Furthermore, because outliers in the dataset can create serious distortions in the DEA, the existence of outliers was also investigated. Since none outlier was found, all 93 hotels were included in the analysis.

Initially, DEA models assumed input minimisation, meaning that hotels aim to maintain at least the same level of outputs (be effective) while minimising inputs (be efficient). However, it does not make sense to use input minimisation when uncontrollable inputs are included in the DEA analysis (Avkiran, 1999, p. 51), since such an assumption is unrealistic given that managers have no control on determining/managing uncontrollable inputs. Thus, output maximisation was assumed at step 4, because an uncontrollable input (demand variability) was included in the DEA model. However, this did not affect the DEA analysis and comparisons across steps. This is because constant returns to scale were also assumed and under constant returns input minimisation and output maximisation give the same DEA scores. It has also been suggested that the number of units in the dataset should be substantially greater than N * M (where N = number of inputs and M = number of outputs) (Dyson, Thanassoulis & Boussofiane, 1990). This is because there are N * M possibilities that units could be efficient and so, one could expect the identification of at least N * M units to be efficient. In this study, the use of 3 outputs and 6 inputs in a dataset of 93 hotels clearly allows suitable discrimination between hotels.

In brief, the stepwise DEA approach in rooms division was applied as follows. At step 1, the following aggregated metrics were used in order to capture the rooms' division outputs and inputs: non-F&B total revenue representing revenue from roomnights, telephone and minor operations (e.g., laundry, souvenir sales, etc.), in other words, revenue from the major activities occupying rooms' division employees; number of rooms representing the capital investment; and total rooms' division payroll and Material and Other (M&O) expenses for accounting the labor resources and other rooms' division inputs. By correlating the DEA scores obtained at step 1 with the disaggregated productivity inputs/outputs, significant positive correlations between DEA scores and ARR ($P = 0.601$, $\alpha = 0.0000$), number of roomnights ($P = 0.495$, $\alpha = 0.0004$) and non-roomnights revenue ($P = 0.562$, $\alpha = 0.0000$) revealed that the latter can significantly enhance and determine productivity levels. This is not surprising and compatible with findings from previous studies (e.g., Johns, 1997; National Economic Development Council, 1992; Van der Hoeven & Thurik, 1984). Thus, in constructing the DEA model at step 2, these three productivity determinant, disaggregated outputs were used instead of the non-F&B total revenue. The DEA score was recalculated and then correlated with disaggregated outputs/inputs. Although the correlations of DEA scores with ARR, roomnights and non-roomnights revenue disappeared (which is not surprising since the productivity impact of the latter was now being considered through the specification of the DEA model), significant negative correlations between DEA scores and front office payroll ($P = -0.811$, $\alpha = 0.0000$) and administration M&O expenses ($P = -0.592$, $\alpha = 0.0000$) were found. In order to include these two productivity determinant factors in the DEA model at step 3, the two inputs, namely total payroll and total M&O expenses, were adjusted to exclude the former. So, total payroll was changed to other payroll, referring to total payroll excluding payroll for front office staff, while total M&O expenses were changed to other M&O expenses, referring to total M&O expenses excluding the administration M&O expenses (Table 3). The DEA score was then recalculated and correlated with disaggregated inputs/outputs. The only significant correlation that was found was between the DEA score and demand variability ($P = -0.203$, $\alpha = 0.0512$), which justified the inclusion of the latter in the DEA model at step 4. The productivity impact of demand variability is widely argued in the literature (e.g., National Economic Development Council, 1992; Johns & Wheeler, 1991; Jones, 1988). The DEA score was then recalculated and correlated. As no correlation was found between the new DEA score and disaggregated inputs/outputs (meaning that none other disaggregated input/output is a significant determinant of productivity), it was concluded that the DEA model at step 4 is a robust productivity metric in rooms division reflecting all inputs/outputs that hotels should effectively manage to be productive. Overall, the following disaggregated inputs/outputs were found to be significant determinants of rooms division productivity: ARR, roomnights, non-roomnights revenue, number of rooms, front office payroll, administration M&O expenses, other rooms' division payroll, other rooms' division M&O expenses and demand variability.

As previously argued, a thorough examination of the DEA scores across the different steps can also indicate the reason for which a hotel is found productive. Specifically, hotels that become efficient from step 1 to step 2 (e.g., hotel 17, 23, 27 in Table 4) become efficient because they can effectively manage and improve their ARR, roomnights (occupancy) as well as non-room revenue (revenue from telephone and minor operations). In this vein, the investigation of the effectiveness and implementation of the yield management practices, distribution and marketing strategies of these hotels becomes of a great interest and importance. Hotels that become efficient from step 2 to step 3 (e.g., hotel 8, 9, 39) achieve this because they can successfully manage their front office payroll and administration M&O expenses. Further investigation of these hotels might reveal best practices, for example, in staff scheduling, information technology applications and paperless office strategies. Finally, hotels that become efficient at step 4 (e.g., hotel 1, 4, 79) achieve this because of demand factors and so, further investigation of such cases might reveal either attractive hotel locations and/or best practices in managing demand fluctuations.

To better illustrate how the disaggregated inputs and outputs determine productivity frontiers, the configuration of inputs/outputs of three groups of hotels was calculated: 100% efficient hotels; inefficient hotels with a DEA score above the median; inefficient hotels with a productive score below the median. The median rather than the average DEA score was used as a cut off point among hotel types, as DEA scores were not normally distributed (none hotel was less than 30% productive). A radar plot was used for visually representing the configuration of the inputs/outputs of the three types of hotels. The dimensions of the radar plot correspond to the ratios of the average input/output scores of the inefficient units to the average input/output scores of the efficient units. These ratios rather than the raw average scores of inputs and outputs for each hotel group were calculated (Table 5) and plotted (Figure 2), because inputs/outputs were measured in different units (e.g., responses varied from one-digit numbers–number of rooms–to five-digit numbers–revenue) and so, average scores would not allow easy illustration in a radar plot.

Figure 2 shows the productivity frontiers and input/output configuration of the three hotel groups. One hundred percent efficient hotels clearly outperform other hotels in the management of all productivity determinant factors. Specifically, although of a smaller room capacity than the efficient units, the inef-

TABLE 5. Average and Ratio Scores of Inputs/Outputs per Efficiency Type of Hotel

	Efficient units (1)	Units above the median score (2)	Units below the median score (3)	Ratio (1)/(1)	Ratio (2)/(1)	Ratio (3)/(1)
Demand variability	2.909091	3.62069	3.741935	1	1.245	1.286
Number of rooms	107.303	100.1034	63.3871	1	0.933	0.591
ARR	64.80364	56.35517	53.91935	1	0.87	0.832
Roomnights	28,760.52	24,967.83	15,943.26	1	0.868	0.554
Non-room revenue	379,005.9	265,789.8	73,044.6	1	0.701	0.193
Front office payroll	96,134.18	140,326.6	139,981.8	1	1.46	1.456
Adm. M&O	92,559.97	177,697.2	113,250.9	1	1.92	1.224
Rooms payroll minus front office payroll	312,605.8	373,208	277,538.5	1	1.194	0.888
Rooms M&O minus administration M&O	254,717.7	258,274.5	116,484.5	1	1.014	0.457

FIGURE 2. Configuration of Productivity Determinant Inputs/Outputs in Step 4 DEA Productivity Model in Rooms Division

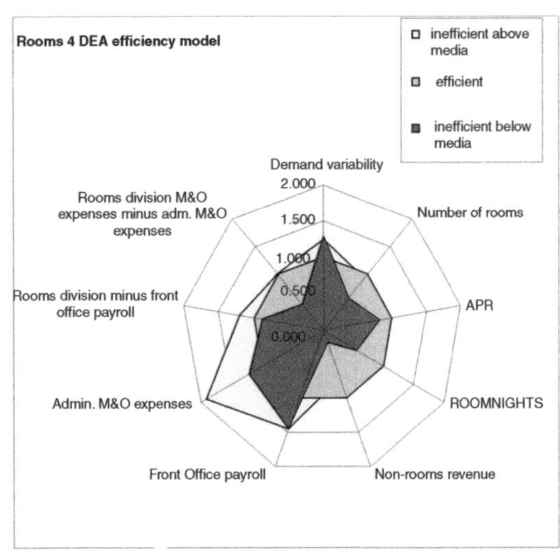

ficient units below the median (59% of the rooms of the efficient units) only achieve 55% of the roomnights of the efficient units, meaning that they achieve 4% less roomnights than would be expected due to their smaller room capacity. The former also achieve only the 83% of the ARR and the 19% of the non-room revenue of the efficient units and despite their smaller size they spend 105.6% and 122.4% of the front office payroll and administration non-payroll expenses of the efficient units. The overspend in resources is less for other payroll and other non-payroll expenses than the previous expenses (88% and 45% of those of the efficient units respectively), which illustrates the fact that it is the former expenses rather than other payroll and other non-payroll expenses that significantly determine efficiency.

On the other hand, relative to the efficient units, inefficient units above the median are doing better than the inefficient units below the median in terms of ARR and non-room revenue (the former achieve 87% of the ARR and 70% of the non-room revenue of the efficient units). The same is true in terms of expenses management. So, the inefficient above the median have similar overspends in terms of front-office payroll, administration non-payroll expenses, other payroll and other expenses as inefficient units below the median. However, as the former are of a greater room capacity than the latter, this overspend is easier justified. However, when comparing the inefficient above the median with the efficient units, it is evident that although the former have 93% of the efficient units room capacity, they achieve proportionally fewer roomnights (86% of the efficient units roomnights meaning 7% fewer roomnights than expected). Moreover, although efficient units are of a smaller size inefficient units, the latter achieve less ARR and non-room revenue than the efficient units (87% and 70% respectively). Overall, inefficiencies are attributed to both underachievement of outputs and overspend of inputs.

However, for an operations manager, it is not only important to find how productive the operation is, but also to identify ways to improve productivity. DEA can also estimate how much outputs could be increased and/or the magnitude of inputs that could be conserved by each unproductive hotel. Table 3 provides (% in parentheses) the average amount of improvement for each productivity determinant input/output in the hotel dataset. Although individual amounts of improvement can be obtained for each individual hotel, average amounts of improvement are provided here (mainly for reasons of economy) to illustrate the value and use of this type of analysis. ARR and roomnights consist the major areas of improvement and so the application of appropriate managerial techniques, e.g., yield management, multi-channel distribution strategies, should be considered. However, because it is unrealistic to argue that a manager should also aim to reduce demand variability (as it is an uncontrollable/external factor), the following analysis is conducted for identifying appropriate improvement strategies for each hotel.

An operational-market productivity matrix was developed in order to categorise hotels based upon their type/reason for being productive (Table 6). The DEA model including demand variability (step 4) reflects combined productivity, which refers to the ability to be operational efficient while also effectively managing/coping with market conditions. On the other hand, when demand variability is not included (step 3), the DEA score reflects only operational productivity measuring the ability

TABLE 6. Operational-Market Productivity Matrix in Rooms Division

Market productivity	Inefficient (In Step 3)	Efficient (In Step 3)
Efficient (In Step 4)	**Cluster 3** *Units:* 19 *Hotels:* 1, 4, 7, 16, 29, 33, 34, 47, 48, 66, 70, 71, 78, 79, 81, 83, 84, 85, 93 *Demand Variability score: Min = 1 Max = 4 Aver. = 1.7*	**Cluster 4** *Units:* 14 *Hotels:* 8, 9, 15, 17, 23, 27, 39, 51, 65, 73, 74, 76, 88, 90 *Demand Variability score: Min = 1 Max = 6 Aver. = 4.5*
Inefficient (In Step 4)	**Cluster 1** *Units:* 58 *Hotels:* 2, 3, 5, 6, 10, 11, 12, 13, 14, 18, 19, 20, 21, 22, 24, 25, 26, 28, 30, 31, 32, 35, 36, 37, 38, 40, 41, 42, 43, 44, 45, 46, 49, 50, 52, 53, 54, 55, 56, 57, 58, 59, 60, 61, 62, 63, 64, 67, 68, 69, 72, 75, 77, 80, 82, 86, 87, 92 *Demand Variability score: Min = 1 Max = 9 Aver. = 3.6*	**Cluster 2** *Units:* 2 *Hotels:* 89, 91 *Demand Variability score: Min = 2 Max = 6 Aver. = 4*
	Operational productivity	

of hotels to efficiently manage their production operations only. In other words, hotels that were inefficient in step 3, but became efficient in step 4 attribute their efficiency to the fact that they can effectively manage demand variability (and so, they are market efficient only), while inefficient hotels in both step 3 and 4 are both operational and market inefficient. Hotels in cluster 3 (operational inefficient hotels, but market efficient–as they became efficient only in step 4) need to improve their operational efficiency by improving their operating system and processes. Hotels in cluster 2 represent hotels that although were found efficient in step 3, they became inefficient in step 4 when demand variations were considered, and so they need to better manage their operating system in light of the market conditions. Hotels in cluster 1 represent hotels that were found inefficient in both step 3 and 4 and so, they need to improve their productivity by configuring a more efficient operating system while also controlling (managing or exploiting) demand levels.

Productivity Measurement in the F&B Division

For developing the DEA productivity metric in the F&B division, the same stepwise process was undertaken (Table 7 and Table 8). Aggregated metrics were used in step 1, DEA scores were calculated and then correlated with disaggregated inputs/outputs. When significant correlations were found and a cause and effect relationship existed between variables, disaggregated inputs/outputs were included into the model. A robust model is concluded (step 3) when no other significant correlations between DEA scores and disaggregated inputs/outputs are found. Findings illustrated that the following factors determine productivity in the F&B division: F&B revenue, percent of banqueting covers to restaurant covers, F&B capacity, F&B payroll, F&B M&O expenses and demand variability.

Specifically, the significant positive correlation between DEA scores and percent of banqueting covers to restaurant covers indicated that banqueting covers contributed to more efficient F&B operations than restaurant covers. The positive productivity impact of banqueting covers is not surprising when considering that banqueting operations are more predicable, standard and streamlined as well as less labor and material consuming operations than restaurant business (Jones, 1988; Levitt, 1972). Because of that, strategies aiming at increasing the percentage of banqueting covers served were found to have the greatest

TABLE 7. Input and Output Metrics Included in the Stepwise DEA in FB

	Step 1 (input min)	Step 2 (output max)	Step 3 (output max)
Outputs			
FB total revenue	*	*	*(37.3%)
Ratio of banqueting to restaurant covers			*(43.2%)
Inputs			
Total FB capacity (banqueting and restaurant seats)	*	*	*(2.3%)
FB payroll	*	*	*(24%)
FB material and other expenses	*	*	*(17.1%)
Demand variability (uncontrollable input)		*	*N.A.
Other inputs/outputs and factors correlated with DEA scores in all steps			
DEA inputs: % of roomnights from: repeat customers, business, leisure, conference and other; occupancy; total capacity; number of restaurant seats; banqueting max capacity; F&B M&O expenses; F&B payroll; roomnights; number of: full time and part time staff; % of payroll for full time staff. **DEA outputs:** number of: restaurant covers served, banqueting covers served; % of: banqueting served to total covers served, restaurant served to total covers served, banqueting served to restaurant covers served; total covers served; F&B revenue; hotel profit.			

*Indicates that a variable is included in the DEA model.

potential for improving F&B productivity (43.2% average improvement). The radar plot illustrating how these disaggregated factors affect the F&B productivity frontiers was also constructed (Figure 3).

Below the median inefficient units have 82% and 89% of the restaurant and banqueting capacity of the efficient units but they achieve proportionally less revenue than the efficient units would have achieved with the same capacity (slack/underused resources); specifically, they achieve 40% of the efficient units' revenue meaning approximately 40% (82% – 40%) less revenue than what they would have been expected to achieve. Below the median inefficient units also make a proportionally greater use of resources. They achieve 40% revenue of efficient units with 52% and 74% of the payroll and non-payroll expenses of the efficient units, meaning that they overspend 12% (52% – 40%) in payroll and 34% (74% – 40%) in non-payroll expenses than they would have expected if they were going to be considered as efficient.

On the other hand, above the median inefficient units are doing better than below the median inefficient units in terms of using their capacity and controlling their expenses. In particular, above the median inefficient units have the 88% and 93% of the restaurant and banqueting capacity of efficient units (they are of greater banqueting capacity than units below the median) but they achieve the 72% of the revenue of the efficient units, meaning approximately 18% less revenue than expected (instead of 40% as the below the median units). In the same vein, the 72% revenue is achieved with 73% of payroll and 94% of the non-payroll of the efficient units, which means that actually units above the median can control their payroll as efficiently as the efficient units (only 73% – 72% = 1% expected difference), while they are overspending in terms of non-payroll expenses (94% – 72% = 22%), but which is still less than that of the below median units.

However, because demand variability was included in the F&B DEA analysis from step 2, it was not possible to distinguish between operational and market efficiency and develop the market-operational productivity matrix.

Productivity Measurement at the Hotel Property Level

Based on the findings of the previous DEA analysis in the rooms and F&B division, a robust DEA hotel property productivity metric was constructed by including in a single DEA model all the previously identified disaggregated inputs/outputs determining departmental productivity. Specifically, the hotel property DEA model considered the following five outputs (ARR, roomnights, non-roomnights

TABLE 8. DEA Scores in F&B Division

Hotel	Step 1	Step 2	Step 3	Hotel	Step 1	Step 2	Step 3
1	84.38	85.34	85.14	50	81.43	100	100
2	25.85	25.82	37.91	51	88.74	100	100
3	69.07	69.23	74.08	52	51.43	55.72	47.57
4	73.5	87.35	94.53	53	72.66	73.98	91.93
5	100	100	87.37	54	80.65	78.72	90.59
6	51.28	71.31	80.06	55	65.14	72.21	74.88
7	76.21	78.2	99.94	56	60.44	62.29	67.92
8	52.03	52.26	100	57	61.42	63.2	53.31
9	95.38	81.02	100	58	62.68	64.26	68.06
10	90.59	92.59	100	59	45.62	45.99	72.67
11	49.42	60.79	65.39	60	82.19	82.91	83.95
12	58.73	60.5	87.2	61	49.76	51.65	80.06
13	65.06	66.98	89.35	62	57.68	82.24	85.1
14	65.7	65.48	72.33	63	52.5	54.03	79.31
15	61.77	61.73	100	64	59.62	60.94	72.95
16	69.61	100	67.91	65	81.35	83.24	100
17	65.7	100	100	66	65.24	73.21	98.58
18	52.03	53	63.77	67	87.58	86.7	86.24
19	77.02	78.36	80.67	68	100	78.01	82.22
20	62.98	63.92	68.19	69	55.86	56.2	82.28
21	86.27	86.23	88.96	70	42.37	43.45	85.42
22	74.24	74.53	76.38	71	41.41	42.02	87.39
23	69.31	73.84	100	72	43.56	100	61.34
24	85.87	88.72	92.82	73	92.28	92.7	100
25	61.02	96.86	96.7	74	100	100	100
26	85.98	88.45	99.11	75	96.66	100	54.42
27	82.34	85.43	100	76	100	100	100
28	97.53	99.13	92.87	77	44.68	46.06	46.73
29	50.87	64.22	85.86	78	51.08	51.58	86.53
30	65.68	66.28	57.01	79	68.67	81.56	87.76
31	63.78	64.65	67.19	80	45.13	57.92	75.25
32	22.13	51.79	39.49	81	66.78	84.88	85.33
33	76.13	79.19	60.6	82	83.73	86.21	82.9
34	53.7	100	60.79	83	44.37	46.21	71.6
35	32.91	39.53	35.16	84	50.5	70.77	86.54
36	55.82	57.39	68.82	85	50.84	51.85	82.14
37	53.96	74.3	74.21	86	72.76	84.38	93.54
38	63.88	65.88	44.66	87	94.78	96.48	99.21
39	43.33	43.32	100	88	70.02	71.1	100
40	72.92	76.34	64.29	89	65.35	66.64	100
41	89.85	100	81.43	90	60.48	62.38	100
42	100	100	61.54	91	92.62	95.1	100
43	37.24	61.29	94.56	92	51.88	61.29	70.86
44	44.69	63.54	49.13	93	56.62	62.27	71.23
45	53.09	54.89	54.07				
46	58.53	58.96	73.84				
47	59.48	79.39	65.95				
48	59.96	85.25	88.36				
49	100	100	51.39				

FIGURE 3. Configuration of Productivity Determinant Inputs/Outputs in Step 3 DEA Productivity Model in F&B Division

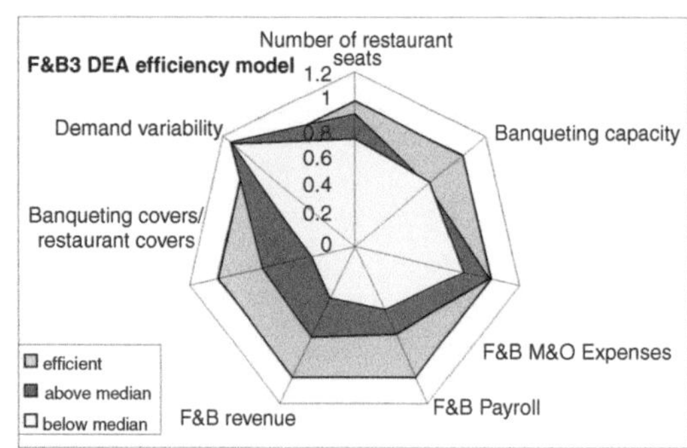

revenue, F&B revenue, ratio of banqueting to restaurant covers) and nine inputs (number of rooms, total F&B capacity, front office payroll, administration M&O expenses, F&B payroll, F&B M&O expenses, other payroll, other M&O expenses, demand variability). Following the same process as described before, the following calculations were conducted for identifying appropriate productivity improvement strategies: average improvement for each factor, combined (demand variability is included in the DEA model), operational (demand variability is not included in the DEA model) productivity scores. The operational-market productivity matrix was also developed in order to identify the hotels that were market efficient or market inefficient.

Impact of Contextual Factors on Productivity

Since the DEA productivity metrics were argued to be robust, productivity differences amongst hotels can be attributed to other factors that the stepwise DEA has not so far considered. Statistical tests were conducted for investigating the productivity impact of the following factors (Table 9): hotel location; hotel design; ownership structure; management arrangement; market segments served; repeat customers; distribution channels used.

Location was not found to affect productivity, which was quite surprising. However, hotel location may significantly determine levels of demand variability. Indeed, an ANOVA test (0.007, $\alpha = 0.05$) revealed that hotels located

TABLE 9. Impact of Contextual Factors on Productivity Metrics

	Rooms division			F&B	Hotel property		
	Oper.	Mark.	Comb.	Comb.	Oper.	Mark.	Comb.
Hotel location (ANOVA test)							
Hotel design (ANOVA test)	* F = 6.910, Sign. 0.002, df = 2 **31 rural hotels** (67.0, 19.7) **25 city cent. hotels** (68.1, 17.7) **37 rural hotels** (81.4, 15.9)				* F = 5.502 Sign. 0.006 df = 2 **31 rural hotels** (85.2, 16.6) **25 city cent. hotels** (89.9, 11.4) **37 rural hotels** (95.3, 8.1)		
Ownership structure (T-test)			* t = −2.541 df = 91 Sign. 0.013 **48 indiv.** (71.1, 18.8) **45 chain** (75.0, 18.9)	* t = −3.305 df = 91 Sign. 0.001 **48 indiv.** (78.4, 19.4) **45 chain** (87.4, 13.9)	* t = −2.878 df = 91 Sign. 0.005 **48 indiv.** (86.9, 14.4) **45 chain** (94.3, 10.0)		
Management arrangement (ANOVA test)			* F = 3.456 Sign. 0.036 **28 indep.** (75.8, 18.9) **47 chain** 86.3, 15.2) **18 ind&consor** (84.5, 18.4)	* F = 3.677 Sign. 0.029 **28 indep.** (75.8, 18.9) **47 chain** 86.3, 15.2) **18 ind&consor** (84.5, 18.4)			
% of roomnights from business, leisure, conference (Pearson correlations)							
% of roomnights from repeat customers (Pearson correlations)							
% of reservations from property owned system, third parties, Internet (Pearson correlations)							

*Indicates a significant effect ($\alpha = 0.05$)
Numbers in parenthesis give Average DEA score and standard deviation.

in rural places faced significantly higher fluctuations in demand than hotels in city centers. Thus, it can be argued that the impact of hotel location on productivity has already been incorporated into productivity scores when demand variability was included into DEA models. In accordance with previous studies (e.g., McKinsey Global Institute, 1998), hotel design was found to significantly affect operational productivity in rooms division and hotel property level. Specifically, purpose built hotels significantly outperformed old and/or traditional properties. Chain owned hotels significantly outperformed independently owned hotels in terms of combined productivity in rooms and F&B and in terms of operational productivity in hotel property level. Independently managed hotels had significantly lower combined DEA productivity scores in rooms and F&B. This might be explained by the fact that chain managed hotels as well as hotels of a consortium have access and are promoted to several distribution and reservation systems that in turn can significantly impact on demand and capacity levels management. Chain managed hotels were also previously found to practice more sophisticated management techniques, e.g., labor scheduling, demand forecasting, that independent hoteliers were not even familiar with (McKinsey Global Institute, 1998; Johns & Wheller, 1991).

However, repeat customers, market segments served and distribution channels used were not found to have a significant impact on productivity. Sigala (2002) also reported that Internet reservations and the use of electronic distribution channels had none impact on hotel productivity for two major reasons. First, electronic channels were not integrated with existing computer systems and databases, which meant that a lot of manual work was required for data entry and updates, while errors were easy to make (e.g., over/under-bookings). Lack of systems integration is also claimed to inhibit the effective practice of yield management across distribution channels as well as the maximization of profit per loyal customer and hotel location in the case of hotel chains (Sigala et al., 2001). Moreover, as the very small percentage of Internet reservations were not found to positively affect productivity, Sigala (2002) concluded that a threshold level of Internet reservations is required in order to counterbalance the new types of expenses involved for online distribution (e.g., website development, maintenance, promotion and online hotel rates discounts/offers).

CONCLUSIONS

The paper aimed to illustrate and advocate the value of using a stepwise approach to DEA for measuring productivity and identifying appropriate productivity improvement strategies in the hotel sector. To that end, the problems of productivity measurement and the different productivity methods were reviewed and debated, while the advantages of the stepwise DEA were analysed and illustrated by gathering data from the three star hotel sector in the UK. DEA provides an overall productivity metric that can be easily interpreted, used as a tool for identifying specific local problems and so, deciding appropriate strategies for improvement. In addition, a stepwise approach to DEA was proposed for identifying and considering only the factors that significantly determine productivity frontiers. In this way, a robust productivity metric is obtained that can discriminate between efficient and inefficient units as well as identify the reasons of efficiency of the former and the areas of improvement of the latter. Overall, the proposed stepwise DEA can overcome productivity measurement problems related with: the simultaneous manipulation of several inputs/outputs and productivity determinant factors irrespective of their units of measurement; the "ceteris paribus" problem; the impact of the level and/or unit of analysis on productivity measurement.

The evidence gathered from the three star hotel sector in the UK revealed that the following factors can significantly determine productivity in the rooms' division: ARR, number of roomnights, non-rooms revenue, number of rooms, front office payroll, administration and general M&O expenses, other payroll, other M&O expenses, demand variability. Findings also revealed that the following factors determine productivity in the F&B division: F&B revenue, percent of banqueting covers to restaurant covers, F&B capacity, F&B payroll, F&B M&O expenses and demand variability. However, the productivity impact of these factors has been confirmed by analyzing data from the three star hotel sector in the UK. Thus, future research could investigate whether the same conclusions can be replicated and generalized in different hotel segments and/or countries. Given the great product differentiation, operational, environmental and clientele diversity of the global hotel industry, the application of DEA across hotel segments and countries can produce interesting results and findings that can have both crucial academic and managerial implications. For example, one would apply DEA for investigating the productivity impact of different hotel locations and operational procedures.

The present paper demonstrated the use of DEA as a diagnostic tool for problems of capacity, demand and utilisation of resources. By using DEA, it was also possible to identify the areas of improvement and so the appropriate strategies that managers could use for increasing productivity. For example, yield management techniques and multi-channel distribution strategies are advisable for hotels that need to improve ARR and roomnights, while ICT applications are advisable for automating/streamlining front office processes and reducing front office expenses. In the F&B division, the pursuit of increasing the provision of banqueting services can significantly increase productivity. The analysis also provided another way that DEA can facilitate decision making. As demand variability was found to be a crucial productivity determinant, an operational-market matrix was developed in order to illustrate how hotel managers can identify the reasons of their inefficiency (operational and/or market inefficiency) and implement appropriate improvement strategies.

DEA productivity scores were robust, meaning that they discriminate between efficient and inefficient units after taking into consideration numerous inputs/outputs but finally including only those that significantly impact productivity. In this way, the "ceteris paribus" problem is overcome and productivity differences among hotels can be attributed to factors that have not so far considered. Thus, statistical tests were conducted for testing the impact of hotel location, design, ownership structure, management arrangement, market segments served, percentage of repeat customers and type of distribution channels used on productivity. Consistent with previous research, findings revealed that hotel design, management arrangement and ownership structure significantly affect productivity levels. Specifically, as independently owned and managed hotels had significantly lower productivity scores than chain managed hotels, it is suggested that the former would need to consider the adaption and implementation of more sophisticated operational and market strategies that the latter may have. To achieve that, independent hoteliers may need to seriously consider a hotel consortia membership that can provide them with access to and transfer them to technological resources and managerial know-how.

However, this study has some limitations that need to be acknowledged, but which at the same time lend themselves nicely towards identifying future research avenues. First, a more accurate metric for labour inputs would have been desirable. The study used the number of full-time and part-time employees as a proxy of labour resources. Full-time equivalent employee (FTE) metrics could have been used, but hotels hardly measure and have such figures (specifically, small independent properties; Sigala, 2002). However, the use of FTE would have more effectively investigated productivity issues regarding labour numerical flexibility. The study also argued that the aggregate, financial productivity outputs (such as revenue, payroll) should encapsulate soft, qualitative dimensions of productivity inputs/outputs such as customer satisfaction and employee skills. Irrespective of the strength of this argument, such an approach did not allow the identification of specific qualitative factors that can significantly determine productivity. Future research could actually try to develop better metrics for such quantitative dimensions and apply DEA for investigating their productivity impact. So, for example, aspects such as customer satisfaction and service quality could be considered. Indeed, because DEA can deal with soft, qualitative data it offers a great potential for redefining service productivity and solving some of the problems of its measurement. However, when soft data are used, issues of instrument reliability and validity become extremely important and so DEA would need to be combined with other research approaches and methodologies.

Despite of the above acknowledged limitations that can provide food for future research, the outcomes and methodology of this study provide useful and valuable findings for both academics and professionals. Research efforts for the replication, enhancement and refinement of the DEA methodology and its findings can significantly contribute to the body of knowledge. At the same time, DEA application requires the collection and analysis of many data and so professionals should seriously consider the establishment of procedures and systems for continuously and periodically gathering, benchmarking and monitoring their businesses' performance in key productivity input and output factors. The implementation of operational and information management systems and techniques is deemed crucial since the hospitality industry has been criticized for its lack of and/or unsophisticated approach to information systems and data collection (e.g., Johns et al., 1997; Sigala, 2002). As the operating environment of the hotel industry is highly competitive and more conducive to efficient operations, productivity measurement and benchmarking is a critical strategic issue, and so methodologies and procedures/systems to achieve the former become a strategic necessity.

REFERENCES

Al-Faraj, T.N., Alidi, A.S., & Bu-Bhsait, K.A. (1993). Evaluation of bank branches by means of Data Envelopment Analysis. *International Journal of Operations and Production Management*, 10 (1): 112-120.

Al-Shammari, M., & Salimi, A. (1998). Modelling the operating efficiency of banks: A non-parametric methodology. *Logistics Information Management*, 11 (l) : 5-17.

Anderson, R. I., Fish M., Xia Y., & Michello, F. (1999). Measuring efficiency in the hotel industry; a stochastic frontier approach. *International Journal of Hospitality Management*, 18: 45-57.

Anderson, R.I., Fok, R., & Scott, J. (2000). Hotel industry efficiency: An advanced linear programming examination. *American Business Review* (January), 40-48.

Andersson, T.D. (1996). Traditional key ratio analysis versus data envelopment analysis: A comparison of various measurements of productivity and efficiency in restaurants. In N. Johns (Ed.), *Productivity management in hospitality and tourism* (pp. 209-226). London: Cassell.

Avkiran, N.K. (1999). *Productivity Analysis in the services sector with Data Envelopment Analysis*. Queensland: Camira.

Baker, M., & Riley, M. (1994). New perspectives on productivity in hotels: Some advances and new directions. *International Journal of Hospitality Management*, 13 (4): 297-311.

Ball, S.D., Johnson, K., & Slattery, P. (1986). Labour productivity in hotels: An empirical analysis. *International Journal of Hospitality Management*, 5(3): 141-147.

Banker, R.D., & Thrall, R. (1992). Estimation of returns to scale using data envelopment analysis. *European Journal of Operational Research*, 17: 74-84.

Brown, J.R., & Dev, C.S. (1999). Looking beyond RevPAR; productivity consequences of hotel strategies. *Cornell Hotel and Restaurant Administration Quarterly*, April: 23-33.

Charnes, A.C., Cooper, W.W., & Rhodes, E. (1978). Measuring the efficiency of decision making units. *European Journal of Operational Research* 2(6): 429-444.

Charnes, A.C., Cooper, W.W., Lewin, A.Y., & Seiford, L.M. (1994). *Data Envelopment Analysis: Theory, Methodology and Applications*. Boston, MA: Kluwer Academic Press.

Charnes, A.C., Cooper, W.W., Lewin, A.Y., Morey, R.C., & Rousseau, J. (1985). Sensitivity and stability analysis in DEA. *Annals of Operations Research*, 2: 139-156.

Chatzoglou, P., & Soteriou, A. (1999). A DEA framework to assess the efficiency of the software requirements capture and analysis process. *Decision Sciences*, 30(2): 503-531.

Chen, T. (1997) An evaluation of the relative performance of university libraries in Taipei. *Asian Libraries*, 6 (1/2): 39-50.

Chew, B.W. (1986). No nonsense guide to measuring productivity. *Harvard Business Review*, 64 (1): 30-89.

Cizmar, S., & Weber, S. (2000). Marketing effectiveness of the hotel industry in Croatia. *International Journal of Hospitality Management*, 19: 227-240.

Cooper, W.W., Seiford, L.M., & Tone, K. (2000). *Data Envelopment Analysis. A Comprehensive Text with Models, Applications, References and DEA-Solver Software*. Boston, MA: Kluwer Academic Publishers.

Dilworth, J.B. (1989). *Production and Operation Management*. New York: Random House.

Dyson, G, Thanassoulis, E., & Boussofiane, A. (1990). *Data Envelopment Analysis*. Tutorial papers in Operational Research by the Operational Research Society.

Heap, J.P. (1992). *Productivity Management: A fresh approach*. London: Cassell.

Johns, N., & Wheeler, K. (1991). Productivity and Performance measurement and monitoring. In R. Teare (Eta), *Strategic Hospitality Management* (pp. 45-71), London: Cassell.

Johns, N., Howcroft, B., & Drake, L. (1997). The use of Data Envelopment Analysis to monitor hotel productivity. *Progress in Tourism and Hospitality Research* 3(2): 119-127.

Jones, P. (1988). Quality, capacity and productivity in service industries. *International Journal of Hospitality Management*, 7 (2): 104-112.

Jones, P., & Hall, M. (1996). Productivity and the new service paradigm, or servicity and the neo-service paradigm. In N. Johns (Ed), *Managing productivity in hospitality and tourism* (pp. 227-240). London: Cassell.

Jones, P., & Lockwood, A. (1989). *The management of hotel operations*. London: Cassell.

Levitt, T. (1972). Production Line Approach to Service. *Harvard Business review*, September/October, 50: 41-52.

Mahoney, T.A. (1988). Productivity defined. In R.J. Campbell & J.P. Campbell (Eta), *Productivity in Organizations: New Perspectives from Industrial and Organizational Psychology* (pp. 101-121). New York: Jossey-Bass.

McKinsey Global Institute (1998). *Driving productivity and growth in the UK economy*. London: McKinsey Global Institute.

Morey, R.C., & Dittman, D.A. (1995). Evaluating a hotel GM's performance. A case study in benchmarking. *Cornell Hotel and Restaurant Administration Quarterly*, 36(5): 30-35.

National Economic Development Council (NEDC) (1992). *Working Party, Competitiveness in tourism and leisure, sub-group report. Costs and manpower productivity in UK hotels*. London: NEDC.

Norman, M., & Stoker, B. (1991). *DEA the assessment of performance*. London: Wiley.

O' Connor, P. (2002). An analysis of the pricing strategies of the International Hotel Chains. In Wober, K., Frew, A. and Hitz, M. (Eds.) *Information and Communication Technologies in Tourism 2002* (pp. 285-293), New York: Springer-Verlag.

Parkin, D., & Hollingsworth, B. (1997). Measuring Productive Efficiency of Acute Hospitals in Scotland, 1991-1994: Validity Issues in Data Envelopment Analysis. *Applied Economics*, 29(11): 1425-1438.

Pickworth, J. (1987). Minding the P's and Q's: Linking quality and productivity. *Cornell Hotel Restaurant and Administration Quarterly*, 28(1): 40-7.

Rimmington, M., & Clark G. (1996). Productivity measurement in food service systems. In N. Johns (Ed.), *Productivity management inhospitality and tourism* (pp. 194-208). London: Cassell.

Sasser, W.E., Olsen, P.R., & Wyckoff, D.D. (1978). *Management of Service Operations*. Boston: Allyn and Bacon.

Schroeder, R.G. (1985). *Operations management; decision making in the organisations function*. New York: McGraw-Hill.

Sengupta, J.K. (1988). A robust approach to the measurement of Farrell efficiency. *Applied Economics*, 20: 273-283.

Sigala, M. (2002). *Assessing the impact of Information and Communication Technologies on productivity in the hotel sector; an operations management approach*. Unpublished PhD thesis, University of Surrey, Guildford, Surrey, UK.

Sigala, M., & Christou, E. (2001). *Applying HOSTQUAL for TQM performance benchmarking: Evidence from the Greek hotel sector*. Conference of the International Council for Hotel, Restaurant and Institutional Education, (CHRIE), Brig, Swisstzerland, 25-27 October, 2001.

Sigala, M., Lockwood, A.. & Jones, P. (2001). Strategic implementation and IT: Gaining competitive advantage from the hotel reservation process. *International Journal of Contemporary Hospitality Management*, 17 (3), 364-371.

Tarim, Ş., Dener, H.I., & Tarim, Ş.A. (2000). Efficiency measurement in the hotel industry: output factor constrained DEA application. *Anatolia: An International Journal of Tourism and Hospitality Research*, 11(2): 111-123.

TRI Hospitality Consulting (2002). *United Kingdom Hotel Industry 2002*. Report. London: TRI Hospitality Consulting.

Van der Hoeven, W., & Thurik, A.R. (1984). Labour productivity in the hotel business. *Service Industries Journal*, 2(2): 161-173.

Witt, C.A., & Witt, S.F. (1989). Why productivity in the hotel sector is low. *International Journal of Contemporary Hospitality Management*, 1 (2): 28-33.

Wöber, K.W. (2000). Benchmarking Hotel Operations on the Internet: A Data Envelopment Analysis Approach. *Information Technology and Tourism* 3(3/4): 195-212.

Wöber, K.W. (2002). *Benchmarking in Tourism and Hospitality Industries: The Selection of Benchmarking Partners*. Wallingford: CAB International.

Modeling Tourism Demand: A Decision Rules Based Approach

Rob Law
Carey Goh
Ray Pine

SUMMARY. Most of the existing studies on tourism demand forecasting apply economic models that use mathematical functions, which require many statistical assumptions and limitations. This paper presents a new approach that applies the rough sets theory to form a forecasting model for tourism demand. The objective of this research is to create patterns which are able to distinguish between the classes of arrivals in terms of volume, based upon differences in the characteristics in each arrival. The information about the arrivals was organized in an Information Table where the number of arrivals corresponds to condition attributes, and the classification was defined by a decision attribute that indicated the forecast categorical value of future arrivals. Utilizing Japanese arrivals data in Hong Kong, empirical results showed the induced decision rules could accurately forecast (86.5%) of the test data. *[Article copies available for a fee from The Haworth Document Delivery Service: 1-800-HAWORTH. E-mail address: <docdelivery@haworthpress.com> Website: <http://www.HaworthPress.com> © 2004 by The Haworth Press, Inc. All rights reserved.]*

KEYWORDS. Tourism demand forecasting, rough sets, Information Table, condition attributes, decision attribute

INTRODUCTION

The tourism industry often possesses many data, which appear in a non-numeric form. These non-numeric data are related to socio-economic and demographic factors and are usually stored in guest history databases, employee files, and airline reservation repositories. At present, there exists a very limited number of published articles that incorporate any non-numeric (categorical) data directly into tourism demand forecasting. While some of the vari-

Rob Law is Associate Professor, Carey Goh is a PhD Candidate, and Ray Pine is Professor, all at the Polytechnic, School of Tourism Management, The Hong Kong University, Hong Kong.

Address correspondence to: Rob Law, School of Hotel & Tourism Management, The Hong Kong Polytechnic University, Hung Hom, Kowloon, Hong Kong (E-mail: hmroblaw@polyu.edu.hk).

The authors acknowledge the constructive comments and suggestions offered by the anonymous reviewers.

This project was partly supported by a research grant funded by RGC of the HKSAR Government and the Hong Kong Polytechnic University (under contract: B-Q398; PolyU5342/00H). An earlier draft of this research paper was presented in the APTA 2001 Conference.

[Haworth co-indexing entry note]: "Modeling Tourism Demand: A Decision Rules Based Approach." Law, Rob, Carey Goh, and Ray Pine. Co-published simultaneously in *Journal of Travel & Tourism Marketing* (The Haworth Hospitality Press, an imprint of The Haworth Press, Inc.) Vol. 16, No. 2/3, 2004, pp. 61-69; and: *Management Science Applications in Tourism and Hospitality* (ed: Zheng Gu) The Haworth Hospitality Press, an imprint of The Haworth Press, Inc., 2004, pp. 61-69. Single or multiple copies of this article are available for a fee from The Haworth Document Delivery Service [1-800-HAWORTH, 9:00 a.m. - 5:00 p.m. (EST). E-mail address: docdelivery@haworthpress.com].

http://www.haworthpress.com/web/JTTM
© 2004 by The Haworth Press, Inc. All rights reserved.
Digital Object Identifier: 10.1300/J073v16n02_05

ables used in the published articles are non-numeric in nature, their values were transformed into numeric ones. In other words, the existing formal tourism demand forecasting techniques fail to maintain the original useful information in the raw tourism data. Originating from Artificial Intelligence, a subdivision of Computer Science, a rough sets approach can model the relationship of a decision attribute and a set of condition attributes in terms of decision rules. More importantly, these decision rules can represent data in a non-numeric (and numeric) form. The rough sets approach has been successful in pattern recognition and object classification in medical and financial fields (McKee and Lensberg, 2002; Miyamoto, 1998; Tanaka and Maeda, 1998; Slowinski & Zopounidis, 1995). In the context of tourism and hospitality research, the applicability of the rough sets theory has been demonstrated in hotel guests expenditures (Law and Au, 1998), shopping (Law and Au, 2000), and sightseeing spending (Au and Law, 2000).

The rough sets approach has proved to be an excellent classification and pattern recognition technique. However, to date, no published work has linked the rough sets theory with relationship modeling and forecasting in tourism demand analysis. This study makes an attempt to bridge this gap. The key challenge of this study is to develop a decision-rule based tourism demand forecasting model for the Hong Kong tourism industry, and to investigate the quality of forecasting accuracy using the induced decision rules. In other words, this research aims to make an attempt to incorporate the rough sets theory into the context of tourism demand forecasting to develop formal relationship modeling and forecasting in international demand for tourist arrivals. This area of study is virtually non-existent in the current tourism demand analysis literature.

This paper presents a methodology for using the rough sets approach for the automated discovery of rules from a set of data samples for Hong Kong tourism demand forecasts. The raw data contain samples that cover information on economic and environmental factors, and their corresponding volume of tourist arrivals in Hong Kong.

THE ROUGH SETS THEORY

Basic Concept

Introduced by Pawlak (1982; 1998), the rough sets theory is developed from the formal concept of sets. In the rough sets theory, objects characterized by the same information are considered to be indiscernible (similar). This indiscernibility relationship constitutes the main mathematical basis of the rough sets theory. Any set of all indiscernible objects is called an elementary set and any set of objects being a union of some elementary sets is referred to as *crisp* (precise); otherwise the set is *rough* (imprecise, vague). Associated with every set X are two crisp sets, called the lower and the upper approximations of set X. The lower approximation of set X is the set of all elements that definitely belongs to X, whereas the upper approximation of X is the set of all elements that possibly belongs to X. The difference of the upper and the lower approximations of X is its boundary region. A set is rough if it has a non-empty boundary region; otherwise the set is crisp. The following subsections present the concepts of approximation classification, Information Table, and information reduction which are pertinent to the rough sets theory.

Approximate Classification

Figure 1 illustrates a set approximation. Let x be a set of objects which represents a concept, X, of universe U and $x \subseteq U$. x is then put into the database (or knowledge base) $K = <U, R>$ where R represents the elementary sets

FIGURE 1. Rough Sets–Set Approximation

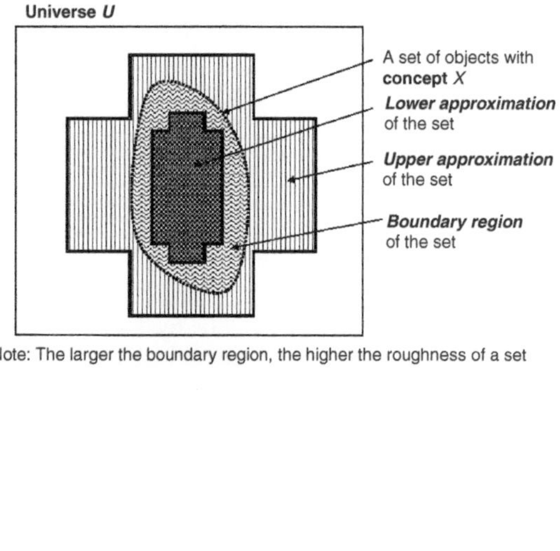

Note: The larger the boundary region, the higher the roughness of a set

or equivalent classes based on knowledge of *P* attributes that describe the objects. Further, the *P*-lower approximation of *X* in *K* = <*U*, *R*> is defined as:

$$\underline{P}X = \cup\{Y \in U \mid R{:}Y \subseteq X\}$$

The lower approximation of *PX* of concept *X* is the union of all those elementary sets each of which is contained by the concept based on knowledge of *P* attributes.

The *P*-upper approximation of *x* in *K* = <*U*, *R*> is defined as:

$$\overline{P}X = \cup\{Y \in U \mid R{:}Y \cap X \neq \varnothing\}$$

where $\overline{P}X$ is the set containing elements that can only possibly has concept *X* based on the same knowledge of *P* attributes.

Finally, the boundary region of concept *X* is defined as:

$$BN_p(X) = \overline{P}X - \underline{P}X$$

For objects belonging to $BN_P(X)$, it is not possible to determine that they have concept *X* based on the description of *P* attributes.

Information Table

The rough sets theory was first introduced as a tool to describe dependencies between attributes, to evaluate the significance of attributes, and to deal with inconsistent data. The rough sets theory is based on the assumption that with every object some information (data, knowledge) is associated. This information involves two types of attributes, namely *condition* and *decision* attributes. *Condition* attributes are those used to describe the characteristics of objects. Examples of *condition* attributes in the context of tourism demand are independent variables in the traditional causal models like income, price, level of promotion, and substitute price. The *decision* attribute(s) defines a partition of objects into classes according to the *condition* attributes. In the case of tourism demand forecast, a *decision* attribute would be number of tourist arrivals or amount of tourism receipts. On the basis of these two types of attributes, an Information Table such as the one shown in Table 1 can then be formed. The categorization of values of attributes in the Information Table will be described in the methodology section of this paper.

TABLE 1. An Information Table of Demand for Tourism

Objects	Condition Attributes						Decision Attribute
	X_1	X_2	X_3	X_4	X_5	X_6	Y
1	M	L	H	L	L	L	L
2	L	L	H	L	L	L	L
3	L	L	H	L	L	L	L
4	L	L	H	L	L	L	L
5	L	M	M	M	M	M	M
6	M	M	M	M	M	M	M
7	M	M	M	M	M	M	M
8	M	H	M	M	M	M	M
9	M	H	M	M	M	M	M
10	H	H	L	H	H	H	H
11	H	M	L	H	H	H	H

Note: Data for attributes have been preprocessed before rough sets analysis, and values of attributes are categorized where L = Low, M = Medium, H = High.

An Information Table represents input data gathered from any domain. The *condition* and *decision* attributes of tourism demand are represented in categorical values (e.g., high, medium, low) in an Information Table. For a time series forecasting approach such as tourism demand forecasting, *objects* in the Information Table are the time periods in which data are collected. *Objects* having the same attribute values are indiscernible with respect to these attributes and belong to the same block of *classification* determined by the set of attributes. Based on data classification, the rough sets theory offers simple algorithms in information reduction and decision rules induction.

Generally speaking, a decision rule is in the form of *IF_condition(s)_THEN_decision(s)*. If the condition(s) in the *IF* part matches with the given fact(s), the decision(s) in the *THEN* part will be performed. Unlike mathematical functions or statistical models in traditional tourism demand forecasting analyses, decision rules induced from a set of raw data can capture and represent non-numeric attributes. In addition, a decision rule always consists of a single and relatively independent piece of information. Different from the mathematically oriented models, the modular nature of decision rules makes it easy for researchers to add new decision rules or to modify existing decision rules without affecting the overall system. So, for example, a general decision rule for, say, arrivals to Hong Kong could be used as a base from which modified rules could be created for specific market sectors arriving in Hong Kong. In addition, it is relatively more intuitive and insightful to comprehend a process by citing the particular rule(s) used in reaching the conclusion than by citing a complex mathematical function. The easy-to-understand characteristic of decision rules is particularly useful for non-technical tourism practitioners. An example of a tourism demand decision rule is:

IF[*Per Capita Income* = High] AND
[*National Educational Level* = High] AND
[*Political System* = Capitalist]
THEN [*Arrivals* = High]

TABLE 2. A Profile of Japanese Tourist Arrivals in Hong Kong

Obj	*SP*	*AHR*	*ER*	*Pop*	*Mkt*	*Inc*	*Avl*
1	M	L	H	L	L	L	L
2	M	L	H	L	L	L	L
3	M	L	H	L	L	L	L
4	L	M	H	L	L	L	L
5	L	M	H	L	L	L	L
6	L	L	H	L	L	L	L
7	M	L	H	L	L	L	M
8	L	L	H	L	L	L	L
9	L	L	H	L	L	L	L
10	L	L	H	L	L	L	L
11	L	L	M	M	M	M	M
12	L	L	M	M	M	M	M
13	L	M	M	M	M	M	M
14	L	M	M	M	M	M	L
15	M	M	M	M	M	M	M
16	M	M	M	M	M	M	M
17	M	M	M	M	M	M	M
18	M	H	M	M	M	M	M
19	M	H	M	M	M	M	M
20	M	H	M	M	M	M	M
21	H	H	L	H	H	H	H
22	H	H	L	H	H	H	H
23	H	H	L	H	H	H	H
24	H	H	L	H	H	H	H
25	H	M	L	H	H	H	H
26	H	M	L	H	H	H	H
27	H	M	L	H	H	H	H
28	H	H	L	H	H	H	H
29	H	H	L	H	H	H	H
30	H	H	L	H	H	H	H

Obj: A particular year in consideration.
SP: Service price in Hong Kong relative to Japan.
AHR: Average hotel rate in Hong Kong.
ER: Foreign exchange rate between Yen and Hong Kong Dollar.
Pop: Population in Japan.
Mkt: Marketing expenses in Hong Kong.
Inc: Income per capita in Japan.
Avl: Number of Japanese visitors to Hong Kong.

Information Reduction

Intuitively, not all information in an attribute-value Information Table is important. More precisely, unique judgements on an Information Table can be made by omitting some attributes. To eliminate the superfluous attributes, the concepts of *reduct* and *core* sets of attributes are introduced. For every R, $R \subseteq C$, if $POS_C(D) \neq POS_R(D)$, C is defined as independent with respect to D. Otherwise, C is defined as dependent with respect to D. Discovering attribute independencies is claimed to have a primary importance in the rough sets approach for relationship modeling (Slowinski and Zopounidis 1995). An example of the *reduct* process occurs later in this paper: of the seven attribute values used in Table 2, only two (Income per capita in Japan/*Inc*) and Service price in Hong Kong relative to Japan/*SP*) remains after the reduction process to appear in Table 3.

The set S is known to be a *reduct* of C, denoted by $RED_D(C)$ if S is an independent subset of C with respect to D and $POS_S(D) = POS_C(D)$. In other words, the reduct $RED_D(C)$ is the minimal subset of C which generates the same classification of objects into an equivalence class of knowledge D as the whole knowledge C. For a set of condition and decision attributes, C and D, $a \in C$ is defined as dispensable in D if $POS_C(D) = POS_B(D)$; where $B = C - \{a\}$. Otherwise, attribute a is said to be indispensable in D.

TABLE 3. Decision Rules

6 out-of-sample forecast:	
IF <GDP = Low>	*THEN* <Arrivals = Low>
IF <GDP = Medium> AND <Service Price = Medium>	*THEN* <Arrivals = Medium>
IF <GDP = High>	*THEN* <Arrivals = High>
9 out-of-sample forecast:	
IF <GDP = Low>	*THEN* <Arrivals = Low>
IF <GDP = Medium> AND <Service Price = Medium>	*THEN* <Arrivals = Medium>
IF <GDP = High>	*THEN* <Arrivals = High>
12 out-of-sample forecast (random sample a)	
IF <GDP = Low>	*THEN* *<Arrivals = Low>*
IF <GDP = Medium>	*THEN* <Arrivals = Medium>
IF <GDP = High>	*THEN* <Arrivals = High>
12 out-of-sample forecast (random sample b)	
IF <GDP = Low>	*THEN* *<Arrivals = Low>*
IF <GDP = Medium>	*THEN* <Arrivals = Medium>
IF <GDP = High>	*THEN* <Arrivals = High>
12 out-of-sample forecast (random sample c)	
IF <GDP = Low>	*THEN* *<Arrivals = Low>*
IF <GDP = Medium>	*THEN* <Arrivals = Medium>
IF <GDP = High>	*THEN* <Arrivals = High>
12 out-of-sample forecast (random sample d)	
IF <GDP = Low>	*THEN* *<Arrivals = Low>*
IF <GDP = Medium>	*THEN* <Arrivals = Medium>
IF <GDP = High>	*THEN* <Arrivals = High>

Note: Only two attributes–GDP and service price–were left in the above six sets of rules. The rest were *superfluous* and were thus eliminated from the system through attribute reduction process.

A *core* is defined as the set of all indispensable attributes in *P*. That is, $CORE_D(C) = \{a \in C:POS_C(D) \neq POS_B(D)\}$. The *core* is a collection of the most significant attributes in an Information Table. In other words, one cannot eliminate a *core* attribute without destroying the ability to classify objects into an equivalence class *D*. However, the *core* set could be empty. Rules can then be induced from the reduced Information Table which contains the *reduct* set. The procedure for capturing decision rules from a set of raw data is known as induction (Pawlak et al., 1995; Pawlak and Slowinski, 1994; Pawlak, 2002).

Outcomes of a rough sets analysis are thus represented in a set of decision rules that is obtained from a reduct. The rules can identify data patterns hidden in a data set that link the value of specific condition attributes with a decision attribute.

METHODOLOGY

Data

This research used secondary data for Japanese arrivals in Hong Kong in the period of 1967 to 1996. Japan was the major source market for Hong Kong's tourism industry during the study period. Data collection and selection were mainly performed based on data availability and reliability. Having searched for various publicly available channels, data from the following sources were chosen for analysis:

- *Statistical Survey of Japan's Economy, 1976-1986,* published by the Economic and Foreign Affairs Research Association of Japan (1976-1986);
- *Commissioner of Inland Revenue Annual Review, 1967-1996,* published by the Hong Kong Government (Hong Kong Statistics Department, 1967-1996).
- *A Statistical Review of Tourism, 1976-1997,* published by the Hong Kong Tourist Association (1967-1997);
- *Statistical Handbook of Japan, 1996-1997,* published by the Statistics Bureau Management and Coordination Agency, Government of Japan (1996-1997);
- *Japan Statistical Yearbook, 1977-1997,* published by the Statistics Bureau Prime Minister's Office of Japan (1977-1997);
- *Hong Kong Tourist Association Annual Report, 1967-1997,* published by the Hong Kong Tourist Association (1976-1997).

Attributes

Similar to previous studies on tourism demand forecasting (Gonzalez and Moral, 1995; Kim and Uysal, 1997; Law, 2000; Lim, 1997a; Lim, 1997b; Witt and Witt, 1995), Japanese demand for travel to Hong Kong, measured in total number of Japanese tourist arrivals, was represented by the following function:

$$Avl_{hjt} = f(AHR_{ht}, SP_{hjt}, ER_{hjt}, Pop_{jt}, Mkt_t, Inc_{jt}) \quad (1)$$

Where Avl_{hjt} = number of Japanese tourist arrivals to Hong Kong in Year *t*;

AHR_{ht} = average hotel rate in Hong Kong in Year t;
SP_{hjt} = relative price for Japanese visitors' services in Hong Kong in Year t;
ER_{hjt} = exchange rate between Yen and Hong Kong Dollar in Year t;
Pop_{jt} = population in Japan in Year i;
Mkt_t = marketing expenses to promote Hong Kong's tourism industry in Year i;
Inc_{jt} = national income per capita in Japan in Year t.

Having obtained the relevant data for Japanese arrival in Hong Kong, the tourism demand attributes were identified. In this research, *Avl* served as the decision attribute for measuring demand for Japanese visitors to Hong Kong; whereas other variables in function (1) were the condition attributes. In other words, values of the decision attribute *Avl* were determined by the condition attributes: *AHR, SP, ER, Pop, Mkt,* and *Inc.* Published articles in the tourism literature have indicated that the number of tourist arrivals can be a suitable indicator of demand for tourism (Fretching, 2001; Law and Au, 1999; Qu and Lam, 1997).

Values for *AHR*, *ER*, and *Pop* were obtained or derived directly from published sources. "Relative price for Japanese visitors' services in Hong Kong" (*SP*) was defined as the ratio of the CPI in Hong Kong to the CPI in Japan (1990 = 100). That is, *SP* served as a proxy that measured the relative prices for Japanese to purchase in Hong Kong. Since it is almost impossible to collect all data for tourism prices, CPI ratios have been used widely in the tourism literature, as a proxy, to represent tourism prices (Carey, 1991; Morley, 1993). Additionally, "Marketing expenses to promote Hong Kong's tourism industry" (*Mkt*) measured the total marketing expenditure on promotional activities used by the Hong Kong Tourist Association (which has been renamed as the Hong Kong Tourism Board since 2001) to encourage potential tourists to visit Hong Kong. Due to data unavailability, *Mkt* was used as the proxy for marketing expenses in Japan to promote Hong Kong's tourism industry. Lastly, in this research, "national income in Japan" (*Inc*) measured the per capita income in Japan calculated by dividing Japan's GDP by Japan's population.

All monetary values were converted to real U.S. dollars, and adjusted by local consumer price index. Specifically, *AHR* and *Mkt* ware adjusted by the Hong Kong CPI (1990 = 100) while *Inc* as deflated by Japan CPI (1990 = 100). After that, the values were transformed to categorical classification in a non-numeric discrete interval form using an equal percentile approach with 3 categories, namely: H (High), M (Medium), and L (Low). These 3 categories were equivalent to the equivalence classes of the decision attribute in an Information Table. Table 2 shows the Information Table which contains the categorical values.

Information reduction and decision rules induction were then performed. The induced decision rules, appearing in a form of IF_condition(s)THEN_decision, described the behavior of demand for Japanese tourist arrivals in Hong Kong and its determining factors.

EMPIRICAL RESULTS

The data entries included in Table 2 were randomly divided into 2 groups for model calibration and model testing. A rough sets based computer program was developed to determine forecasting quality. Six different tests were performed which included one 6 out-of-sample, one 9 out-of-sample, and four 12 out-of-sample forecasts. Table 3 presents the induced decision rules using rough sets algorithm. As stated earlier, the primary objective of this paper is to investigate the feasibility of incorporating the rough sets theory into tourism demand forecasting. The in-depth analysis of the induced decision rules, albeit useful to tourism practitioners and policy makers, are beyond the discussion scope of this paper. Future studies can examine these rules and their industrial applicability in detail. The induced decision rules which modeled the relationship between the decision attribute and its associated condition attributes were then used to compute the forecast value of tourist arrivals. The forecast value and actual value of tourist arrivals were subsequently compared to evaluate the forecasting quality. The quality of forecasting performance, measured in the percentage of correctly classified cases, were presented in Table 4.

TABLE 4. Summary of Forecasting Performance

	6 out-of-sample forecast		9 out-of-sample forecast		12 out-of-sample forecast							
					(random selection a)		(random selection b)		(random selection c)		(random selection d)	
	Prediction	Actual	Prediction	Actual	Prediction	Actual	Prediction	Actual	Prediction	Actual	Prediction	Actual
	H	H	L	L	L	L	L	L	L	L	L	L
	H	H	L	M	L	M	L	M	L	L	L	M
	H	H	L	L	L	L	L	L	L	M	L	L
	H	H	L	L	L	L	M	M	L	L	M	M
	H	H	*ND	M	L	L	M	M	L	L	M	M
	H	H	*ND	M	M	M	M	M	M	M	M	M
			M	M	M	M	M	L	M	M	M	L
			M	M	M	M	M	M	M	L	M	M
			M	M	M	L	M	M	M	M	M	M
					M	M	M	M	M	M	M	M
					M	M	H	H	M	M	M	M
					H	H	H	H	M	M	H	H
Classified case	6		7		12		12		12		12	
No. of match	6		6		10		10		10		10	
match %	100%		85.7%		83.3%							
Overall accuracy	86.5%											

*ND = No Decision.

As revealed in Table 4, the induced rules could generate good forecasting results. In particular, the 6 out-of-sample test achieved 100% forecasting accuracy; whereas the corresponding values for 9 out-of-sample and 12 out-of-sample tests were 85.7% and 83.3% respectively. Overall, the forecasting quality could attain an 86.5% accuracy in this research. In other words, almost 90% of the forecast values and actual values were in the same category, showing the accurate forecasting results of the approach.

CONCLUSIONS AND FUTURE RESEARCH

The Hong Kong tourism industry has experienced a difficult time in the period 1997 to 1999 due to the Asian economic crisis. Although Hong Kong has recently recovered from the drop in tourist arrivals and tourism receipts, the market structure has significantly changed. In view of this non-trivial market change, there is a pressing need for policy makers and industry practitioners to better understand the demand for tourist arrivals so that more accurate planning at strategic, tactical, and operational levels could then be carried out. The research outcomes as presented in this paper indeed contribute to such a planning process.

The potential advantages and long term significance offered by this research are multi-fold. First, it is much easier for tourism practitioners and policy makers to understand the relationship of tourism demand and its determinants from a set of decision rules rather than from a complex mathematical function. Tourism professionals can then confidently apply the rough sets approach as an alternative forecasting technique to handle non-numeric categorical data. Without any loss in meaning of the original discrete categories, non-numeric data are simply difficult to handle using the existing mathematical functions based tourism demand forecasting models. Knowing the interaction of tourism demand and its determining factors, tourism decision-makers in

Hong Kong can carry out more accurate planning activities. Most importantly, traditional mathematical functions based tourism demand forecasting models have long been known and widely exploited. Only marginal improvements in tourism demand forecasting can be achieved with large additional development efforts on these traditional techniques. Consequently, new evolutionary or revolutionary forecasting techniques are needed to enhance, if not to revolutionize, tourism demand forecasting capability. The introduction of a decision rules based tourism demand forecasting model undoubtedly contributes to meeting this challenge.

The application of the rough sets theory to tourism demand forecasting, albeit appearing technically sound and empirically promising in this research, needs to demonstrate its general applicability in future studies. This generalization of knowledge could be achieved at both macro and micro levels using time series data alone or simultaneously with cross sectional data. For example, at the macro level, it could be used to analyze relationships between travel demand from each individual origin country and its determinants using time series data such as what has been investigated in this study. It could also be utilized to study cross sectional or panel data. That is to use pooled data on demand determining factors of multiple origin countries over a period of time. Because of the nature of the algorithm, which the rough sets theory is based on, non-numeric variables such as political system and cultural differences, could also be included in the demand analysis without having to transform their values to numeric ones. At the micro level, the approach could be used to study demand for a particular tourism product in many ways. For instance, a food and beverage operator could use cross sectional survey data to identify the target market for a specific restaurant product using the rough sets approach. Also, a tour operator could make use of information in its database to discover taste and preferences of customers in different demographic categories, and hence the demand for a particular type of products and services. Similarly, when planning strategies to increase room occupancy rate, a hotel operator could exploit historical data in a customer database to induce decision rules for sales promotion. These rules not only discover the demographic factors of potential customers but also classify the potential customers into groups in terms of expenditure levels. Unlike traditional demand analyses, which are carried out through statistical inferential techniques that follow many statistical assumptions, the only assumption made under this approach is that the values of attributes could be categorized. This unique advantage potentially makes the decision rules based approach a promising tool in a variety of demand analyses.

Although the objective of this study is not to focus on analyzing the methods of discretizing continuous-values, it has to be emphasized that the question of how to optimally discretize the attribute values is a topic of ongoing research. Future studies should look into various methods of discretization both static and dynamic ones, and compare and analyze how they could make a difference to the rules induced.

REFERENCES

Au, N. and Law, R. (2000). Application of rough sets to sightseeing expenditures. *Journal of Travel Research*, 39(1), 70-77.

Carey, K. (1991). "Estimation of Caribbean tourism demand: Issues in measurement and methodology", *Atlantic Economic Journal*, 19(3), 32-40.

Economic and Foreign Affairs Research Association of Japan (1976-1986). *Statistical Survey of Japan's Economy*, Economic and Foreign Affairs Research Association of Japan.

Fretching, D.C. (2001). *Forecasting Tourism Demand.* Oxford: Butterworth-Heinemann.

Gonzalez, P. and Moral, P. (1995). An analysis of the international tourism demand in Spain. *International Journal of Forecasting*, 11, 233-251.

Hong Kong Statistics Department (1967-1996). *Commissioner of Inland Revenue Annual Review,* Hong Kong: Hong Kong Statistic Department.

Hong Kong Tourist Association (1976-1997). *A Statistical Review of Tourism*, Hong Kong: Hong Kong Tourist Association.

Hong Kong Tourist Association (1967-1997). *Hong Kong Tourist Association Annual Report*, Hong Kong: Hong Kong Tourist Association.

Kim, Y. and Uysal, M. (1997). The endogenous nature of price variables in tourism demand studies. *Tourism Analysis*, 2, 9-16.

Law, R. (2000). Back-propagation learning in improving the accuracy of neural network-based tourism demand forecasting, *Tourism Management*, 21(4), 331-340.

Law, R. and Au, N. (1998). A rough set approach to hotel expenditure decision rules induction. *Journal of Hospitality & Tourism Research*, 22(4), 359-375.

Law, R. and Au, N. (1999). A neural network model to forecast Japanese demand for travel to Hong Kong. *Tourism Management*. 20(1), 89-97.

Law, R. and Au, N. (2000). Relationship modeling in tourism shopping: A decision rules induction approach. *Tourism Management*, 21(3), 241-249.

Lim, C. (1997a). Review of international tourism demand models. *Annals of Tourism Research*, 24(4), 835-849.

Lim, C. (1997b). An econometric classification and review of international tourism demand models. *Tourism Economics*, 3(1), 69-81.

McKee, T.E. and Lensberg, T. (2002). Genetic programming and rough sets: A hybrid approach to bankruptcy classification. *European Journal of Operational Research*, 138, 436-451.

Miyamoto, S. (1998). Application of rough sets to information retrieval. *Journal of the American Society for Information Science*, 49(3), 195-205.

Morley, C.L. (1993). Forecasting tourism demand using extrapolative time series methods, *Journal of Tourism Studies*, 4(1), 19-25.

Pawlak, Z. (1982). Rough-sets. *International Journal of Information and Computer Science*, 11, 341-356.

Pawlak, Z. (1998). Rough Set Elements. In Polkowski, L. & Skowron, A. (Eds.) *Rough Sets in Knowledge Discovery*, Vol. 1, 10-30. Warsaw: Physica-Verlag.

Pawlak, Z. (2002) Rough sets, decision algorithms and Bayes' theorem. *European Journal of Operational Research*, 136, 181-189.

Pawlak, Z., Grzymala-Busse, J., Slowinski, R., and Ziarko, W. (1995). Rough sets. *Communications of the ACM*, 38(11), 89-95.

Pawlak, Z. and Slowinski, R. (1994). Rough set approach to multi-attribute decision analysis. *European Journal of Operational Research*, 72, 443-459.

Qu, H. and Lam, S. (1997). A travel demand model for Mainland Chinese tourists to Hong Kong. *Tourism Management*, 18(8), 593-597.

Slowinski, R. and Zopounidis, C. (1995). Application of the rough Set approach to evaluation of bankruptcy risk. *Intelligent Systems in Accounting, Finance and Management*, 4(1), 27-42.

Statistics Bureau Management and Coordination Agency (1996-1997). *Statistical Handbook of Japan*, Statistics Bureau Management and Coordination Agency, Government of Japan.

Statistics Bureau Prime Minister's Office of Japan (1977-1997). *Japan Statistical Yearbook*, Statistics Bureau Prime Minister's Office of Japan.

Tanaka, H. and Maeda, Y. (1998). Reduction Methods for Medical Data. In Polkowski, L. & Skowron, A. (Eds.) *Rough Sets in Knowledge Discovery*, Vol. 2, 295-306. Warsaw: Physica-Verlag.

Witt, S.F. and Witt, C.A., (1995). Forecasting tourism demand: A review of empirical research. *International Journal of Forecasting*, 11(3), 447-475.

Initially Testing an Improved Extrapolative Hotel Room Occupancy Rate Forecasting Technique

Rob Law

SUMMARY. The existing time series forecasting models either capture the information of the last few data in the data series or the entire data series is used for projecting future values. In other words, the time series forecasting models are unable to take advantage of the last trend in the data series, which always have a direct influence on the estimated values. This paper proposes an improved extrapolative time series forecasting technique to compute future hotel occupancy rates. The performance of this new technique was tested with officially published room occupancy rates in Hong Kong. Forecasted room occupancy rates were compared with actual room occupancy rates in several accuracy performance dimensions. Empirical results indicate that the new technique is promising with reasonably good forecasting results. *[Article copies available for a fee from The Haworth Document Delivery Service: 1-800-HAWORTH. E-mail address: <docdelivery@haworthpress.com> Website: <http://www.HaworthPress.com> © 2004 by The Haworth Press, Inc. All rights reserved.]*

KEYWORDS. Room occupancy rates, time series forecasting, forecasting accuracy

INTRODUCTION

The accurate forecasting of hotel occupancy rates is crucial in most, if not all, departments of hotel operations. If accurate information about future demand for hotel rooms is not available, either overbooking or underbooking will occur, and both are very costly to the hotel business. Deveau et al. (1996) argue that overbooking is very damaging to the reputation of the hotel involved; whereas underbooking is always associated with financial loss that can never be recaptured. Similarly, Donaghy, McMahon-Beatie, and McDowell (1997) state that improvement in room occupancy forecast can facilitate management and financial strategies. Therefore, an accurate forecast of hotel room occupancy helps in shaping demand in planning for future supply of personnel, facilities, and services for the hotel

Rob Law is Associate Professor of Information Technology, School of Hotel & Tourism Management, The Hong Kong Polytechnic University, Hong Kong.

Address correspondence to: Rob Law, School of Hotel and Tourism Management, The Hong Kong Polytechnic University, Hung Hom, Kowloon, Hong Kong (E-mail: hmroblaw@polyu.edu.hk).

The author acknowledges the Hong Kong Polytechnic University research grant (G-T456), which partly supported this research.

The constructive comments and suggestions offered by the anonymous reviewers about an early draft of this paper are greatly appreciated.

[Haworth co-indexing entry note]: "Initially Testing an Improved Extrapolative Hotel Room Occupancy Rate Forecasting Technique." Law, Rob. Co-published simultaneously in *Journal of Travel & Tourism Marketing* (The Haworth Hospitality Press, an imprint of The Haworth Press, Inc.) Vol. 16, No. 2/3, 2004, pp. 71-77; and: *Management Science Applications in Tourism and Hospitality* (ed: Zheng Gu) The Haworth Hospitality Press, an imprint of The Haworth Press, Inc., 2004, pp. 71-77. Single or multiple copies of this article are available for a fee from The Haworth Document Delivery Service [1-800-HAWORTH, 9:00 a.m. - 5:00 p.m. (EST). E-mail address: docdelivery@haworthpress.com].

http://www.haworthpress.com/web/JTTM

© 2004 by The Haworth Press, Inc. All rights reserved.

Digital Object Identifier: 10.1300/J073v16n02_06

guests. This, in turn, leads to the reduction of heavy costs of excess supply and the opportunity costs of unfulfilled demand.

Other than the informal qualitative guesswork, traditional hospitality and tourism forecasting literature has predominantly concentrated on multivariate regression analyses and univariate time series models (Andrew et al., 1990; Frechtling, 1996; Witt and Witt, 1995). In multivariate regression analyses (sometimes known as econometric models), the relationship of a dependent variable and a set of independent variables is identified and represented using a multivariate mathematical function. This function is then used to predict future values of the dependent variable (Icoz et al., 1998; Lee et al., 1996). To illustrate, Law (1998) performed a study of multivariate regression analysis in room occupancy rate forecast. In his study, Law (1998) used six independent variables of microeconomic and macroeconomic factors to determine the room occupancy rates in Hong Kong and obtained significant results of forecasting performance. Despite their relatively high explanatory power and prediction accuracy, multivariate regression models have their own fundamental limitations. In particular, Frechtling (1996, 2001) comments the disadvantages of using regression models include the large costs involved, the required substantial skill, and the need to forecast the independent variables in order to obtain forecasts of the dependent variable.

Univariate time series models are non-causal quantitative techniques, which assume that a variable can be predicted without referring to the determining factors that affect the level of the variable (Witt and Witt, 1992; Frechtling, 2001). In other words, past history of the variable is simply extrapolated. Univariate time series models estimate future values for a single variable through a process of identifying a relationship, using mathematical functions, for past values of the variable. The natural advantages of a time series forecasting model are that the model is simple to apply and requires no more than a data series. Researchers claimed time series forecasting models are able to produce accurate results in hospitality and tourism forecasts (Athiyaman and Robertson, 1992; Witt and Witt, 1995). In particular, Andrew et al. (1990) examined the forecasting accuracy of monthly occupancy rates for a major center-city hotel using two time series forecasting models. Experimental results in Andrew et al.'s (1990) study showed that time series forecasting models had a high level of predictive accuracy.

The simple nature of time series forecasting models can lead to accurate results in tourism forecast. However, the existing time series forecasting models either capture the information of a few numbers towards the ending period of the data series or the entire data series is used for projecting future values. The problems associated with the approaches which take the last few numbers in the data series, such as the Moving Average or Naïve techniques, may induce a loss of relevant information in a trend. Nevertheless, considering the entire data series, such as the ARIMA or Autoregressive techniques, is very expensive to compute and uneasy to use. In other words, the existing time series forecasting models are unable to take advantage of the last trend in the data series, which always have a direct influence on the estimated values. Kasavana and Cahill (1997) state hospitality practitioners should consider the recent trend, instead of all historical trends, when projecting future revenue.

This paper presents a new time series forecasting technique for hotel room occupancy rates, named Improved Extrapolative Room Occupancy Rate Forecasting Model (IERORFM). An IERORFM uses past annual room occupancy rates in a data series to compute future values. The unique feature of an IERORFM is that it uses an incremental approach to calculate the growth rate in the last trend of the data series. In this paper, a trend is defined as the data range in a data series, and in this range the sum of deviations of the estimated and actual values of each data point is less than a user-defined preset threshold value. Specifically, an IERORFM makes an attempt to improve the forecasting accuracy by incorporating a certain degree of specified discrepancy that the previous forecasts have produced. The following section of this paper introduces the IERORFM approach. Next, there is a section to compare the forecasting performance of the commonly used time series forecasting models with a comparable computational efficiency as the IERORFM. The last section of this paper discusses the empirical findings and provides concluding comments.

THE MODEL

For a data series of annual room occupancy rates (measured in percentages) represented in $r_1, r_2, \ldots, r_y$ where r_y is the entry of the last time period in the series whereas r_1 is the entry of the first time period in the series, the IERORFM proceeds in the following way:

Transformation Stage

The series $r_1, r2, \ldots, r_y$ is transformed to the Cartesian Coordinate System in the form of $f(X_{first}, Y_{first}), f(X_{first+1}, Y_{first+1}), \ldots, f(X_{last}, Y_{last})$. In this new representation, an abscissa (x-coordinate) represents a specific time period whereas an ordinate (y-coordinate) denotes the magnitude (value) of a particular room occupancy rate.

Modeling Stage

The modeling stage starts from the point $f(X_{last-1}, Y_{last-1})$. Such a starting point is temporary and it is assumed to be the first point of the extrapolative trend, i.e., $f(X_{start}, Y_{start})$. Then, the point $f(X_{last}, Y_{last})$ is taken as the ending point of the trend under construction. The sum of deviations ($\sum Dev$) between the actual and estimated room occupancy rates obtained from the *trend* (growth rate) linking the start and end points is computed by:

$$f'(X_i, Y_i) = trend * (X_i - X_{start}) + f(X_{start}, Y_{start})$$

where

$$\sum Dev = \sum_{i=X_{start}}^{X_{last}} |f(X_i, Y_i) - f'(X_i, Y_i)|$$

$$trend = \frac{f(X_{last}, Y_{last}) - f(X_{start}, Y_{start})}{X_{last} - X_{start}}$$

A positive value of *trend* represents an increasing growth rate in room occupancy, whereas a negative value of *trend* indicates a decreasing growth rate in room occupancy. $f(X_i, Y_i)$ and $f'(X_i, Y_i)$ represent the original and forecasted room occupancy rates at time period *i*. The sum of deviations computed for the *trend* under construction is compared with a preset threshold limit for error tolerance ($\propto$). For instance, a value of 2 will be assigned to $\propto$ if the tolerance of maximum cumulative deviations is 2. If the sum of deviations is less than the deviation tolerance limit for the current $f(X_i, Y_i)$, then $f(X_{i-1}, Y_{i-1})$ is taken as the temporary start point. This procedure repeats until the sum of deviations is larger than $\propto$. At this point, the previous value of room occupancy rate examined will be taken as the start point of the trend. The value of $\propto$, which is chosen by the user, largely determines the computation speed and forecasting accuracy. A large value of $\propto$ allows for a higher computational efficiency at the expense of a lower forecasting accuracy. A small value of $\propto$ will produce a lower distortion between original series and the reconstructed series. The drawback for a small value of $\propto$ is that it takes a longer time to complete the iteration procedure.

Extrapolative Stage

To forecast room occupancy rate in *k* time periods ahead, with respect to $f(X_{last}, Y_{last})$, the estimated value of $f(X_{last+k}, Y_{last+k})$ is calculated by:

$$f(X_{last+k}, Y_{last+k}) = f(X_{last}, Y_{last}) + k * trend$$

EMPIRICAL FINDINGS

Officially published hotel occupancy rates, as shown in Figure 1 and Table 1, in Hong Kong (HKTA 1967-1998) were used to test for the forecasting accuracy of the IERORFM. A computer program was implemented for the IERORFM. Forecasting accuracy of the IERORFM was then compared with the commonly used extrapolative time series forecasting models (Athiyaman and Robertson 1992; Frechtling, 1996; Witt and Witt, 1992). The time series forecasting models included for comparison consist of Holt's Two-Parameter Exponential Smooth-

FIGURE 1. Hotel Occupancy Rates in Hong Kong

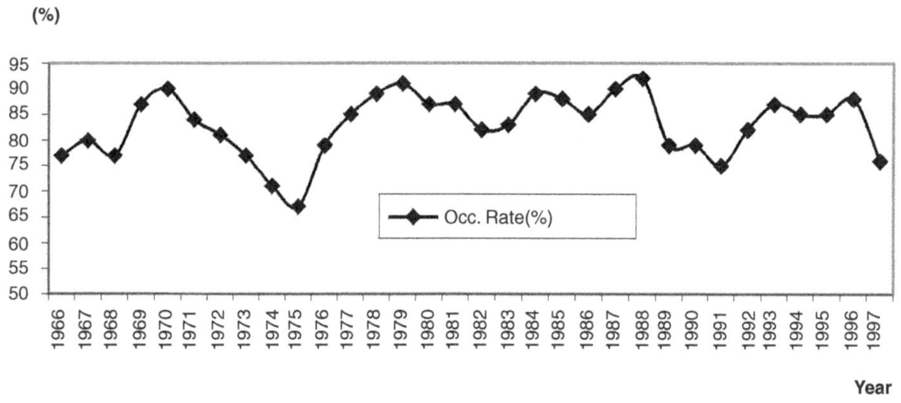

ing (1.0, 0) where 1.0 and 0 represent the values of base coefficient and trend of the series, Single Exponential Smoothing (1.0), Order 3 Moving Average, Naïve 1, and Naïve 2 models. These time series forecasting models are all simple in nature and easy to compute. In other words, they are comparable in terms of understandability and computation efficiency to the IERORFM introduced in this paper. Appendix A provides an overview of these time series forecasting models.

Among the 32 numbers in the years 1966 to 1997, the first 29 numbers (i.e., 1966 to 1994) were used to forecast the hotel occupancy rates in 1995 to 1997. Hong Kong experienced a big decrease in tourist arrivals in 1997 (Granitsas, 1998; HKTA, 1998). Therefore, it would be worthwhile to observe whether the aforementioned time series forecasting models can predict this directional change. Table 2 shows the experimental results of the actual values and the forecasted values and Table 3 illustrates the accuracy measurements. Forecasting accuracy was measured in terms of mean absolute error (*MAD*), mean square error (*MSE*), mean absolute percentage error (*MAPE*), and root mean square percentage error (*RMSPE*). According to Law (2000), *MAD* measures the overall accuracy, and provides an indication of the overall spread, where all errors are given equal weights. *MSE* also measures the overall accuracy by providing an indication of spreading level, but large errors are assigned larger weights. *MAPE* is a relative measurement that corresponds to *MAD*. Finally, *RMSPE* is a relative measurement, corresponding to *MSE*. Each of these measurements is defined next (for 1995-1997, n = 1, 2, 3).

$err_t = f'(X_t, Y_t) - f(X_t, Y_t)$ where $f'(X_t, Y_t)$ and $f(X_t, Y_t)$ represent the forecasted value and actual value, respectively.

$$MAD = \frac{1}{n}\sum_{t=1}^{n}|err_t|$$

$$MSE = \frac{1}{n}\sum_{t=1}^{n}err_t^{\,2}$$

$$MAPE = \frac{1}{n}\sum_{t=1}^{n}\frac{|err_t|}{f(X_t, Y_t)} * 100\%$$

$$RMSPE = \sqrt{\frac{1}{n}\sum_{t=1}^{n}\left[\frac{err_t}{f(X_t, Y_t)}\right]^2} * 100\%$$

DISCUSSION AND CONCLUSIONS

In Table 2, the estimated room occupancy rates as computed by the IERORFM are very close to their actual counterparts. In other words, the forecasting output from an IERORFM is accurate with a small amount of error. In addition, Table 3 reveals the forecasting quality for the selected forecasting models in terms of *MAD, MSE, MAPE*, and *RMSPE*. In particular, the *MAPE* of the IERORFM is only 4.77%. Witt and Witt (1992) and Frechtling (2001)

TABLE 1. Hotel Occupancy Rates in Hong Kong (1966-1997)

Year	Hotel Occupancy Rate (%)
1966	77
1967	80
1968	77
1969	87
1970	90
1971	84
1972	81
1973	77
1974	71
1975	67
1976	79
1977	85
1978	89
1979	91
1980	87
1981	87
1982	82
1983	83
1984	89
1985	88
1986	85
1987	90
1988	92
1989	79
1990	79
1991	75
1992	82
1993	87
1994	85
1995	85
1996	88
1997	76

categorize such a low MAPE value as "highly accurate forecasting."

Previous studies reveal that it is crucial to forecast the direction of change of a data series instead of its actual magnitude (Frechtling, 1996; Witt and Witt, 1995). In the context of this research, the challenge is to investigate whether there will be more or fewer rooms to be sold in the future. Hotel managers can then receive an indication as to whether to plan for an increase or decrease in hotel rooms demand, despite the magnitude of the change is somewhat unsure. Based on the forecasted directional change, hotel managers can then decide whether to increase or decrease room rates, staffing, and facilities. As indicated in Table 2, only the IERORFM can accurately forecast the most critical downturn in 1997 during that year Hong Kong was facing the worst slump in its tourism industry, which the local hotels depended almost entirely on. The result Moving Average was not included as the decreasing value is negligible.

To summarize, the IERORFM is inexpensive to calculate and easy to understand. More importantly, the IERORFM can produce more accurate forecasting results than the other comparable time series forecasting models. An accurate forecast in hospitality and tourism is always emphasized by previous studies (Chan 1993; Witt and Witt, 1992). Hotel managers can benefit from the outcomes of this research to improve strategic planning aimed at the provision of rooms to be sold in the next several years. To recap, an inaccurate forecast creates excess supply and therefore results in extra costs if the estimation of room occupancy rate is too high; whereas an underestimation of room occupancy rate is always associated with losing businesses.

Determining room occupancy and hence room availability in the hotel business is an ongoing process for both long-term and short-term planning. The time frame for forecasting is, in fact, not a very important factor. The most important factor for performing a room occupancy forecast is that an accurate and reliable method is needed when a hotel manager attempts to ascertain the answer to his/her query for future room occupancy. The IERORFM approach presented in this paper certainly contributes to meet this challenge.

The IERORFM introduced in this paper deals with annual room occupancy rates which assumes a data series with no seasonal fluctuations. To handle a data series with seasonal patterns, a decomposition method can be performed to remove such patterns (Frechtling, 2001). Besides, the applicability of the IERORFM in strategic long-term room occupancy rate forecasting has been shown. However, it is unknown whether the IERORFM can maintain its reliability in short-term room occupancy rate

TABLE 2. An Overview of Actual and Forecasted Room Occupancy Rates

Actual	IERORFM	Holt's Exponential Smoothing (1.0, 0)	Single Exponential Smoothing (1.0)	Moving Average (3)	Naïve 1	Naïve 2
85.00	83.09	85.29	85.00	84.67	85.00	83.05
88.00	81.18	85.57	85.00	85.56	85.00	85.00
76.00	79.27	85.86	85.00	85.08	85.00	91.11

TABLE 3. Comparisons of Forecasting Accuracy Measurements

Measurement	IERORFM	Holt's Exponential Smoothing (1.0, 0)	Single Exponential Smoothing (1.0)	Moving Average (3)	Naïve 1	Naïve 2
MAD	4.00	4.19	4.00	3.95	4.00	6.69
MSE	20.28	34.40	30.00	29.50	30.00	80.37
MAPE	4.77%	5.36%	5.08%	5.04%	5.08%	8.53%
RMSPE	5.28%	7.66%	7.11%	7.08%	7.11%	11.72%

forecasting. An interesting future research possibility is to investigate such reliability.

This study has shown the feasibility and accuracy of applying the IERORFM model to forecast hotel occupancy rates for the Hong Kong hotel industry. While the empirical results appear promising, further work needs to be done to test the general applicability of the model. A major area open for future research is to investigate the standardization and optimization procedures for defining the threshold value. In this present study, the chosen threshold value was made on a subjective basis. Since the value of the threshold limit will largely influence the behavior of the procedure, a commonly agreed approach for choosing (or calculating) the threshold will help standardize the approach. Another limitation of this research is that it used the Hong Kong case as the only example as a benchmark for initial comparison, making it unknown whether the technique can handle complex series. After the standardization process, it will be beneficial to test the model more extensively and thoroughly with different types of time series which include various trends and patterns.

REFERENCES

Andrew, W.P., Cranage, D.A., & Lee, C.K. (1990). Forecasting Hotel Occupancy Rates with Time Series Models: An Empirical Analysis. *Hospitality Research Journal*, 14(2): 173-181.

Athiyaman, A., & Robertson, R.W. (1992). Time Series Forecasting Techniques: Short-Term Planning in Tourism. *International Journal of Contemporary Hospitality Management*, 4(4): 8-11.

Chan, Y.M. (1993). Forecasting Tourism: A Sine Wave Time Series Regression Approach. *Journal of Travel Research*, Fall: 58-69.

Deveau, L.T., Deveau, P.M., Portocarrero, N.D.J., & Escoffier, M. (1996). *Front Office Management and Operation*. NJ: Prentice Hall.

Donaghy, K., McMahon-Beatie, U., and McDowell, D. (1997). Yield Management Practices. In I. Yeoman and A. Ingold (Eds.) *Yield Management–Strategies for the Service Industries* (pp. 183-201). London: Cassell.

Frechtling, D.C. (1996). *Practical Tourism Forecasting*. Oxford: Butterworth-Heinemann.

Frechtling, D.C. (2001). *Forecasting Tourism Demand: Methods and Strategies*. Oxford: Butterworth-Heinemann.

Granitsas, A. (1998, January 15). Wish You Were Here: Hong Kong's Tourist Industry Is Getting Hammered. *Far Eastern Economic Review*, p. 51.

HKTA (1967-1998). *A Statistical Review of Tourism*. Hong Kong: Hong Kong Tourist Association.

Icoz, O., Var, T., & Kozak, M. (1998). Tourism Demand in Turkey. *Annals of Tourism Research*, 25(1): 236-239.

Kasavana, M., & Cahill, J. (1997). *Managing Computers in the Hospitality Industry*, Lansing: American Hotel & Lodging Association.

Law, R. (1988). Room Occupancy Rate Forecasting: A Neural Network Approach. *International Journal of Contemporary Hospitality Management*, 10(6): 234-239.

Law, R. (2000). Back-propagation learning in improving the accuracy of neural network-based tourism demand forecasting. *Tourism Management*, 21(4): 331-340.

Lee, C.K., Var, T., & Blaine, T.W. (1996). Determinants of inbound tourist expenditures. *Annals of Tourism Research*, 23(3): 527-542.

Witt, S.F., & Witt, C.A. (1992). *Modeling and Forecasting Demand in Tourism.* London: Academic Press.

Witt, S.F., & Witt, C.A. (1995). Forecasting tourism demand: A review of empirical research. *International Journal of Forecasting*, 11: 447-475.

APPENDIX A

Time Series Forecasting Models

Among the chosen forecasting models, a Naïve 1 model is the simplest to understand and the easiest to compute. Assuming there is no change, a Naïve 1 model assigns the value of *a* at time *t* to the value of α' at time period *t* + 1. That is:

$$\alpha'_{t+1} = \alpha_t.$$

A Naïve 2 model assumes no change in growth rate. The value of α' at time period *t* + 1 is calculated by multiplying the value of α at time period *t* by the growth rate over the previous period:

$$\alpha'_{t+1} = \alpha_t * \left[1 + \frac{\alpha_t - \alpha_{t-1}}{\alpha_{t-1}}\right]$$

For an Order N Moving Average forecasting model, the value of α' at time period *t* + 1 is calculated as the average of the last N numbers. In other words, a Moving Average forecast model is an extension of the Naïve 1 model by including N previous numbers. Therefore, a Moving Average (3) projects α'_{t+1} as:

$$\alpha'_{t+1} = (\alpha_t + \alpha_{t-1} + \alpha_{t-2}) / 3$$

While a Moving Average forecasting model gives equal weight to all of the included past values, a Single Exponential Smoothing model attempts to improve the forecasting accuracy by incorporating a portion of the error that the previous forecast produced. In this approach, the value of *a'* at time *t*+1 is calculated as:

$\alpha'_{t+1} = \alpha'_t + \beta(\alpha_{t-}\ \alpha'_t)$ where β is a smoothing constant, such that $0 < \beta < 1$.

As an extension of the Single Exponential Smoothing method, the Holt's Two-Parameter Exponential Smoothing approach assumes the existence of a linear trend. At the end of time period *t*, the Holt's method generates an estimate of the base level (L_t) and the per-period trend (T_t) of the series. The value of *a'* at period *t* + 1 then is calculated as:

$$L_t = \alpha(\alpha_t) + (1 - \alpha)(L_{t-1} + T_{t-1})$$

$$Tt = \beta(L_t - L_{t-1}) + (1 - \beta)\, T_{t-1}$$

$a'_t = L_t + T_t$ where α and β are smoothing constants, such that $0 < \alpha, \beta < 1$.

Forecasting in Short-Term Planning and Management for a Casino Buffet Restaurant

Clark Hu
Ming Chen
Shiang-Lih Chen McCain

SUMMARY. Demand fluctuation accounts for an important consideration in a restaurant's daily operational decisions. Good short-term planning and management require accurate forecasts of daily demand. The objective of this study is three-fold: (1) to apply, evaluate, and compare different methods of forecasting customer counts for an on-premises buffet restaurant of a local casino in Las Vegas, (2) to describe and propose a combined forecasting approach for this casino buffet restaurant, and (3) to explore the concept of revenue and capacity management for this buffet restaurant. Eight forecasting models were tested and evaluated by two common error measures. The results suggest that a double moving average model was the most accurate model with the smallest MAPE and RMSPE. Extensive discussions on forecasting and planning/management in buffet operations are provided along with recommended future research. *[Article copies available for a fee from The Haworth Document Delivery Service: 1-800-HAWORTH. E-mail address: <docdelivery@haworthpress.com> Website: <http://www.HaworthPress. com> © 2004 by The Haworth Press, Inc. All rights reserved.]*

KEYWORDS. Casino buffet restaurant, combined forecasting, demand forecasting, restaurant revenue management (RRM), short-term planning, time series

BACKGROUND

Casinos are well known for aggressive marketing programs that attract vacationers to the casino floor and keep them there for more gaming opportunities. However, casino hotel managers often find that enticing guests to visit their properties can be very challenging, especially in Las Vegas, where visitors have a wide range of dining and entertainment venues to choose. Local casinos focusing on repeat clients have been known to entice customers to the casino floor via their attractive price/value restaurants. Although fine dining has evolved to be a trendy attraction for Las Vegas casinos (Mack, 1999; Tasoulas, 1999),

Clark Hu is Assistant Professor, School of Tourism & Hospitality Management, Temple University, 316L Vivacqua Hall (062-62), Philadelphia, PA 19122-0840 (E-mail: clark.hu@temple.edu). Ming Chen is a Doctoral Student, College of Hotel Administration, University of Nevada at Las Vegas, 4505 Maryland Parkway, Las Vegas, NV 89154 (E-mail: mingchenmichael@hotmail.com). Shiang-Lih Chen McCain is Assistant Professor, School of Hospitality Management, Widener University, One University Place, Chester, PA 19013-5792 (E-mail: Shianglih@yahoo.com).

[Haworth co-indexing entry note]: "Forecasting in Short-Term Planning and Management for a Casino Buffet Restaurant." Hu, Clark, Ming Chen, and Shiang-Lih Chen McCain. Co-published simultaneously in *Journal of Travel & Tourism Marketing* (The Haworth Hospitality Press, an imprint of The Haworth Press, Inc.) Vol. 16, No. 2/3, 2004, pp. 79-98; and: *Management Science Applications in Tourism and Hospitality* (ed: Zheng Gu) The Haworth Hospitality Press, an imprint of The Haworth Press, Inc., 2004, pp. 79-98. Single or multiple copies of this article are available for a fee from The Haworth Document Delivery Service [1-800-HAWORTH, 9:00 a.m. - 5:00 p.m. (EST). E-mail address: docdelivery@haworthpress.com].

http://www.haworthpress.com/web/JTTM
© 2004 by The Haworth Press, Inc. All rights reserved.
Digital Object Identifier: 10.1300/J073v16n02_07

buffet restaurants have remained an excellent bargain for casino guests among different types of restaurants offered in casinos. Many local casino operators designed their on-premises restaurants with less intention to make profits but as a draw to lure customers to their properties. They hope that once customers are exposed to the gaming environment, the chances to engage customers in gaming activities will be higher (Lucas & Santos, 2002). This longstanding approach to foodservice as a subsidized amenity still exists in the industry (Anonymous, 1996). This is particularly true for in-house buffet restaurants through discount-priced meals or "comps" (giveaways) based on guests' levels of play.

Some evidence has provided support for the argument that casino restaurants may serve as a necessary determinant for a customer's visitation decision to casinos. In a study conducted by Roehl (1996) to examine customers' use of casino amenities, 56.5% of respondents reported that they usually patronized buffet restaurants while only 8.8% of respondents reported that they usually patronized gourmet restaurants. Although Roehl did not find a significant relationship between casino restaurant use and frequency of casino visitations, he recognized a positive contribution of the buffet restaurant to a casino's success if (1) the revenue generated by the buffet restaurant exceeded the cost of its operation, and/or (2) customers would not have visited the casino if the buffet restaurant was not offered (available). Richard and Adrian (1996) found that the features of casino restaurants positively influenced customers' revisit intentions. According to the latest Clark County Residents Study (Las Vegas Convention & Visitor Authority, 2001), 73% of residents who gambled in casinos usually ate in a casino restaurant and 38 % of local residents reported that they were most likely to eat at a buffet when gambling in a casino. Hence, casino buffet restaurants are considered as a significant part of casino operations and often used as a marketing feature to attract visitors.

Messersmith and Miller (1991) correctly acknowledged that the forecasting of a food operation influences food production, inventory, staffing, financial status, manager confidence, employee morale, and customer satisfaction. Forecasting business volume for the next day plays an important role in buffet restaurant operations. Figure 1 illustrates the problems, consequences, and likely remedies in daily operations management of a typical buffet restaurant. The restaurant manager coordinates with the head chef to schedule the front-house and kitchen staff for the next-day operation based on the estimation of the food covers for the next day. Most casino hotels keep a certain percentage of on-call/part-time employees for contingency operations in case of situational needs. This gives managers more flexibility in scheduling staff based on market demand but the execution of this flexibility comes with higher costs (e.g., paying for the employees' overtime hours). This can be avoided if the forecasting of short-term demand in daily planning is accurate.

Currently, most buffet restaurant managers rely on their own intuition and experience to estimate the food covers. If their estimates are accurate, then the operation of the next day will be smooth. However, this is often not the case. They either over-forecast or under-forecast daily food covers. Either overproduction or underproduction can be detrimental to buffet operations. Overproduction leads to costly food waste, which is particularly evident in buffet restaurants where a substantial amount of food is prepared and served in advance instead of being cooked after customers place their orders. Although many casinos redistribute their buffet leftovers to the employees' cafeterias, it takes efforts to make the surplus food remain safe and still possess acceptable quality. On the other hand, when managers under-forecast the food covers and therefore under-staff employees, buffet customers often receive unsatisfactory buffet services as a result of slow operations (e.g., longer waiting times for seating and slow food refills). In addition, employees' morale will be lowered under the stress of last-minute preparation and/or customer complaints. Consequently, the quality and value of buffet offerings are discounted and customers are driven to competing casinos or other local restaurants. Furthermore, when managers under-forecast the buffet covers, overtime pay (usually 1.5 times normal pay) and higher food purchasing costs will occur if the management wants to keep the customers

FIGURE 1. An Illustration of Forecasting Challenges in a Typical Buffet Restaurant's Daily Operations

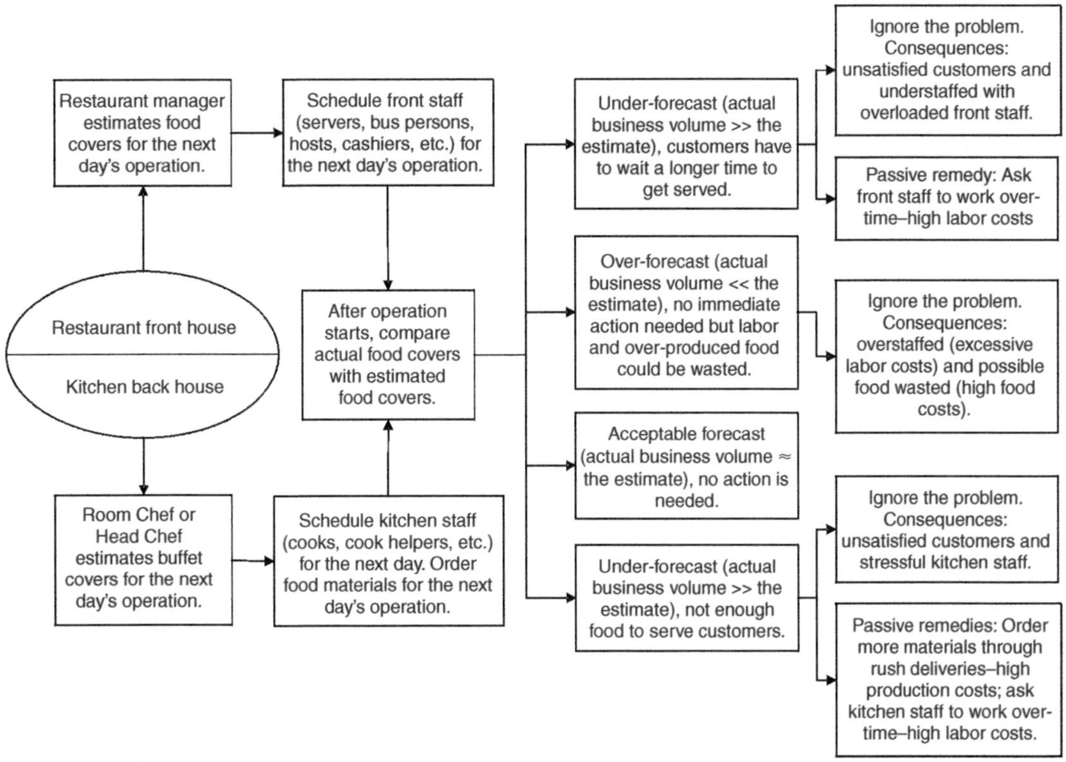

Restaurant manager estimates food covers for the next day's operation.

Schedule front staff (servers, bus persons, hosts, cashiers, etc.) for the next day's operation.

Restaurant front house

Kitchen back house

Room Chef or Head Chef estimates buffet covers for the next day's operation.

Schedule kitchen staff (cooks, cook helpers, etc.) for the next day. Order food materials for the next day's operation.

After operation starts, compare actual food covers with estimated food covers.

Under-forecast (actual business volume >> the estimate), customers have to wait a longer time to get served.

Ignore the problem. Consequences: unsatisfied customers and understaffed with overloaded front staff.

Passive remedy: Ask front staff to work over-time–high labor costs

Over-forecast (actual business volume << the estimate), no immediate action needed but labor and over-produced food could be wasted.

Ignore the problem. Consequences: overstaffed (excessive labor costs) and possible food wasted (high food costs).

Acceptable forecast (actual business volume ≈ the estimate), no action is needed.

Under-forecast (actual business volume >> the estimate), not enough food to serve customers.

Ignore the problem. Consequences: unsatisfied customers and stressful kitchen staff.

Passive remedies: Order more materials through rush deliveries–high production costs; ask kitchen staff to work over-time–high labor costs.

satisfied under this particular situation. The long-term consequence will be a high employee turnover rate and higher costs in hiring/training new employees. Before new employees become skillful at their jobs, the lost productivity will impose an extra burden on their fellow workers.

The problems of over- and under-production usually result from incorrect operational decisions during ineffective planning. Makridakis (1996) argued that the prerequisite for effective planning is accurate forecasting and that forecasts are the best estimates about the future at the short-term operational level. Forecasting is also an integral part of the operations management because accurate forecasts can provide valuable information for managers' decision making (Athiyaman & Robertson, 1992; Makridakis, Wheelwright, & Hyndman, 1998). In order to achieve good short-term planning, buffet chefs/managers need to anticipate daily demand fluctuation in the operation.

Forecasting is particularly important in the foodservice industry where perishability is a major concern (Kimes, Chase, Choi, Lee, & Ngonzi, 1998). Accurate forecasting can ensure adequate food production; improve inventory/staffing precision; and increase manager confidence and employee morale, and customer satisfaction. Based on the authors' observations and work experiences, many casino restaurants' operators currently predict customer counts solely based on their managers' intuition or guess-estimation from past experiences. Nevertheless, even simple mathematical methods, such as a naïve model, a simple moving average model, or a single exponential smoothing model have been suggested to outperform the intuitive experts' assessments (Chandler, Norton, Hoover, & Moore, 1982; Georgoff & Murdick, 1986; J. J. Miller, McCahon, & Miller, 1991a). In spite of the importance of accurate forecasting, most foodservice operators still only rely on their intuition or experience to estimate the future demand in the foodservice industry (J. J. Miller, McCahon, & Miller, 1991a; J. L.

Miller, McCahon, & Bloss, 1991; Ryu & Sánchez, 2002). Yet, researchers have recognized the need for the foodservice industry to apply mathematical or quantitative methods to forecast the future demand and conducted several studies to forecast food production in university dining halls, hospitals, and hotel restaurants by using mathematical models (J. J. Miller, McCahon, & Miller, 1991a; J. L. Miller, McCahon, & Bloss, 1991; J. L. Miller, Thompson, & Orabella, 1991; Ryu & Sánchez, 2002). Why does the gap exist between academic researchers and industry practitioners? The authors believe the answers line with three possible reasons: (1) Arguably, researchers' mathematical or quantitative forecasting methods may still be incomprehensible to industry practitioners. (2) These forecasting methods may be perceived by industry managers too cumbersome or intimidated to apply even with relatively accessible software. (3) More convincingly, researchers have not provided a more comprehensive and practical coverage to guide industry managers through these methods' applications.

RESEARCH OBJECTIVES

To the authors' knowledge, virtually no research has been conducted to examine the roles of forecasting and operational planning played in the casino restaurant setting. In responding to the need for accurate forecasting expressed by casino restaurants' operators, this study examined eight forecasting methods ranging from the simplest naïve models to slightly complicated Holt-Winters model and multiple regression models that are applicable and relatively available for managers' practical use. The objectives of this study were to (1) apply, evaluate, and compare different methods of forecasting customer counts for an on-premises buffet restaurant of a local casino in Las Vegas, (2) describe and propose a combined forecasting approach for this casino buffet restaurant, and (3) explore the concept of revenue and capacity management for this buffet restaurant. Forecasting methods were intentionally chosen for their simplicity and applicability for industry practitioners to replicate. Using the actual casino buffet restaurant's time series data, the authors attempted to demonstrate the usefulness and applicability of forecasting models in short-term planning. A "combined forecasting" concept was proposed to be integrated into the buffet restaurant's planning and operation. Finally, this forecasting approach was linked to the concept of revenue and capacity management for this buffet restaurant to explore possible operational improvements. By achieving the objectives of this research, the authors hope to bridge the gap between academic researchers and industry practitioners.

FORECASTING METHODOLOGY

Data and the Casino Hotel

A total of 610 daily observations of buffet covers (or customer counts) along with relevant data, from June 1, 2000, to January 31, 2002, were obtained and analyzed in this study. All data were secondary in nature and queried from the marketing/financial database of a casino hotel located in Las Vegas, Nevada (Hereafter, this unidentified property will be referred to as "LV Casino"). This particular property was a medium-sized operation, in terms of hotel rooms and annual gaming revenues, with a significant position in the local market. In addition to 3 fast-food outlets, the LV Casino operated five full-service restaurants at the time of the study: a 410-seat buffet restaurant, a 300-seat café, an 140-seat steak and seafood restaurant, a 149-seat Italian restaurant, and a 220-seat Mexican restaurant. The buffet restaurant was operated on a daily basis and served daily buffet covers between 1,500 and 2,500. To the authors' knowledge, this study was the first work in forecasting casino buffet counts. The authors' literature review indicated that prior studies in foodservice forecasting applied univariate methods to estimate the guest or meal counts. For instance, Miller, McCahon, and Miller (1991a; 1991b; 1993), Miller, McCahon, and Bloss (1991), and Miller, Thompson, and Orabella (1991) applied univariate methods to forecast the guest covers in the university dinning halls and restaurants. Miller and Shanklin (1988), Morgan and Chintagunta (1997), and Ryu and Sánchez (2002) also only considered the current meal counts and their lagged values to estimate future forecasts of meal counts in the restaurant, health care and university dining facilities. No variable other than the "demand" variables (guest/meal counts and their lagged values) can be followed by this study. Therefore, the selection of the independent variables for regression models was based on the authors' work experience and personal in-depth interviews with casino managers and internal analysts. Available variables considered to have the predicting power to the buffet covers (as the dependent variable being forecasted) were the number of occupied hotel rooms, the occurrence of marketing events, and weekly fluctuating patterns (as dummy variables). Although most experts agreed that some external factors such as competitors' promotion efforts would influence the buffet covers, competition data were unobtainable. Due to the limitation on the data availability, this study utilized only available internal data. The following few sections describe all variables used in the study.

Buffet Covers (BC)

Used by the restaurant industry, "cover" is a term that stands for the number (or the number of times) of customers dining at a restaurant. In this study, a cover is defined as the number of customers dining at a restaurant. On a typical day, buffet covers consist of 40% of the total food covers of this LV Casino. Because of this significance in serving the dining needs of mass casino visitors (including hotel and nonhotel guests), buffet covers were chosen as the forecasting subject of this study. Figure 2 provides a time series plot showing both buffet covers and the number of occupied hotel rooms during the 87-week studied period.

Numbers of Occupied Rooms (NOR)

It was believed by LV Casino's restaurant managers that the more hotel rooms occupied, the larger demand would be for LV Casino's dining services. According to the casino restaurants' managers' collective wisdom, the number of occupied hotel rooms (estimated by reservation data) could be a good indicator for forecasting buffet covers.

Marketing Events (ME)

Special events are one of the most important marketing tools employed by casino hotels to attract more guest/player visits. Restaurants of a casino hotel are operated to meet dining needs of both hotel guests and casino players. The commonly used marketing events in the LV Casino have been gift give-aways, slot tournaments, blackjack tournaments, player club members' birthday parties, and cash drawings, etc. These marketing events might have an impact on buffet covers for two reasons. First, participants in these marketing events could dine conveniently at either the buffet restaurant or other types of restaurants inside the LV Casino. Second, free buffet coupons were frequently used in these marketing events to attract more casino visits. Consequently, the occurrence of the marketing events was considered to influence the fluctuation of buffet covers. In this study, this variable was a dummy variable that was coded as 1 if there was a special event on that day and 0 otherwise.

Weekly Fluctuating Patterns

The LV Casino had weekly fluctuating patterns in most of service operations. Therefore, days of the week were used as dummy variables (TU, W, TH, F, SA, and SU) to accommodate possible pattern shifts during a week. These dummies were coded as binary variables. For example, TU (Tuesday) was coded as 1 if it was Tuesday and 0 otherwise in the data. In this study, Monday was treated as the reference day during a week. Any other days in the week were referenced (compared) to Monday when their impact and significance were assessed and interpreted in the regression models.

Forecasting Models

In this section, the authors discuss eight forecasting models, six univariate time series models and two multivariate regression models, examined in this study. They were respectively: (1) naïve model 1 (n = 1, no-change model), (2) naïve model 2 (n = 7, same-as-last-week model), (3) single moving average model,

FIGURE 2. Time Series Plot of Buffet Covers and the Number of Rooms Occupied During 88 Week Periods

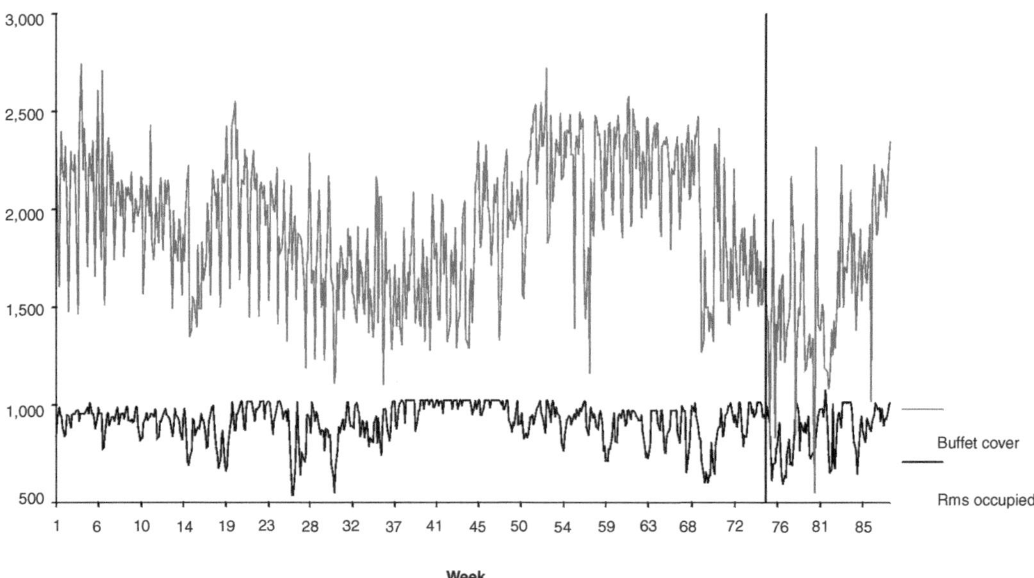

(4) double moving average model, (5) single exponential smoothing model (α = 0.3), (6) Holt-Winters method, (7) regression model 1, and (8) regression model 2 (the log-linear form of regression model 1). Data were partitioned into two sets. The first 17-months' observations (from June 2000 to October 2001) were used to build each forecasting model and the remaining three-months' data (from November 2001 to January 2002) were used as a hold-out sample to test for the accuracy of each forecasting model.

Naïve Models

The naïve method is the simplest to implement. Naïve forecasts assume that the recent periods are the best predictors of the future (Hanke, Reitsch, & Wichern, 2001). In this study, the authors examined naïve with $n = 1$ where the naïve forecast for each period is the immediately preceding observation. Thus, the model can be written as Equation 1. Since 100% of the weight is given to the current value in the series, this model is sometimes called "no-change" model.

$$\hat{y}_{t+1} = y_t \qquad (1)$$

where $\hat{y}_{t+1}$ is the forecast made at time t (the forecast origin) for time $t + 1$.

In addition, the authors also examined the naïve with $n = 7$, where the naïve forecast for each period is the most recent available same-weekday observation in last week. This was to reflect the weekly demand fluctuation in the casino buffet restaurant. This model can be written as Equation 2 below.

$$\hat{y}_{t+7} = y_t \qquad (2)$$

where $\hat{y}_{t+7}$ is the forecast made at time t (the forecast origin) for time $t + 7$.

Moving Average Models

Single moving average (SMA) is a very simple short-term forecasting tool that averages/smooths the most recent actual values to remove the unwanted randomness (DeLurgio, 1998). In single moving average method, each past observation is equally weighted and the average moves through time. Hence, the oldest observations are removed once new data points are observed (Hanke, Reitsch, & Wichern, 2001; J. L. Miller, McCahon, & Bloss, 1991). The single moving average SMA(k) model can be written as Equation 3.

$$\hat{y}_{t+1} = \frac{1}{k}\sum_{t=1}^{k} y_t \qquad (3)$$

where $\hat{y}_{t+1}$ is forecast made at time t (the forecast origin) for time $t + 1$, and k is the number of periods in the moving window (size of moving window).

The numbers of periods (size of the moving window) used for averaging influences the responsiveness of the model. For instance, the fewer number of periods used for averaging, the more responsive of the forecast to immediate demand shifts. On the contrary, the more number of periods used for averaging, the less responsive of forecast. In this study, the casino restaurant managers generally predict the buffet covers in a weekly basis (7 days). Therefore, the size of moving window was set to $k = 7$ for averaging in the SMA(7) model.

When the single moving averages were generated from time series data with a linear trend, a systematic error occurs between actual data and single moving averages. Applying double moving averages can avoid these errors. In single moving average model, the moving averages are calculated from the actual data. In double moving averages, the moving averages are calculated from the moving averages in the single moving averages model (Hanke, Reitsch, & Wichern, 2001, pp. 104-106). The lag time (moving window) between the actual and single moving averages are the same as the lag time between single moving averages and double moving averages. In this study $k = 7$ and the model was DMA(7). The double moving average model can be understood as follows involving Equations 4-8:

$$M_t = \hat{y}_{t+1} = \frac{1}{k}\sum_{t=1}^{k} y_t = \frac{1}{k}(y_t + y_{t-1} + \ldots + y_{t-k+1}) \quad (4)$$

Equation 4 above is the same as SMA(k) model in Equation 3 and M_t represents the single moving average. Equation 5 below is used to compute the second moving average (M_t') with moving window size = k.

$$M_t' = \frac{1}{k}(M_t + M_{t-1} + M_{t-2} + \ldots + M_{t-k+1}) \quad (5)$$

Equation 6 is used to develop a forecast from M_t by adding the difference between the single and second moving averages.

$$\alpha_t + M_t + (M_t - M_t') = 2M_t - M_t' \quad (6)$$

Equation 7 is an adjustment similar to a slope measure that can change over the time series. Finally, the forecast ($\hat{y}_{t+p}$) for the time period p into the future can be made in Equation 8.

$$b_{\pm} = \frac{2}{k-1}(M_t - M_t') \quad (7)$$

$$\hat{Y}_{t+p} = \alpha_t + b_{\pm}p \quad (8)$$

Although moving averages methods can smooth the trending data, there are two main limitations of applying this method. First, when forecast a large number of items, the past observed values need to be available. Thus, considerable storage space will be occupied for storing the data. For a forecasting task involving averaging over many thousands of time series, this data storage requirement may be a big computation burden (Makridakis, Wheelwright, & Hyndman, 1998). Secondly, moving averages methods consider each of the past time series value carry the same weight. This disregards the possibility that the most recent data contain more information about the future forecasts than do the older data.

Exponential Smoothing Models

The single exponential smoothing model takes the latest forecast, generated from the current period, and adds a proportion of its forecast error to predict the value of the next period. The proportion of the forecast error is denoted by a smoothing constant α, which ranges from 0 to 1. Generally speaking, the greater the α value, the more of the forecast error will be used to adjust the next period's forecast (J. L. Miller, McCahon, & Bloss, 1991). In this study, multiple α values were assessed and the best α with lowest Mean Squared Error (MSE), $\alpha = 0.3$, was used in the single exponential smoothing model. The single exponential smoothing model can be expressed as Equation 9 below.

$$\hat{y}_{t+1} = \hat{y}_t + \alpha(y_t - \hat{y}_t) = \alpha y_t + (1-\alpha)\hat{y}_{\pm} \quad (9)$$

where:

- $\hat{y}_{t+1}$ is the forecasted value for time $t + 1$,
- $\hat{y}_t$ is the forecasted value for time t,
- y_t is the actual value observed at time t, and
- α is the smoothing constant ($0 < \alpha < 1$).

A more advanced exponential smoothing method, Holt-Winters additive seasonal method, was also tested in this study. This method was extended by Winters (1960) from the original Holt's two-parameter exponential smoothing model (Holt, 1957) to adjust for seasonality directly. The Holt-Winters' general models are based on three smoothing equations that associated with three parameters: level parameter (α), trend parameter (β), and seasonal parameter (γ). The trend and seasonal components of these models can be additive or multiplicative. The additive trends are more popular than multiplicative trends because long-horizon forecasts that modeled by extrapolating a multiplicative trend tend to significantly over- or under-forecast demand (DeLurgio, 1998, p. 230). Therefore, the Holt-Winters additive seasonal method was selected as the last univariate model in this study to account for weekly fluctuating patterns.

The Holt-Winters additive seasonal model used in this study can be specified as the Equation 10 in which the forecasted value is the sum of three components (level, trend, and seasonal components):

$$\hat{y}_{t+k} = \alpha_t + b_t k + c_{t+k-s} \tag{10}$$

where $\hat{y}_{t+k}$ is the forecasted value for time $t + k$, α_t and b_t are the intercept term (level component) and trend component at time t, and c_{t+k-s} is the additive seasonal components or indices at time $t + k - s$ where s is seasonal frequency.

The above three components are defined by the following recursions in Equation 11.

$$\begin{aligned} \alpha_t &= \alpha(y_t - c_{t-s}) + (1-\alpha)(\alpha_{t-1} + b_{t-1}) \\ b_t &= \beta(\alpha_t - \alpha_{t-1}) + 1 - \beta b_{t-1} \\ c_t &= \gamma(y_t - \alpha_{t+1}) - \gamma c_{t-s} \end{aligned} \tag{11}$$

where all parameters (level (α), trend (β), and seasonality (γ)) are between 0 and 1, and s = seasonal frequency (i.e., the seasonal components are estimated from the last s observations).

The computation of optimizing three parameters is an iterative process to minimize the model's root mean squared error via a non- linear optimization algorithm. The parameters in this study were optimized at level (α) = .26, trend (β) = 0, and seasonality (γ) = .23 where s = 7.

Multiple Regression Models

Two multiple regression models with buffet cover (*BC*) and its natural log form as dependent variables were examined. Multiple regressions use causal methods to predict the future and allow forecasters to experiment the effects of the different combination of the explanatory variables on the forecasts. In the multiple regression model 1, weekly dummy variables (TU, W, TH, F, SA, SU), NOR (number of occupied rooms), and marketing events (ME) were independent variables. The initial test of such model indicated that there was a serious auto-correlation problem. Therefore, two autoregressive terms, AR(1) and AR(7), were added to the model to correct the problem. Additionally, variables TU, W, F, and NOR were dropped from the model due to their redundancy with a redundant test ($p = 0.07$). The final equation for the first multiple regression model is expressed as Equation 12:

$$\begin{aligned} BC &= \underset{(28.84^{**})}{1915.569} + \underset{(3.37^{**})}{110.820TH} - \underset{(-6.72^{**})}{256.406SA} - \underset{(-3.91^{**})}{148.447SU} \\ &+ \underset{(3.55^{**})}{84.826ME} + \underset{(13.73^{**})}{.478AR(1)} + \underset{(10.56^{**})}{.368AR(7)} \end{aligned} \tag{12}$$

The F statistic for regression model 1 was 116.59, with a p-value less than .0001. All the t-tests of the coefficients were significant at $\alpha = .01$ level a + $\alpha = .01$ level (**). The adjusted R^2 for the model was 0.581, which indicted that 58.1% of variation in buffet covers was explained by the model. The p-value (.25) of the Breusch- Godfrey serial correlation LM test and the Durbin-Watson statistic (2.01) for this regression model indicated that autocorrelations were not presented in this model. According to this equation, there is a positive relationship between buffet covers and independent variables TH and Marketing Events. Negative relationships between buffet covers and independent variables SA and SU were also found. Buffet covers would increase by 85 units if there was a marketing event, *ceteris paribus*. Holding other things constant, buffet covers would increase by 111 units more than Monday if it was a Thursday. On the other hand, the buffet covers would be 256 units less than the Monday's number if it was a Saturday. Similarly, if it was a Sunday, the buffet covers would decrease by 148 units from the Monday's number, *ceteris paribus*. The possible reason for the higher demand on weekdays than that during the weekend might be in that the buffet menus on weekdays were more attractive than those offered during the weekend. Restaurant managers' explanation was that the management tried to lure more customers with more attractive menus when they commonly anticipated less customer counts on weekdays.

The authors also examined a log-linear multiple regression model (the multiple regression model 2) with the natural log of buffet cover ($\ln BC$) as the dependent variable. The final equation for the second multiple regression model is as Equation 13:

$$\begin{aligned} \ln BC &= 7.54 + .056TH - .141SA - .078SU \\ &(217.17^{**})(3.06^{**})(-6.68^{**})(-3.72^{**}) \\ &\quad + .05ME + .465AR(1) + .373AR(7) \\ &\quad (3.81^{**})\ \ (13.28^{**})\ \ (10.64^{**}) \end{aligned} \tag{13}$$

The F statistic for the regression model 2 was 217.17, with a p-value less than .0001. All the t-tests of the coefficients were significant at $\alpha = .01$. The adjusted R^2 for the model was 0.565 and explained 56.5% of data variation. The p-value of the Breusch-Godfrey serial correlation LM test was .12 and the Durbin-Watson statistic for this regression model was 2.04. These statistics suggested that autocorrelations did not significantly exist in this model. Although this model could be used for forecasting the buffet covers, the interpretation of independent variables' impacts on buffet covers in this model was more cumbersome than that in the earlier multiple regression model.

VALIDATING FORECASTING MODELS

The buffet-cover forecasts for the *ex post* period from November 1, 2001 to January 31, 2002 were generated by using the aforementioned eight forecasting models. The accuracy of these forecasting models was evaluated in terms of mean absolute percentage error (MAPE) and root mean squared percentage error (RMSPE). Both MAPE and RMSPE are relative measures and widely employed in forecasting studies to facilitate the comparison of accuracy among different methods. The following two sections discuss these two error measures and their validation results that are summarized in Table 1.

Mean Absolute Percentage Error (MAPE)

The percentage error (PE) is the proportion of error at a particular time t in the series. The mean percentage error (MPE) is the average of

TABLE 1. Holdout-Sample[a] (*ex post*) Forecasting Performance

Forecasting Models	MAPE % (Rankings)	RMSPE % (Rankings)
Naïve Model 1 (n = 1)	18.78 (4)	30.38 (5)
Naïve Model 2 (n = 7)	21.081 (7)	30.99 (6)
Single Moving Average Model; SMA(7)	16.40 (3)	26.40 (3)
Double Moving Average Model; DMA(7)	6.68 (1)	8.92 (1)
Single Exponential Smoothing Model ($\alpha = .3$)	15.86 (2)	27.10 (4)
Holt-Winters Additive Seasonal Model ($\alpha = .26, \beta = 0, \gamma = .23$)	21.077 (6)	32.26 (7)
Multiple Regression Model 1[b]	28.34 (8)	42.52 (8)
Multiple Regression Model 2[c]	19.11 (5)	23.57 (2)

Note: a. *Ex post* forecasting period: 11/1/2001 to 1/31/2002
b. The dependent variable was buffet covers; independent variables were 4 dummy variables (TH, SA, SU) and marketing events (ME), and 2 autoregression terms, AR(1) and AR(7).
c. Same as Multiple Regression Model 1 except the dependent variable was transformed to the natural log of buffet covers.

all PEs in the time series and it is a useful measure to compare the fits of different models. To prevent positive and negative PEs from canceling out each other, the mean absolute percentage error (MAPE) takes the absolute value of all MPEs. The calculation of MAPE is shown in Equation 14:

$$MAPE = \frac{1}{n}\sum_{t=1}^{n}\left|\frac{y_t - \hat{y}_t}{y_t}\right| \times 100 \qquad (14)$$

where y_t is the value of the observation at time t in the time series, and $\hat{y}_t$ is the fitted value for the observation at time t.

MAPE is a common measure for evaluating the accuracy of forecasting models. Suggested by Lewis (1982, p. 40), this error measure can be interpreted as follows: (1) MAPE smaller than 10% indicates a highly accurate model, (2) MAPE between 10% and 20% indicates a good and accurate model, (3) MAPE between 21% and 50% indicates a reasonably accurate model, and (4) MAPE greater than 50% indicates an inaccurate model.

As indicated in Table 1, the double moving average model produced the best (smallest) MAPE (6.68%), followed by the single exponential smoothing model (15.86%), the single moving average model (16.4%), the naïve model 1 (18.78%), the multiple regression model 2 (19.11%), the Holt-Winters' additive seasonal model (21.077%), and the naïve model 2 (21.081%). The multiple regression model 1 generated the worst (largest) MAPE value (28.34%).

Root Mean Square Percentage Error (RMSPE)

Another relative error measure is the root mean square percentage error (RMSPE) that takes square root of the average sum of squared errors (RMSE) and expresses it as a percentage term in relation to observed value in Equation 15 below:

$$RMSPE = \sqrt{\frac{1}{n}\sum_{t=1}^{n}\left(\frac{y_t - \hat{y}_t}{y_t}\right)^2} \times 100 = \sqrt{\frac{1}{n}\sum_{t=1}^{n}\left(\frac{e_t}{y_t}\right)^2} \times 100 \qquad (15)$$

where n is the number of observation in the time series, and e_t is the error occurs at time t between fitted value ($\hat{y}_t$) and observed value (y_t).

An examination of RMSPE values (in Table 1) disclosed that the double moving average model was still the best forecasting model with the smallest RMSPE (8.92%). It was followed by the multiple regression model 2 (23.57%), the single moving average model (26.4%), the single exponential smoothing model (27.1%), the naïve model 1 (30.38%), the naïve model 2 (30.99%), and the Holt-Winters' additive seasonal model (32.26%). The largest MAPE value (42.52%) was again produced by the multiple regression model 1.

The *ex post* validation results indicated that the double moving average model was the best model among all the proposed ones and that three univariate time series models–double moving average model, single moving average model, and single exponential smoothing model–outperformed the benchmark naïve model 1 in terms of forecasting accuracy measured by MAPE and RMSPE. Despite its ability and convenience to explain dependent variables' impacts on buffet covers, the multiple regression model 1 was considered as the most inferior model in forecasting the buffet covers in the study. Both accuracy measures of this model were worse than those of the naïve model 1. However, the log-linear multiple regression model 2 performed better than the multiple regression model 1. The results of this study demonstrated that applying simple mathematical forecasting techniques (such as double moving average method) could indeed obtain highly accurate forecasts within 10% error. Moreover, the findings of this study were consistent with those from many previous food production forecasting studies in which their authors supported that simple models sometimes produce as accurate results as do their complex counterparts and that there is no indication that more complex methods provide more accurate forecasts (J. J. Miller, McCahon, & Miller, 1991a; J. L. Miller, McCahon, & Bloss, 1991; Schnaars, 1984). In addition, the results of this study particularly substantiated the discussion of applying moving average forecasting in Chandler et al.'s study (1982). According to them, foodservice operators are encouraged to use moving average forecasting techniques to perform demand forecasting tasks so that more time can be spent in improving labor utilization and food quality.

APPLICATION: BETTER FORECASTING APPROACHES

In this section, the authors discuss the concept and the use of different forecasting approaches in the (casino buffet) restaurants. Figure 3 conceptually illustrates the basic ideas of three forecasting approaches in both under-forecast and over-forecast situations in the buffet restaurant setting. Using forecasting errors as a measurement, costs of under-forecast and over-forecast are represented by the triangular area covered. This figure shows that the larger the forecasting errors, the greater the incurred costs (including both labor and food costs). Adopting accurate forecasting models can help reduce the costs of both over-estimation and under-estimation of food covers. Judgmental forecasting solely based on restaurant managers' intuition and experience often produces the largest forecasting errors and incurs the greatest costs. Demonstrated by the authors in this study, the use of simple time series forecasting model (i.e., double moving average method) could achieve highly accurate forecasts. The utilization of a time series forecasting approach can reduce forecasting errors and lessen associated costs. The shaded area A indicates the gains of using time series forecasting models over judgment-based forecasting approach. Armstrong (2001b, p. 365) argues two important points: first, given enough data, quantitative methods are more accurate than judgmental methods; second, when large fluctuations are expected, simple methods are preferable to complex methods because they are easier to understand, less expensive, and seldom less accurate. The LV Casino restaurant operators have employed spreadsheet software, such as Excel or Lotus 123, to store their historical data. However, they seldom utilize their databases for their food production forecasting. Based on one author's personal conversations with the casino restaurant managers, many managers indicated that they felt that applying mathematical models to forecast demand (guest counts) was too complicated

FIGURE 3. A Conceptual Illustration of Using Different Forecasting Approaches for the Casino Buffet Restaurant

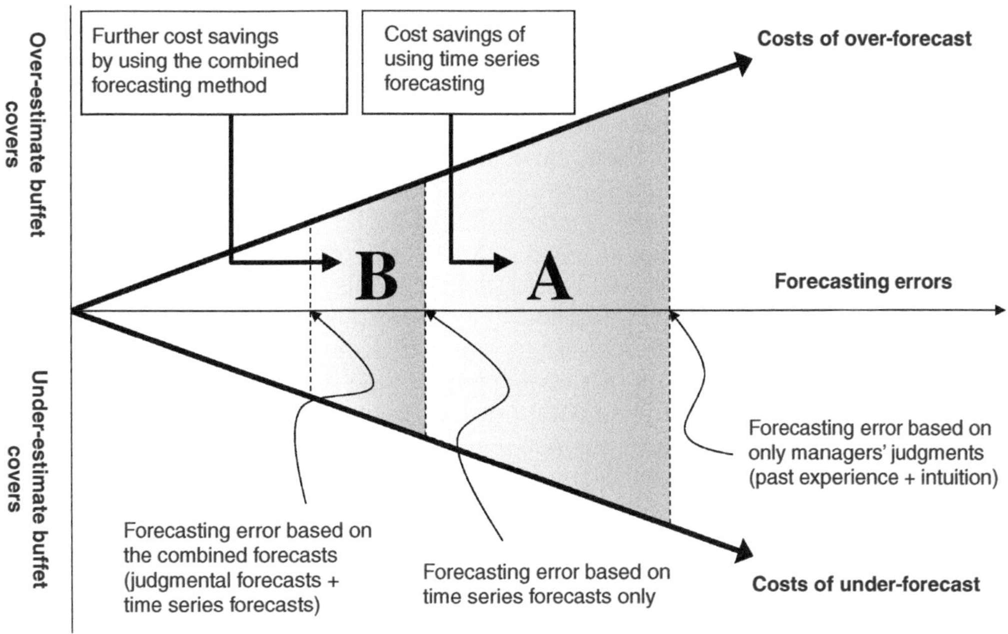

and extremely time-consuming. They had the impression that every method involving mathematical theories or equations must be complex and time-consuming. Most managers never thought about applying mathematical models in their daily operations because they were intimidated by the terminology in and unfamiliarity with "mathematical models."

The results of this study proved that by using historical data with the simple double moving average method, highly accurate demand forecasts could be obtained. This encouraging result inspired casino restaurant operators to consider applying the simple mathematical forecasting methods to their operations. The potential benefits of applying these simple mathematical models are promising and the investment of implementation is minimal in the casino restaurant settings. Several factors such as cost, technical sophistication, accuracy, and data availability, may influence managers to choose the best forecasting technique. However, casino restaurants are armed with all the necessary elements for applying simple forecasting models (Georgoff & Murdick, 1986). First, casinos do not have to purchase new computer software for using these simple forecasting models since most casinos have been using generic spreadsheet software to store their available data. Most simple time series forecasting models assessed in this study can be performed by generic spreadsheet software. Second, most casinos' analysts/managers with bachelor or master's degrees possess sufficient knowledge of conducting these simple mathematical forecasting models. Third, because the F&B department is usually not a major profit center for a casino hotel's operations, not all the casino hotels have an F&B analyst. In such case, the restaurant manager carries the responsibility of an analyst. The authors believe that the three best forecasting models (double moving average, single moving average, and simple exponential smoothing models) identified in this study are not very complicated. If buffet restaurant managers receive some training on these forecasting methods, they should be able to perform the forecasting tasks using these models. Once the restaurant managers conquer their fears of applying mathematical models and find those models indeed help them, it is more likely that they will be willing to try more complicated mathematical models in the future.

However, managerial intuition and experiences (domain knowledge) should not be discredited. Good managers with long working experiences can sometimes predict relatively accurate demand. Research has shown that combined forecasts (through multiple forecasting methods) are generally more accurate than those obtained by a single forecasting method (Armstrong, 2001a; Geurts & Whitlark, 1999-2000; Gupta & Wilton, 1987; Lawrence, Edmundson, & O'Connor, 1986). In fact, experts have suggested the use of judgmental adjustment in time-series forecasting (Sanders & Ritzman, 1992, 2001; Webby & O'Connor, 1996; Webby, O'Connor, & Lawrence, 2001). The authors propose a combined forecasting approach by integrating time series forecasting (double moving average modeling in this case) with buffet restaurant manager's management judgmental forecasting. Using this combined approach, the restaurant management can expect to further trim the forecasting errors. Graphically, this is shown as the shaded area B where even more cost savings can be achieved.

To realize this "hybrid" forecasting approach, a simple procedure can be taken to combine the human judgmental forecasting with the time series forecasting. Figure 4 illustrates the concept of using this combined forecasting approach in the buffet restaurant planning. This approach is relatively easy and practical to apply. First of all, the procedure is initiated with using time series forecasting (i.e., double moving average method) for predicting buffet covers for the next day's operation. Buffet restaurant managers and chefs can then schedule their staffing and order their service materials based on this starting estimate for both front-house and back-house operations. At the final stage of the daily operation, actual business volume is compared with the earlier estimate. Three possible conditions can be expected from this assessment:

- Condition 1: If the actual business volume is greater than the earlier estimate by 5% or more, the restaurant manager should adjust the forecast downward by a small percentage (a 2% adjustment is recommended) in his/her judgmental forecasting.

- Condition 2: In contrast, if the actual business volume is smaller than the earlier estimate by 5% or more, the restaurant manager should anticipate an upward- adjustment by a small percentage (again, a 2% adjustment is recommended) in his/her judgmental forecasting.
- Condition 3: If the actual business volume is within 5% range of the earlier estimate, the restaurant manager will record the result of the comparison and accumulate the knowledge and experience to improve his/her judgmental forecasting abilities. No adjustment is required under this condition.

For the next day's forecasting task, the process starts again with time series forecasting but this time it accounts for any adjustment from a previous condition in judgmental forecasting from the restaurant manager. The restaurant manager should examine the forecast produced by the time series forecasting model and apply any judgmental adjustments. The new forecast for the next day's demand will then be used for subsequent operational planning and management. From here, the procedure becomes a continuous looping system and the demand forecasting will be expected to improve in the long run. The longer the system is operated, the more stable the procedure should be expected due to accumulated historical data and human learning experience. Forecasting errors should be diminishing to an acceptable level as the system matures. Note that this procedure does not have a termination condition as found in most programming cases where the loop is terminated if a satisfactory (e.g., optimal, maximum, or minimum) output is desired. As described in Figure 4, today's forecast becomes the input for tomorrow's planning and forecasting tasks. The buffet restaurant is operated year round in a continuous fashion. The continuous looping enables the restaurant manager to monitor the forecasting performance and stabilize the system within the 5% error range. Although this unique forecasting approach has not been tested, the authors proposed it to the LV Casino buffet restaurant and hoped this new method would improve its forecasting and planning efforts. The decisions to choose the ±5% error range and ±2% adjustments were a practical concern. The buffet restaurant in the study served 1,500-2,500 customers daily in the data. The

FIGURE 4. Buffet Restaurant Planning and the Combined Forecasting Approach

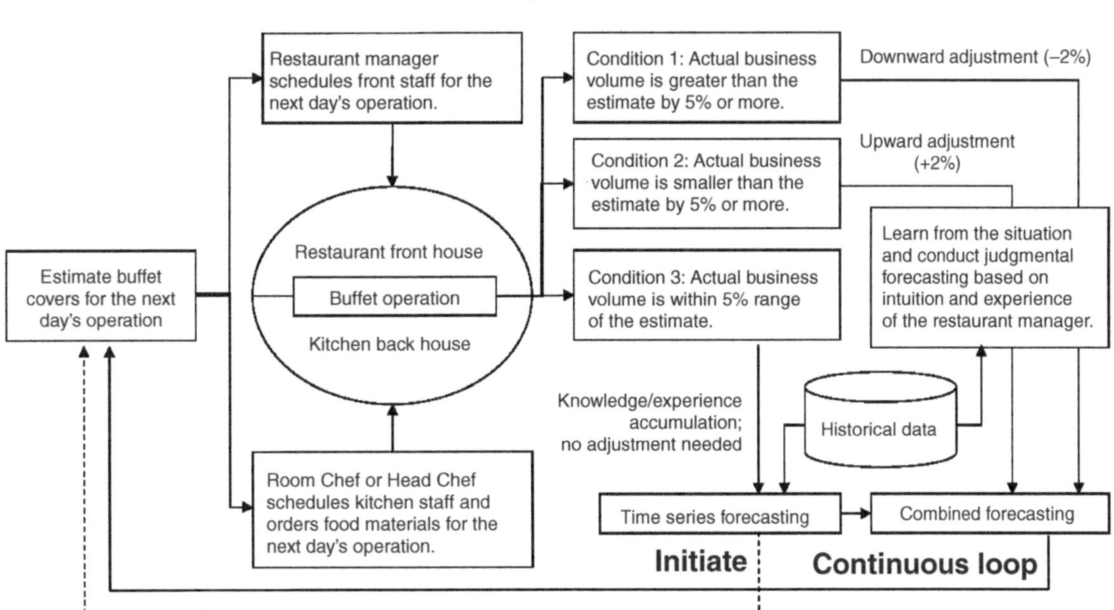

authors believe that a 5% deviation from the actual serving (75-125 food covers) represents a significant cost concern and needs the manager's special attention. This approach allows for some degree of flexibility and a systematic fine-tuning opportunity for long-term improvement as the manager's knowledge/experiences accumulate over time. Obviously this practical concern was addressed to this particular restaurant or similar-size buffet restaurants. The "economies of scale" consideration may factor in if larger-size restaurants are concerned.

FORECASTING AND CASINO BUFFET RESTAURANT MANAGEMENT

Having discussed the proposed forecasting approach in casino buffet restaurant's short-term planning, the authors in this section further discuss the role of forecasting played in buffet restaurant management with a focus on restaurant revenue management (RRM).

Although the casino buffet restaurant may be considered as a cost center rather than a profit center, it does not prevent the casino from pursuing a revenue management practice. In fact, the recent business trend seems to suggest developing a profit-center concept for casino restaurants (Tasoulas, 1999) and makes revenue management an important issue for buffet restaurant operations. According to Kimes and her colleagues (Kimes, 1999; Kimes, Barrash, & Alexander, 1999), the concept of restaurant revenue management is to sell the right seat to the right customers at right price and for the right (meal) duration. To ensure a successful RRM, the buffet manager not only has to conduct accurate daily forecasting (a proposed approach in this study) but also need to become familiar with demand patterns during the day. The former provides an overall planning boundary for the daily operation and the latter facilitates the manager's fine-tuning the hourly operation during the day.

Kimes and McGuire (2001) discussed how to maximize the revenue contribution of each function space for each time period that the space is available. In their study, the duration of function space was defined by day parts (a.m. and p.m.). Different pricing strategies were developed for each day parts based on the demand characteristics for each day parts. The same approach can be applied on the casino buffet restaurant, too. Some casino hotels equip with computerized systems that track the food covers by the hour. It is possible to refine the definition of duration for buffet restaurant into hours or hourly blocks (e.g., 3 or 4 hours) instead of day parts. Then, different operational or pricing strategies can be developed based on the demand characteristics for each hourly block. Some demand characteristics such as the room occupancy or the casino guest mix may be considered in the forecasting equation. The hourly occupancy data provide the management more insights into the operation than the daily data do. The assumptions here are that room guests tend to use in-house restaurants more frequently than visiting guests, and that timing of their check-ins may indicate their possible in-house meal patronages. For instance, a guest checks in at 1:00 PM has more opportunities to use in-house restaurants than another guest who checks in at 7:30 PM. In addition to the hourly occupancy data, the data of the casino guest mix for each hour also presents a valuable piece of information. The guests of casino buffet restaurants can be categorized into gambling guests and non-gambling guests. Gambling guests, who contribute both gaming revenues and food revenues to the casino hotels, are the most valuable clients for the casino hotels. On the other hand, non-gambling guests, who only contribute food revenue, are less attractive to most casino hotels, especially when the buffet restaurants are not operated as profit centers. The casino restaurants can distinguish the non-gambling clients from the gambling clients by utilizing frequent player programs. Most casino hotels have frequent player programs in which frequent player club cards are issued to the members. The hourly data of the composition of gambling and non-gambling guests can be obtained by check their membership cards at the all restaurant entrances or electronic player tracking systems. Once the hourly client-mix patterns is learned and monitored, the buffet restaurant can increase its price to discourage non-gambling guests and provide a discounted price for gambling guest as additional membership benefits. Working with other in-house restaurants, the buffet restaurant can re-distribute non-gambling guests to other in-house restaurants and make more seats available for gambling members. The idea is to let gambling members consume buffet meals (which usually take less time than other table services) quickly and be back on the gambling floors. By refining the definition of duration for buffet restaurant into hours instead of days, the management can have an in-depth picture of the operations and develop better strategies to maximize the revenue contribution to the casino hotel.

The following few sections systematically relate the RRM concept to casino buffet restaurant management and discuss how casino buffet restaurant managers can practically integrate short-term forecasting (at both daily and hourly level) with their management of capacity, demand, meal duration, price, and queuing. These discussions are summarized and illustrated in Figure 5.

Capacity Management

Buffet managers are responsible for matching the restaurant's capacity with fluctuations in short-term demand. The fundamental issue here is to ensure sufficient capacity at all time to meet demand (Metters, King-Metters, & Pullman, 2003, p. 18). Buffet managers should learn to familiarize themselves with when the peak and slow times for each day are and effectively schedule staff and prepare the food to prevent from under-production or over-production. In the meantime, accurate forecasting can facilitate buffet managers' decisions on service hours. For example, the service hours for most casino buffet restaurants are between 6:00 a.m. to 10:00 p.m. If the results of forecasting and managerial experience indicate a consistent drop of demand between 3:00 p.m. to 4:00 p.m., the buffet managers may consider altering capacity as needed (e.g., slowing down the operation for an hour) to save some

FIGURE 5. Integrating Forecasting with Casino Buffet Restaurant Management

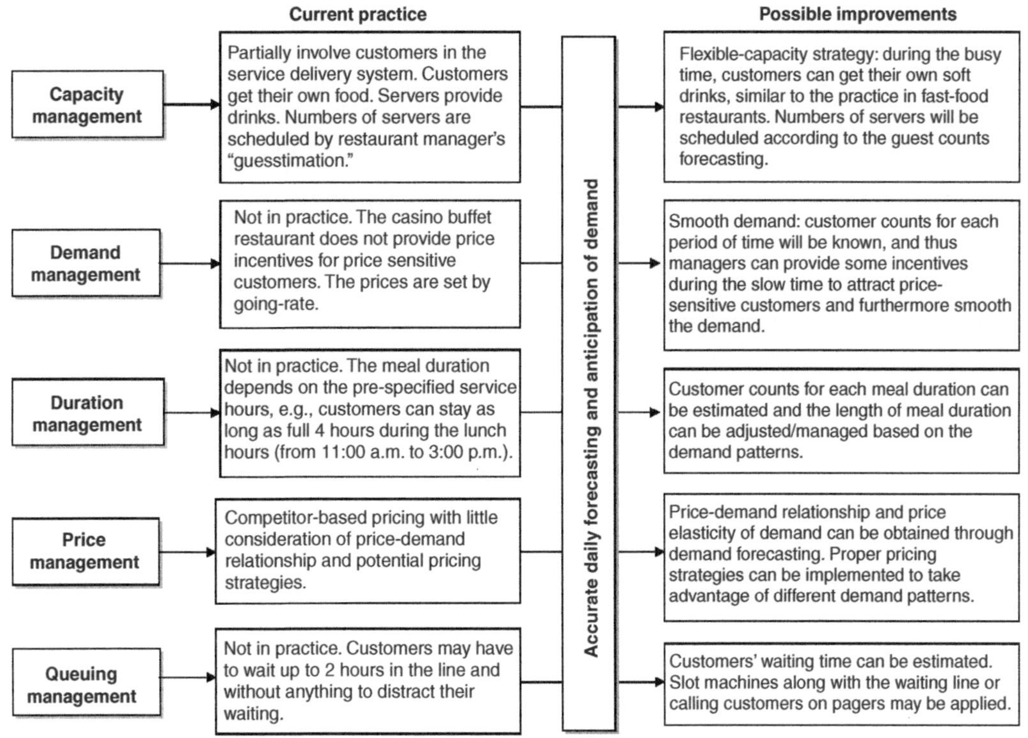

Modified from Sill (1991) and Kimes et al. (1999; 1998).

variable costs or increase "inventory" of employee time (e.g., encouraging more/longer break times for employees) in this duration. Accurate forecasting can provide useful information for buffet managers to decide the level of customers' involvement in the service delivery system. For instance, if the forecasting results indicate that it happens very often that guest counts will jump dramatically on Friday night when the bus tour crowd swarms in, the buffet manager may consider increasing customers' involvement/participation in the buffet service by switching the service mode to self-serving (e.g., allowing customers to get their drinks by themselves in the beginning) (Hoffman & Bateson, 2001, p. 148; Kotler, Bowen, & Makens, 2003, pp. 411-412).

Demand Management

Buffet restaurant managers can also benefit from accurate forecasting for managing the demand. For example, buffet restaurants in general serve breakfast from 6:00 a.m. to 11:00 a.m., lunch from 11:00 a.m. to 3:00 p.m., and dinner from 3:00 p.m. to 10:00 p.m. during the weekday (with about 2 hours standard deviation). If the forecasting result and management judgment indicate that the customer counts are relative low between 3:00 p.m. to 5:00 p.m., the buffet manager may consider providing incentives such as expanding the lunch hour to 5:00 p.m. or using "early-bird" coupon to encourage customers' use of the restaurant during the slow hours so that customers who come in the restaurant before 5:00 p.m. can pay for the lunch's price and avoid later slow services due to crowded guests. The target customers of this tactic are those who are price-sensitive and/or value more in time for gambling than for waiting in line. This effort may fill up the restaurant's slow time before 5:00 p.m. and smooth the dinner crowd after 5:00 p.m. This demand management tactic is called demand shifting that often involves using prices to create or reduce demand (Hoffman & Bateson, 2001, p. 148; Kotler, Bowen, & Makens, 2003, pp. 415-416).

Duration Management

Research has shown that meal durations are a crucial part of the RRM (Kimes, Barrash, & Alexander, 1999). The durations of meals are especially important to casino buffet restaurants. From the restaurant's viewpoint, a slow seat turnover rate greatly influences the restaurant's bottom line. The buffet restaurants manager must find out the possible reasons why meals last as long as they do and identify the most important problems in controlling meal durations (Kimes, 1999). The longer the customers stay in the restaurant, the less time they will gamble in the casino floor. This lesser gambling time is regarded as opportunity costs for the casino operators. Therefore, buffet managers may forecast buffet covers for each meal and gain a better idea about the demand patterns in different meal durations during the operation. Buffet and gaming managers should work together to assess the length of the meal durations in relation to their corresponding demand patterns. If the duration is so long that it decreases customers' gambling time, buffet managers need to work on a solution to shorten the meal duration. For example, the buffet managers can remove the menu items (e.g., fresh made pasta) that require customers to wait a considerable time for the dish to be cooked. In addition, the buffet manager can instruct servers to drop some hints such as offering coffee to customers to signal the end of their consumption and speed up the meal duration. Therefore, buffet managers can utilize the results of forecasting to manage the meal durations.

Price Management

As mentioned in "demand management," discounted prices can be used to smooth demand. Pricing strategies are often used to (1) create new demand in off-peak low-capacity utilization periods, and (2) flatten peaks by shifting existing customers to less busy times (Bateson & Hoffman, 1999, p. 178). Generally speaking, the prices for local casinos' buffets are $4.99 for breakfast, $6.99 for lunch, and $8.99 for dinner during the week, and $8.99 for weekend brunch and $10.99 for dinner (with $2 standard deviation). Most local casino buffet restaurants apply the going-rate pricing approach (i.e., buffet restaurant managers set up their prices based on what prices their competitors offer). They do not put the relationship between price and demand into the consideration when setting the price. Accurate forecasting can help managers to evaluate their pricing strategies based on forecasted demand patterns. For example, if the forecasting results reveal that actual guest covers are much more for Friday lunch than for Sunday brunch, the buffet manager may consider adjusting the price structure to reflect the higher lunch demand on Friday. The other scenario may be that when the food offerings are the same and the cut off time for weekend dinner is 4:00 p.m., customers who get into the restaurant at 3:59 p.m. may pay $8.99, and customers who get into the restaurant at 4:01 p.m. may pay $10.99. If the results of the forecasting reveal that the demand patterns of the guest counts do not fluctuate because of that $2 difference, the buffet restaurant managers should consider the possibility that the demand on weekends is inelastic (i.e., customers do not differentiated over the $2 difference between brunch and dinner). The buffet managers should test the market for a $1 or $2 increase on the brunch price to increase revenues. This pricing strategy is derived from the concept of "time-based price (in) discrimination" where customers may or may not be sensitive to changes in buffet prices at the time of service consumption. Knowing consumers' responses (shown as demand patterns) to prices is essential to the buffet restaurant operation in casinos. Forecasting contributes to the understanding of this important managerial issue.

Queuing Management

Queues are basically a symptom of unresolved capacity management problems in the service delivery system (Lovelock & Wright, 2002, pp. 304-305). In many tourism or hospitality services, queues are often referred to waiting lines that occur whenever the number of customer arrivals at a service facility exceeds the capacity of the operation to process them. Forecasting can help buffet managers in managing queues by predicting customer arrivals and providing good information on arrival patterns for managerial decisions. For example, from the results of the forecasting task, the buffet manager can estimate the number of customer arrivals and compare it with the planned operating capacity (e.g., the number of hosts and servers and the number of seats) to anticipate (1) whether there will be a waiting line, (2) when the waiting line will most likely to occur, and (3) how long the waiting line will be. The buffet manager can then adjust operating capacity/speed or adopt some managerial tactics to manage anticipated queues. The goal of queuing management is to either reduce the length of waiting lines/time or minimize the perceived length of the wait. Managing waiting lines is an important task for casino operations because casino operators want customers to spend as much time as possible on gambling and spend as little time as possible on anything else. Long waiting lines before casino restaurants certainly waste the customers' times and agonize them. Currently, some casinos give customers pagers and notify them when the seats are available. Other casinos mobile some slot machines along with the long buffet lines. However, the majority of the casinos do not take any actions in managing their buffet waiting lines. Buffet managers need to work with other managers on either shortening customers' waiting times or providing gambling devices along their waiting lines.

CONCLUSION AND RECOMMENDATIONS FOR FUTURE RESEARCH

In conclusion, forecasting is the foundation for many operational functions, such as discussed revenue management and capacity management. This study was the first research looking into the casino buffet restaurants. The authors not only identified suitable forecasting methods for the casino buffet restaurant's managers but also extended a practical connection between forecasting and casino buffet operations management. Furthermore, the results of this study suggested that highly accurate forecasts could be obtained through several user-friendly simple forecasting models. However, convincing casino buffet managers to apply simple models for their forecasting is just a starting point. Once the managers learn to adopt an optimal forecasting approach (such as the combined forecasting approach proposed by the authors), more research needs to be conducted to help them more effectively integrate their optimal forecasting approach with their revenue and capacity management. The authors hope this study can provide casino restaurant managers with a good understanding of the ease of applying mathematical models and the combined forecasting method for accurate forecasting. Future research should work on searching for the most appropriate sets of forecasting tools and integrating forecasting with other operational concepts. More importantly, the authors advocate that academia should better communicate with industry operators using practical examples and methods. The final section of this paper discusses possible directions for future research.

Future research should take multiple forecasting models into considerations. Although the results of this study indicated that single moving method, double moving method, and single exponential smoothing possessed the highest level of accuracy, it does not guarantee that these three methods will produce the same level of accuracy when different datasets are evaluated (Makridakis, 1996). An interesting research will be actually testing the proposed combined forecasting method and comparing forecasting performance against other simpler time series methods. Similarly, further research is strongly recommended to investigate the underlying reasons for the inferior performance of multiple regressions analyzed in this study. Although the independent variables in this study were generated from in-depth interviews with several casino operation analysts and financial analysts, other factors (i.e., competitors' promotion) contributing to guest counts need to be examined in future research. Replications of this study to other types of casino restaurants are also desirable. When gambling in casinos, seventy-four percent of Clark County's residents eat in a casino restaurant, including buffet, coffee shop, gourmet restaurant, and fast food restaurant (Las Vegas Convention & Visitor Authority, 2001). Therefore, other types of casino restaurants should also make efforts to attain accurate forecasting to advance their businesses, even though the consequences of inaccurate forecasting may not affect other types of casino restaurants as evidently as they do to buffet restaurants. Future research can replicate this study for other types of casino restaurants.

REFERENCES

Anonymous. (1996). Feeding the slots: Are casino restaurants an amenity or a profit center? *Restaurant Business*, *95*(6), 135-136.

Armstrong, J. S. (2001a). Combining forecasts. In J. S. Armstrong (Ed.), *Principles of forecasting: A handbook for researchers and practitioners* (pp. 417-439). Norwell, MA: Kluwer Academic Publishers.

Armstrong, J. S. (2001b). Selecting forecasting methods. In J. S. Armstrong (Ed.), *Principles of forecasting: A handbook for researchers and practitioners* (pp. 365-386). Norwell, MA: Kluwer Academic Publishers.

Athiyaman, A., & Robertson, R. W. (1992). Time series forecasting techniques: Short-term planning in tourism. *International Journal of Contemporary Hospitality Management*, *4*(4), 8-11.

Bateson, J. E. G., & Hoffman, K. D. (1999). *Managing services marketing: Text and readings* (4th ed.). Fort Worth, TX: The Drydan Press.

Chandler, S. J., Norton, L. C., Hoover, L. W., & Moore, A. M. (1982). Analysis of meal census patterns for forecasting menu item demand. *Journal of the American Dietetic Association*, *80*(4), 317-323.

DeLurgio, S. A. (1998). *Forecasting, principles, and application.* Columbus, OH: McGraw-Hill Companies.

Georgoff, D. M., & Murdick, R. G. (1986). Manager's guide to forecasting. *Harvard Business Review*, *64*(1), 110-120.

Geurts, M. D., & Whitlark, D. B. (1999-2000). Six ways to make sales forecasts more accurate. *Journal of Business Forecasting Methods & Systems*, *18*(4), 21-24.

Gupta, S., & Wilton, P. C. (1987). Combination of forecasts: An extension. *Management Science*, *33*(3), 356-372.

Hanke, J. E., Reitsch, A. G., & Wichern, D. W. (2001). *Business forecasting* (7th ed.). Upper Saddle River, NJ: Prentice Hall Inc.

Hoffman, K. D., & Bateson, J. E. G. (2001). *Essentials of services marketing: Concepts, strategies, & cases* (2nd ed.). Mason, OH: South-Western College Publishing.

Holt, C. C. (1957). *Forecasting seasonal and trends by exponentially weighted moving averages* (ONR Research memorandum No. 52). Pittsburgh, PA: Carnegie Institute of Technology.

Kimes, S. E. (1999). Implementing restaurant revenue management: A five-step approach. *Cornell Hotel* and Restaurant Administration Quarterly, *40*(3), 16-21.

Kimes, S. E., Barrash, D. I., & Alexander, J. E. (1999). Developing a restaurant revenue-management strategy. *Cornell Hotel and Restaurant Administration Quarterly*, *40*(5), 18-29.

Kimes, S. E., Chase, R. B., Choi, S., Lee, P. Y., & Ngonzi, E. N. (1998). Restaurant revenue management: Applying yield management to the restaurant industry. *Cornell Hotel and Restaurant Administration Quarterly*, *39*(3), 32-39.

Kimes, S. E., & McGuire, K. A. (2001). Function-space revenue management: A case study from Singapore. *Cornell Hotel and Restaurant Administration Quarterly*, *42*(6), 33-46.

Kotler, P., Bowen, J. T., & Makens, J. (2003). Chapter 11–Building customer loyalty through quality. In *Marketing for hospitality and tourism* (3rd ed., pp. 381-440). Upper Saddle River, NJ: Prentice Hall, Inc.

Las Vegas Convention & Visitor Authority. (2001). *1999-2000 Clark County Residents Study*. Las Vegas, NV: Las Vegas Convention & Visitor Authority.

Lawrence, M. J., Edmundson, R. H., & O'Connor, M. J. (1986). The accuracy of combining judgmental and statistical forecasts. *Management Science*, *32*(12), 1521-1532.

Lewis, C. D. (1982). *Industrial and business forecasting methods: A practical guide to exponential smoothing and curve fitting*. London, UK: Butterworth Scientific.

Lovelock, C., & Wright, L. (2002). *Principles of service marketing and management* (2nd ed.). Upper Saddle River, NJ: Prentice Hall, Inc.

Lucas, T., & Santos, J. (2003). Measuring the effects of casino-operated restaurant volume on slot machine business. *Journal of Hospitality & Tourism Research*, *27*(1), 101-117.

Mack, D. (1999). What's your sign? Designing facades to get customers in Bellagio's door. *Nation's Restaurant News*, *33*(19), 36-37.

Makridakis, S. G. (1996). Forecasting: Its role and value for planning and strategy. *International Journal of Forecasting*, *12*(4), 513-537.

Makridakis, S. G., Wheelwright, S. C., & Hyndman, R. J. (1998). *Forecasting: Methods and applications* (3rd ed.). New York, NY: John Wiley & Sons, Inc.

Messersmith, A. M., & Miller, J. L. (1991). *Forecasting in foodservice*. New York, NY: John Wiley & Sons, Inc.

Metters, R., King-Metters, K., & Pullman, M. (2003). *Successful service operations management*. Mason, OH: South-Western.

Miller, J. J., McCahon, C. S., & Miller, J. L. (1991a). Foodservice forecasting using simple mathematical models. *Hospitality Research Journal*, *15*(1), 43-58.

Miller, J. J., McCahon, C. S., & Miller, J. L. (1991b). Forecasting food production demand in school foodservice. *School Food Service Research*, *15*(2), 117-122.

Miller, J. J., McCahon, C. S., & Miller, J. L. (1993). Foodservice forecasting: Differences in selection of simple mathematical models based on. *Hospitality Research Journal*, *16*(2), 95-102.

Miller, J. L., McCahon, C. S., & Bloss, B. K. (1991). Food production forecasting with simple time series models. *Hospitality Research Journal*, *14*(3), 9-21.

Miller, J. L., & Shanklin, C. W. (1988). Forecasting the menu-item demand in foodservice operations. *Journal of the American Dietetic Association*, *88*(4), 443-449.

Miller, J. L., Thompson, P. A., & Orabella, M. M. (1991). Forecasting in foodservice: Model development, testing, and evaluation. *Journal of the American Dietetic Association*, *91*(5), 569-574.

Morgan, M. S., & Chintagunta, P. K. (1997). Forecasting restaurant sales using self-selectivity models. *Journal of Retailing and Consumer Services*, *4*(2), 117-128.

Richard, M. D., & Adrian, C. M. (1996). Determinants of casino repeat purchase intentions. *Journal of Hospitality & Leisure Marketing*, *4*(3), 25-39.

Roehl, W. S. (1996). Competition, casino spending, and use of casino amenities. *Journal of Travel Research*, *34*(3), 57-62.

Ryu, K., & Sánchez, A. (2002). The evaluation of the forecasting methods in the institutional foodservice facilities. In A. DeFranco & J. A. Abbott (Eds.), *Proceedings of the Seventh Annual Graduate Education and Graduate Students Research Conference in Hospitality and Tourism: Advances in Hospitality and Tourism Research, January 3-5, Houston, TX* (Vol. 7, pp. 491-493). Houston, TX: University of Houston.

Sanders, N. R., & Ritzman, L. P. (1992). The need for contextual and technical knowledge in judgmental forecasting. *Journal of Behavioral Decision Making*, *5*(1), 39-52.

Sanders, N. R., & Ritzman, L. P. (2001). Judgmental adjustment of statistical forecasts. In J. S. Armstrong (Ed.), *Principles of forecasting: A handbook for researchers and practitioners* (pp. 405-416). Norwell, MA: Kluwer Academic Publishers.

Schnaars, S. P. (1984). Situational factors affecting forecast accuracy. *Journal of Marketing Research*, *21*(3), 290-297.

Sill, B. T. (1991). Capacity management: Making your service delivery more productive. *Cornell Hotel and Restaurant Administration Quarterly*, *31*(4), 76-87.

Tasoulas, M. A. (1999). Betting on a sure thing: Gone are the days when fine dining in a gaming establishment was a no-win proposition. *Restaurant Business*, *98*(13), 32-37.

Webby, R., & O'Connor, M. (1996). Judgmental and statistical time series forecasting: A review of the literature. *International Journal of Forecasting*, *12*(1), 91-118.

Webby, R., O'Connor, M., & Lawrence, M. (2001). Judgmental time-series forecasting using domain knowledge. In J. S. Armstrong (Ed.), *Principles of forecasting: A handbook for researchers and practitioners* (pp. 389-403). Norwell, MA: Kluwer Academic Publishers.

Winters, P. R. (1960). Forecasting sales by exponentially weighted moving averages. *Management Science*, *6*(3), 324-342.

Applying City Perception Analysis (CPA) for Destination Positioning Decisions

Sara Dolnicar
Klaus Grabler

SUMMARY. Typically, the image of a destination is studied by questioning a sample of tourists about their perceptions using a list of attributes and then condensing the data into average values for each individual destination. The city perception analysis (CPA) presented in this article, which is based on the perceptions-based market segmentation concept (PBMS, Dolnicar, Grabler & Mazanec 1999; Mazanec & Strasser 2000; Buchta, Dolnicar, & Reutterer 2000), approaches the positioning task from a completely different perspective. The fundamental assumption is that different consumers harbor different perceptions of various destinations in their minds. Therefore, averaging the perceptions and ignoring inter-individual differences in city image perceptions dramatically distorts the results. The CPA approach uses a three-way data structure and identifies archetypal destination perceptions *before* revealing information on which cities they were associated with, thus avoiding the false assumption of homogeneous consumers. The information on which perception was classified with respect to which brand is disclosed afterwards, thus allowing specific destination image insights. On the basis of CPA results, destination management can analyze the destination images as perceived by the tourists, choose attractive image positions for the future and deduce strategic policies. For the final positioning strategy, segments underlying the single perceptual positions have to be studied in detail. The CPA approach is illustrated using an empirical image study of six European city destinations, followed by a discussion of the managerial implications and advantages over traditional methods. *[Article copies available for a fee from The Haworth Document Delivery Service: 1-800-HAWORTH. E-mail address: <docdelivery@ haworthpress.com> Website: <http:// www.HaworthPress.com> © 2004 by The Haworth Press, Inc. All rights reserved.]*

KEYWORDS. Perceptual charting, city image analysis, positioning

INTRODUCTION

The tourism industry is becoming more and more global and is seeing fiercer competition among different (city) destinations. If competition is defined as the perceived substitutability of products from the perspective of consumers (a common approach described in Day, Shocker and Srivastava 1979), all destinations compete with each other at different levels of intensity. In addition, travel experience among consumers has grown in the last

Sara Dolnicar is Associate Professor, School of Management, Marketing & Employment Relations, University of Wollongong, Wollongong, North South Wales, Australia (E-mail: sarad@uow.edu.au). Klaus Grabler is affiliated with MANOVA Market Research & Consulting, Loewengasse, Vienna, Austria (E-mail: klaus.grabler@ manova.at).

[Haworth co-indexing entry note]: "Applying City Perception Analysis (CPA) for Destination Positioning Decisions." Dolnicar, Sara, and Klaus Grabler. Co-published simultaneously in *Journal of Travel & Tourism Marketing* (The Haworth Hospitality Press, an imprint of The Haworth Press, Inc.) Vol. 16, No. 2/3, 2004, pp. 99-111; and: *Management Science Applications in Tourism and Hospitality* (ed: Zheng Gu) The Haworth Hospitality Press, an imprint of The Haworth Press, Inc., 2004, pp. 99-111. Single or multiple copies of this article are available for a fee from The Haworth Document Delivery Service [1-800-HAWORTH, 9:00 a.m. - 5:00 p.m. (EST). E-mail address: docdelivery@ haworthpress.com].

http://www.haworthpress.com/web/JTTM
© 2004 by The Haworth Press, Inc. All rights reserved.
Digital Object Identifier: 10.1300/J073v16n02_08

few years, resulting in more specific expectations. This development makes destination branding an increasingly important competitive factor in the tourism marketplace. As a consequence, the relevance of image measurement for city destination management is rising, as a city's image heavily influences destination choices, creates destination brand value and serves as an indicator for the substitutability of destinations. For this reason, the main managerial emphasis is no longer placed on hard facts but on the perceptions of consumers or potential visitors, or the images in their minds when thinking of two destinations and choosing one for a holiday. This market knowledge therefore forms the basis for strategic decision-making, for deciding which image should be reinforced in the minds of the consumers by means of advertising.

Since the late '80s, destination positioning has attracted a lot of attention (Calantone et al. 1989; Gartner 1989). Most applications base on the implicit hypothesis that favourable perceptions of a particular destination lead to higher preference for this city. This implicit hypothesis was found valid for regions (Goodrich 1978). The most popular traditional methods used in destination positioning studies include factor analysis, t-tests, perceptual mapping, analysis of means and cluster analysis (a detailed count is provided by Pike, 2002). Another technique that has been used in tourism studies of this kind that is designed for nominal data is correspondence analysis (one of the rare applications has been published by Calantone et al. 1989). All these techniques have advantages and disadvantages and produce perceptual and preference spaces with different meanings (Myers 1992). There is no technique that has proven superior for all purposes. The application of a specific technique heavily depends on the data structure and the managerial aim of the exercise. Despite the long tradition of image studies, they show a number of weaknesses:

The typical approach taken is to design a questionnaire and ask respondents to state the perceptions they associate with a number of destinations or brands. Based on the answers, the mean values over all respondents are computed for each brand. These values are interpreted as the "image profile" or "semantic differential plot" and believed to mirror the tourists' opinion concerning a particular destination or brand. This process is perfectly suited to tackling the problem as long as all individuals agree with the image of the objects rated and share the same picture. As soon as different opinions exist, computing the mean value distorts the results and might lead to the conclusion that a destination or brand is not profiled, although very clear and precise yet different profiles can be revealed within certain subgroups of consumers. This assumption might be appropriate for the consumer goods industry with its high advertising budgets, as they can actively create images for products and brands easily and accurately. In the field of tourism, it is not that simple to construct "artificially engineered images," bearing in mind how consumer decisions are made in this particular industry (see Woodside and Lysonski 1989 for a frequently cited general destination decision model) and the strong "organic" image of a destination. A number of factors such as travel distance, travel experience, etc., interfere with the destination image as defined, engineered and communicated by destination management. The image of destinations is thus unlikely to be homogeneous among tourists. Therefore the traditional approach of computing mean values is inappropriate and can easily lead to false conclusions and subsequent mistakes in managerial decision-making.

The standardization of attributes and objects (destinations) in the data collection process does not account for the fact that respondents will differ in their knowledge of destinations and use different words to describe or differentiate them. Classical approaches implicitly assume that the same set of attributes is applicable to all consumers. The problem of asking for evaluations of objects which are irrelevant to the customer may be tackled by the family of "pick-any" procedures (Holbrook, Moore and Winer 1982) where only destinations within one's consideration set are compared. This also accounts for the fact that alternatives are compared on an attribute level only after a general holistic pre-selection phase (DeSarbo and Jedidi 1995). The problem of using irrelevant and too many attributes was handled by applying self-selected idiosyncratic lists of attributes in the family of adaptive perceptual mapping (Steenkamp and van Trijp 1996; Huber 1988).

This paper does not further address weaknesses in the data collection process, nor does it investigate the nature of destination image: it deals with new ways of improving data analysis in the perceptual mapping of three-way data. The exploratory data analysis approach presented is able to avoid the pitfall of aggregating heterogeneous consumers by using a three-way data structure (this implies that the image of more than one destination is measured questioning the same individuals, a situation not often reported in tourism literature as indicated by the fact that 53 percent of all publications on destination image in tourism only measure the image on one single destination: Pike, 2002). A perceptual chart based on the answers of 226 respondents regarding six European city destinations is constructed. The fundamental idea (comprehensively described in the perceptions based market segmentation concept (PBMS) by Mazanec & Strasser 2000 and Buchta, Dolnicar & Reutterer 2000) is to explore three-way consumer perceptions data and to extract both positioning and segmentation insight which can be used as a basis for strategic marketing decisions.

CPA is thus positioned at the crossroads of three very strong lines of strategic marketing research: positioning, segmentation and competition analysis. In contrast to market segmentation research (Frank, Massy, & Wind 1972; Myers & Tauber 1977; Wedel & Kamakura 1998), CPA does not focus on improving the partitioning task or recommending the most appropriate segmentation base. Instead, the emphasis lies on the integrated treatment of segmentation, positioning and competition, thus avoiding non-harmonized market structure analysis within the fundamental field of strategic marketing. Compared to the rich toolbox of positioning methods (mainly perceptual and preference maps), CPA does not make any rigid assumptions about the nature of the data. The partitioning task is purely exploratory and subsequent testing procedures can all be conducted in an entirely non-parametric way, making use of permutation testing. In addition, it automatically accounts for Myers' demand (1996, p. 232) that perceptual maps be constructed separately for *a priori* preference segments in order not to confound positioning and segmentation (consumer heterogeneity). An excellent example for this procedure is provided by Manrai and Manrai (1993). Furthermore, the relationship between the original space and the projected space is simpler than in the case of traditional methods. Brand positions are not profiled in a reduced space, but in the original space with as many dimensions as there are variables in the data set. As opposed to competition literature, this investigation goes beyond examining competition as interrelated to differentiation (under very rigid assumptions studied by Hotelling (cited in Moorthy 1985), d'Aspremont, Gabszewicz and Thisse (1979) and later extended by Hauser (1988) to account for consumer heterogeneity). Competition is investigated on a completely disaggregate level, simultaneously accounting for heterogeneity among consumers and the existence of different perceptual positions among brands in the marketplace.

CPA thus represents a useful addition to the exploratory toolbox for market structure analysis which (1) integrates three major issues in strategic marketing, (2) provides insights into the data for subsequent model building, (3) avoids oversimplification in analysis, (4) allows for fully non-parametric testing, thus making minimal assumptions about the data, and (5) is characterized by a simple relationship between the original and projected space.

ILLUSTRATING CPA: PERCEPTUALLY CHARTING SIX EUROPEAN CITIES

A positioning analysis for a city tourist destination basically examines the perceptual positions of different and probably competing cities. When perceptual positions alone are examined, the information provided by three-way data is not exploited to its full potential. Ideally, a perceptual positioning approach should also convey information about the heterogeneity of consumer perceptions. CPA reveals various archetypal positions associated with different city destinations by tourists who do not necessarily share the same perception of the cities. In addition, the attractiveness of various image positions can be evaluated by integrating information about consumer preferences, if available.

The aim of this empirical application of the CPA approach is to demonstrate the managerial knowledge gained by applying this methodology. It gives insight into generic city destination images as well as the association of these generic images with particular European city destinations. In our CPA application, we have taken the perspective of Vienna destination management.[1]

METHODOLOGY

Data Set

The data was not collected for the purpose of illustrating the usefulness of CPA; it was the result of a larger exploratory research project on European city tourism with special emphasis on decision-making and positioning. Therefore, it has not been optimized to provide all pieces of information a manager would certainly include in the survey in order to derive the maximum insight from CPA. But due to its three-way format (the most common format used in branded consumer goods industry to learn about image positioning) it is perfectly suited and was therefore chosen for this illustration. Respondents are a convenience sample of ferry trip travelers from the Netherlands to Great Britain who were questioned using standardized face to face interviews in summer 1996. The cities included were selected on the basis of the results of guest-mix analyses where these cities emerged as strongly competing destinations and 28 items (city attributes) were included (for details on the data set see Grabler, Mazanec & Wöber 1996). The respondents were asked to indicate how much they thought each city offered on a rating scale from 1 (the destination offers nothing with regard to the attribute) to 6 (the destination offers the attribute to a very large extent). The variables/items used are attributes considered relevant in the process of a city tourist destination decision such as price level, accessibility or quality of accommodation. The final sample amounted to 226 respondents, revealing their attitude towards six European cities (Barcelona, Budapest, Paris, Prague, Venice and Vienna). This sample size is clearly too small for real CPA application in the segmentation-positioning task due to the typically large number of variables included in an image study.[2] Furthermore, the convenience sample makes it impossible to draw final conclusions on the cities. Thus the sample merely serves as an example of how CPA methodology is applied. In its elongated, stacked version, the final data set used for the CPA approach consists of 1,356 rows (226 judgements on six cities) and 12 columns representing variable information (see Grabler 1997 for the typical pre-processing of three- way data before perceptual mapping by factor analysis and similar methods).

City Perception Analysis

The general CPA procedure is as follows: In the first step, respondents' perception patterns are grouped, disregarding brand information and using any appropriate partitioning algorithm. This means that the patterns of answers given by the respondents with regard to the cities evaluated are partitioned without taking the city judged by any particular answer pattern into account. This yields insights into generic city perceptions which exist in the marketplace. In the second step, brand information is revealed, thus allowing the analysis of city-specific images.

The partitioning algorithm applied in this study is the self-organizing feature map (SOFM), an unsupervised neural network pioneered by Kohonen (1984). SOFMs not only compress the information by partitioning the data, they also arrange the resulting groups or clusters according to similarity (for earlier applications, see Dolnicar 1997; Mazanec 1994, 1995a, 1995b, 1999). This additional information is especially useful in the application of positioning, for example, if certain similar regions of perceptions can be revealed (however, neural networks do not represent an integral part of CPA; any partitioning algorithm could be used instead the SOFM procedure chosen here). The starting points for this iterative procedure are drawn at random. As SOFMs are not very strongly influenced by the starting vectors (Dolnicar 1996), pre-processing or a high number of random draws are the only means of preventing a very bad starting position for learning. Once a predefined number of starting points (prototypes, nodes, cluster representatives) is determined, each answer pattern from the data set is assigned to the starting point with the lowest Euclidean distance. After each case is presented to the network, the closest node is relocated towards the newly assigned case. This iterative procedure ends either when only minimal changes can be detected from one case presentation to the next or a predefined number of iteration steps has been completed. The final prototypes represent an entire group of city perception patterns. The unique feature of arranging the prototypes in a way which mirrors the similarity is achieved by updating not only these representing points but also the neighboring nodes to a lesser extent. The grid resulting from partitioning by means of SOFMs thus allows topological interpretation of the city images.

For the European city CPA, the starting point for the SOFM training run with 16 nodes (arranged in a four-by-four grid) was a random solution of the prototype vectors with 100 trials.[3] The SOFM was calculated using the SOMnia program (1995, available at http://charly.wu-wien.ac.at/software/).[4]

RESULTS

The Perceptual Chart

The result of the partitioning task can be presented as a perceptual chart as shown in Figure 1. The 16 pies represent the 16 prototypes used in the self-organizing feature map. The perceptual chart enables management to both (1) analyze the present image situation on the city-destination market and (2) deduce positioning strategies for the future. The diameter of each pie indicates the number of city perceptions underlying each position. From a managerial standpoint, this can be interpreted as the frequency of city images perceived by tourists in general. Large pies represent commonly perceived generic city image positions, whereas small pies stand for very unusual images of city destinations. The perceptual chart thus enables the management to detect rather unique image positions (niches) easily by focusing on the small pies. The size of the slices indicates how many respondent perceptions within each pie concerned which one of the cities included in the questionnaire. The larger the slice, the higher the proportion of perceptions of one particular city. Larger slices can be interpreted by management as a strong association of an image position with a city. The stronger the association, the better the starting point for an image campaign supporting this particular picture of the destination in the tourists' minds. On the other hand, a low level of association does not necessarily mean that this position should not be chosen as a future target if it is promising for other reasons (e.g., preference). Finally, the arrangement of the image positions within the SOFM reveals the similarity of neighboring prototypes. This knowledge can be of practical use if single positions turn out not to be supported by a sufficient number of consumers, which would make it necessary to merge positions. In this case, adjacent regions would represent candidates for merging.

Compared to traditional positioning charts, the position is not deduced from the coordinates of a product, brand or city destination in the two-dimensional representation of attribute space. Instead, the prototypes represent generic perceptual positions of city destinations in the respondents' minds. The answer to the question of which city is perceived in which manner is provided by exploring the distribution of brands over these generic positions. (The answer to the question of whether competition exists and how intense it is given by computing pairwise Kappa coefficients, assuming competition to exist between two brands if one person perceives two city destinations as located at the same generic perceptual position.) Thus the interpretation of the perceptual chart is more intricate than in the case of traditional perceptual charts, but it is less misleading, as (1) the distances which results from one of many possible projections of highly dimensional data in two- or three-dimensional space are not over-interpreted, and (2) heterogeneity of perceptions among consumers is automatically accounted for.

After the first interpretation of the chart, two further issues have to be investigated in a second step: (1) Which city images are "hid-

FIGURE 1. Perceptual Chart of Six European City Destinations

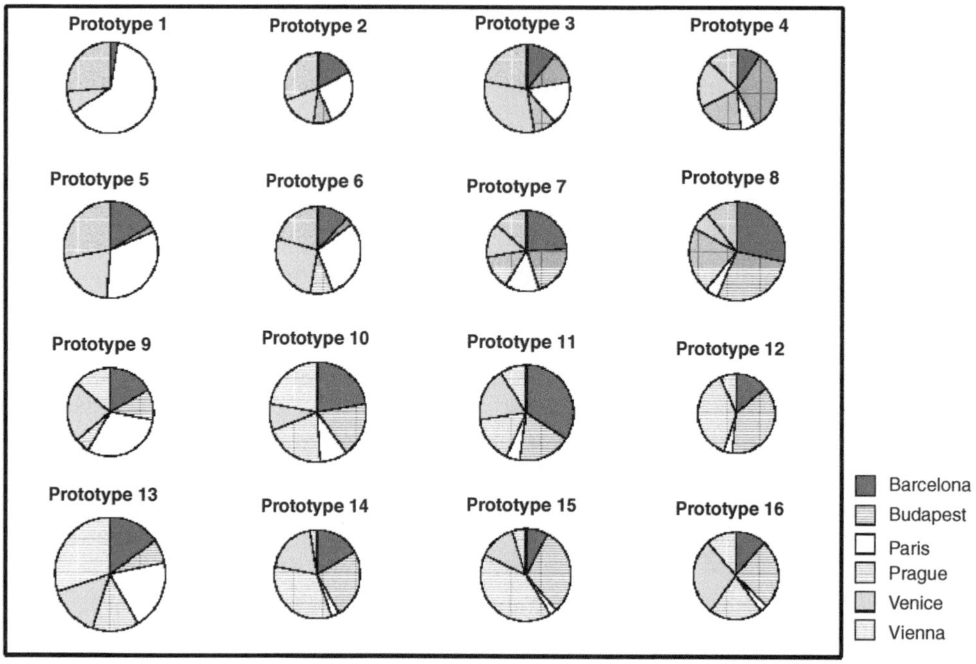

den" behind these prototypes (i.e., which generic images of cities exist in the respondents' minds)? (2) Which market segments/individuals hold these particular perceptions of the cities and are "hidden" behind these positions (i.e., which market segments could be targeted)?

Generic City Images

Instead of inspecting all positions in detail, a rough pre-selection accounting for the attractiveness of specific positions was performed. This attractiveness may be due to a strong image position (reflected in the size of the specific city slice), competitive pressure (diameter as an indicator of poorly occupied positions) or the overall preference for a generic position. The last item is measured in this case study by the number of top rankings aggregated over all city perceptions in the specific prototype. Generally, there is a high correlation between the prototype number and the overall preference structure, which is mirrored in a contingency coefficient of 0.339 (sig. < 0.001). The favorite is number 13, with about 15% of top rankings, followed by prototypes 1, 5, and 9 (each at about 12%). The least preferred positions are numbers 4 and 16.

From the Vienna destination management perspective, three image positions seem to be of relevance and are therefore studied in detail. These three positions are number 13 as the most typical Viennese position and the one enjoying the highest overall preference. Secondly, number one is inspected because of its high overall preference and its tough competitive position with Paris. For demonstration purposes, number 4 is inspected due to its low level of preference.

The one position that attracts the most attention from Vienna destination management is position or prototype 13, because its proportion of perceptions concerning Vienna is higher than at any other position (40 people, or 17.7%) and it is the most preferred generic city destination image. Figure 2 provides the profile of prototype 13. The line indicates the average over all answer patterns (all cities judged by all respondents) and the bars represent the average over the answer pattern for the individual position.

Obviously, cities at this position are perceived to provide all the attributes presented to a very high extent. At the same time, profiles of this kind are suspected to include answer tendencies. In order to prevent such answer tendencies from distorting the interpretation of the prototypes and consequently leading to inaccurate findings, it was assumed that–in the case of answer tendencies–one respondent would evaluate all cities in the same way (agreeing to all attributes). If the number of these individuals is high in prototype 13, it cannot be interpreted in a useful way. If, however, the number of respondents with such answer tendencies is low, the position is relevant for deducing market structure insights. Seven individuals out of 134 in the complete sample were characterized by such an answer pattern. They were excluded from the subsequent analysis of descriptive information in order to avoid distorting results. Thus position 13 actually does represent the image of all applicable attributes, making it a "perfect destination," which explains its highest preference value.

The second position of interest for Vienna is number 1. Actually, this interest could be extended to cover the group of prototypes 1, 2, 5 and 6, since this region indicates possible areas of competition with Paris. Please note that the grid represents a topological map which conveys information on similarity in neighboring regions. The average judgements of respondents grouped in prototype number one are shown in Figure 3.

This position is best characterized by generally associating a large number of attributes with the city, with only the typical negative attributes of mature destinations–high price level and unpleasant attitudes among local population–appearing as disadvantages.

The right-hand side of the perceptual chart (Figure 1) demonstrates the strong perceptual presence of Prague and Budapest. It is therefore worthwhile to take a closer look at these images as well, although preference for such cities is rather low. Position 4 (shown in Figure 4) indicates a generally low perception of the given attributes. The relatively high value concerning the price-level of these cities allows us to describe this position roughly as one that is not satisfactory in general, but nevertheless gets credit for its affordable price levels.

Market Segments Derived

After identifying typical perceptions of the European cities under study and revealing interesting image campaign candidates for Vienna as a destination, the underlying individuals have to be studied as thoroughly as possible in order to customize marketing activities to segment, be it in a concentrated or differentiated manner. For the purpose of demonstrating the methodology, the focus of our segment description lies on preference and attitudes, as they convey important information for targeting the right segments. The typical profiling of the segments using socio-demographic characteristics is not conducted, as this makes no difference to the classic segmentation process. Clearly this would be of great importance for practical applications.

As the sample is rather small (226 evaluations of Vienna) and further split up in 16 groups, which makes statistical tests impossible on a single position level, the following

FIGURE 2. Profile of Active Variables (Segment 13)

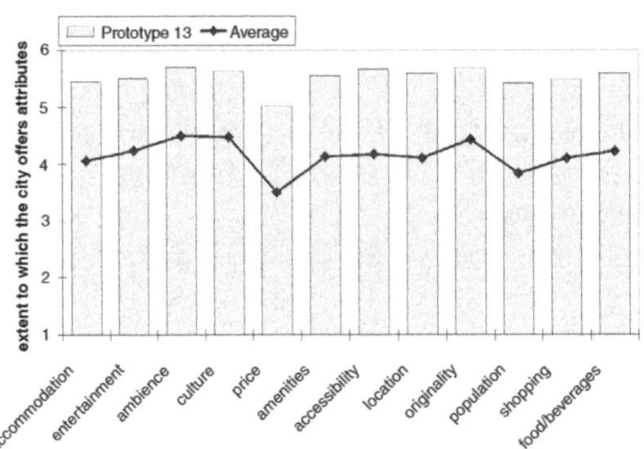

FIGURE 3. Profile of Active Variables (Segment 1)

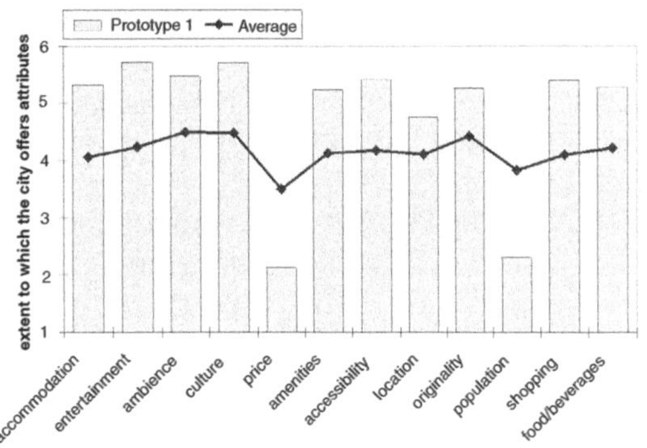

FIGURE 4. Profile of Active Variables (Segment 4)

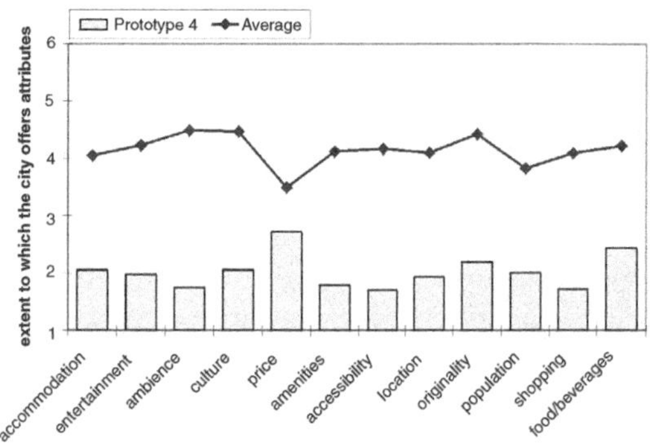

segment groups are constructed and subsequently described in detail: prototype 13 with 40 (17.7%) respondents, an additional group of prototypes forming a potential competition region with Paris and consisting of prototypes 1, 2, 5 and 6 (in sum: 78 answers, which is equal to 34.5% of the Vienna sample), and finally the group of Budapest and Prague-oriented segments numbered 4 and 8, consisting of 20 travellers (8.8%). With larger data sets, of course, the merging of segments according to SOFM regions is not necessary but may be useful for certain purposes such as campaign management, where a larger number of segments cannot be served economically.

"Vienna Is Fabulous" Tourists: Vienna at Perceptual Position 13

The indicator used to evaluate the preference tourists have for city attribute profiles was a ranking order of attractiveness provided by each respondent for all cities. Forty-two percent of the members of this segment stated that Paris is their most preferred city, followed by 24% who voted for Vienna. Venice is ranked third with 21%, while Prague and Barcelona are both below 10% and Budapest was not mentioned by a single respondent. This indicates that the segment which perceives Vienna as "fabulous" has very similar feelings about Paris as well. A number of possible hypotheses can be formulated as to why the preference for Paris is higher in this segment (e.g., more prior experience with Vienna and thus more interest in visiting Paris in the future), but pinpointing the exact reason would call for further analysis. At this stage, disaggregate competition analysis would allow further insights, which is not the main focus of this article and therefore not included (an example of this procedure is provided by Dolnicar, Grabler & Mazanec 1999).

These tourists are familiar with Vienna more than any of the groups compared (significance values and ranks are given in Table 1). They know what to expect, and we may expect them to have a fairly realistic view of Austria's capital as a city destination.

When questioned about the general importance of the aspects used as active variables, the "Vienna is fabulous" tourists placed the greatest emphasis on the ambience and the originality of the city compared to the segment clusters under study.

Segment 13 is the most concerned about possible negative surprises during their stay in Vienna: disliking the population's attitude, feeling that Vienna is too dangerous, feeling anxious about their health, and finally worrying about their friends having a bad impression of them/the city.

As far as activities during their stay in Vienna are concerned, the three segments under study vary in only two variables: visiting markets and going to museums and exhibitions. In both cases "Vienna is fabulous" tourists spend most of their time on these pastimes, followed by the "Vienna as a mass destination" tourists. When asked about the extent to which Vienna offers diverse activities, the former group feels that this city offers little, meaning that it ranks third in 10 of 13 variables.

"Mass Destination Vienna" Tourists: Vienna at Perceptual Positions 1, 2, 5 and 6

Members of this image position perceive Vienna in a more differentiated manner, including negative aspects of a mature city destination. The city preferences shift accordingly: Paris is still in the lead with 33%, followed by Vienna at 19%. The remaining four cities are ranked number one by more than 10% of group members. Obviously, some critical aspects associated with Vienna and Paris make alternative destinations appear more attractive to this segment.

In second place after the "Vienna is fabulous" tourists, these tourists still seem to be

TABLE 1. Test Statistics for Selected Variables

Question	Segments	Mean Ranks[a]	p-value
How familiar are you with Vienna?	segment 13 segments 1, 2, 5 and 6 segments 4 and 8	74.42 69.58 45.24	0.016*
How much would a lack of cultural resources annoy you? (1 = not at all)	segment 13 segments 1, 2, 5 and 6 segments 4 and 8	63.64 76.45 46.53	0.007*
How likely is it to occur in Vienna that you would dislike the population's attitude? (1 = unlikely)	segment 13 segments 1, 2, 5 and 6 segments 4 and 8	72.89 55.70 70.50	0.036*
How likely is it to occur in Vienna that the city would be too dangerous? (1 = unlikely)	segment 13 segments 1, 2, 5 and 6 segments 4 and 8	70.12 54.28 68.37	0.050
How likely is it to occur in Vienna that you would feel anxious about your health? (1 = unlikely)	segment 13 segments 1, 2, 5 and 6 segments 4 and 8	80.13 58.83 68.29	0.011*
How likely is it to occur in Vienna that friend would have a bad impression of the city? (1 = unlikely)	segment 13 segments 1, 2, 5 and 6 segments 4 and 8	78.69 60.59 54.68	0.020*
Importance of quality and type of accommodations (1 = not at all important)	segment 13 segments 1, 2, 5 and 6 segments 4 and 8	80.10 60.09 81.10	0.010*
Importance of the ambience of the city (1 = not at all important)	segment 13 segments 1, 2, 5 and 6 segments 4 and 8	83.97 69.10 42.13	0.000*
Importance of the city's originality (1 = not at all important)	segment 13 segments 1, 2, 5 and 6 segments 4 and 8	77.46 71.04 44.22	0.006*
Time spent on: going to museums and exhibitions (1 = no time at all)	segment 13 segments 1, 2, 5 and 6 segments 4 and 8	70.21 68.25 48.06	0.063
Time spent on: visiting market visits (1 = no time at all)	segment 13 segments 1, 2, 5 and 6 segments 4 and 8	71.93 68.50 45.50	0.029*
How much "shopping" does Vienna offer? (1 = nothing)	segment 13 segments 1, 2, 5 and 6 segments 4 and 8	52.59 68.01 72.07	0.067
How many "cultural events" does Vienna offer? (1 = nothing)	segment 13 segments 1, 2, 5 and 6 segments 4 and 8	55.54 64.11 78.59	0.085
How many "day trips to other amenities" does Vienna offer? (1 = nothing)	segment 13 segments 1, 2, 5 and 6 segments 4 and 8	51.82 67.03 77.19	0.033*
How much "sightseeing of man-made attractions" does Vienna offer? (1 = nothing)	segment 13 segments 1, 2, 5 and 6 segments 4 and 8	46.39 69.57 73.94	0.002*
How much "going to museums and exhibitions" does Vienna offer? (1 = nothing)	segment 13 segments 1, 2, 5 and 6 segments 4 and 8	52.88 65.74 73.28	0.083

[a]The mean ranks (Kruskal Wallis test) are calculated as the sum of ranks divided by the number of cases where ranks are used rather than means to account for the non-metric property of the data.
*Significant at the 95% level.

fairly experienced with Vienna as a city destination.

Among the theoretically possible problems occurring during the city trip, the "lack of cultural resources" very much annoys the segment under investigation. When asked how likely it is for a number of other problems to occur in Vienna, the number of statements which significantly differentiate segments rises, with the "Mass destination Vienna" tourists most strongly feeling that the hostility of the population, excessive danger in the city and friends having a bad impression are unlikely.

"Mass destination Vienna" tourists take an in-between position on the importance of certain city tourism factors as well as the evaluation of whether Vienna actually provides sufficient leisure activities of interest. The term "in-between position" is a defining characteristic of this group in general: they have fairly high prior experience with Vienna, few extremes in their city judgements, and they are open-minded as far as the choice of their next travel destination is concerned.

"Faceless Vienna" Tourists: Vienna at Perceptual Positions 4 and 8

Segments which feel that Vienna offers only very few important vacation aspects have the most characteristic preference structure, with more than half of their votes ranking Paris number 1 (53%). Venice was chosen as the most preferred city destination by 26%, Budapest by 11%, Vienna and Barcelona by 5% each, and Prague was not mentioned as destination number one a single time. When judging Vienna, this group of tourists evaluate cognitive image more than experience, as the latter is fairly low for this segment.

"Faceless Vienna" tourists are hardly ever annoyed by a 'lack of cultural resources'. As far as their judgement of Vienna is concerned, they believe (more than any other segment) that it is unlikely that visiting Vienna would lead to a bad impression when discussing vacation experiences with friends. The quality and type of accommodations are very important to this group, whereas the originality and ambience of the city are ranked lowest. This profile is almost the exact opposite of segment 13.

As mentioned above, the amount of time spent on "visiting markets," "museums and exhibitions" when visiting a city destination differs among the three segments. It turns out that the "faceless Vienna" tourists demonstrate fairly little interest in these leisure activities. On the other hand, Vienna is given most credit for offering leisure-time opportunities, especially in the form of "day trips to other amenities" and "sightseeing of man-made attractions."

To summarize the main characteristics of this group, interest in visiting Vienna is extremely low although the image of this city is very positive; a difficult problem for marketing managers.

Table 1 summarizes mean ranks and the p-value of the non-parametric, k-independent Kruskal Wallis test for the background information describing the segments in more detail. In an application of CPA with a particular managerial goal in mind, the number and kind of background variables could be extended.

STRATEGIC RECOMMENDATIONS FOR VIENNA CITY DESTINATION MANAGEMENT

CPA is introduced as a tool that aims at extracting the maximum amount of information relevant for strategic positioning decisions from typical empirical three-way image data, thus providing solid grounds for management decisions.

The findings from CPA support the city's destination management in two steps:

1. Based on the perceptual chart, the attractiveness of different image positions can be evaluated. The criteria used are the strength of a brand's claim to a certain position (e.g., Vienna is perceived as being located at the top and bottom left-hand side of the perceptual map by many respondents, so these particular images are already strongly associated with the city and thus represent a strong claim), the uniqueness of positions (the smaller the pie in the perceptual chart, the more likely the position represents a niche that might

offer future market potential) and the preference for each position, if available.

2. Depending on a destination's general segmentation strategy (concentrated or differentiated), it is possible to formulate precisely the optimal image strategy for the segment(s) chosen (the individuals placing Vienna at the image positions to be targeted). This goal is achieved by analyzing the perceived city image attributes as well as segment characteristics.

These steps lead to a comprehensive strategic destination image plan, as illustrated in Table 2 for the Vienna example, assuming that a differentiated segmentation strategy is chosen.

The benefit to destination management is that interpretational mistakes are avoided that are typically made when analyzing market data in a sequential manner. In this example entirely different results would have been arrived at if–on the basis of attribute-wise destination evaluation–segments would have been formed in the first step and building on this segmentation solution a positioning decision would have been taken and finally competition would have been taken into account (or in any other order). The fundamental danger of this traditional step- wise procedure is that segmentation and positioning decision are made conditionally upon one another thus reducing space for optimization, whereas CPA assures simultaneous treatment of both issues. The practical value for destination management therefore lies in avoidance of fundamentally flawed interpretation of results in consequence leading to sub-optimal strategic marketing decisions.

CONCLUSIONS, LIMITATIONS AND FUTURE WORK

CPA provides a simple tool for the analysis of typical empirical three-way image data, allowing market structure analysis simultaneously from the segmentation and positioning perspective as well as deductive reasons for strategic positioning decisions without implying homogeneity among consumers or making excessively strong assumptions about the nature of the data. CPA is easy to handle and flexible in terms of the partitioning algorithm applied.

The CPA approach was illustrated using European city data: 16 image positions with unequal city distributions of tourist perceptions were constructed. Image positions/regions relevant from the Viennese point of view were revealed and described in detail, as were the underlying market segments. Two positions turned out to be particularly interesting for Vienna.

TABLE 2. Positioning Strategy Plan for Vienna

Segment	Target tourists perceiving Vienna at position(s)	Central characteristics	Claim intensity of Vienna at this position	Attractiveness of the position (preference)	Communication (marketing) strategy
"Vienna is fabulous" tourists	13	Assign all attributes to Vienna, very familiar with Vienna, care about ambience and originality, like to go to markets, museums and exhibitions	High	High	Support existing image, build up relationship marketing
"Mass destination Vienna" tourists	1, 2, 5 and 6	Critical about value-for-money and friendliness of local population, fairly high prior experience with Vienna, open to other city destinations	High	High	Differentiation from Paris, point out value for money and friendliness of local population
"Faceless Vienna" tourists	4 and 8	No differentiated image of Vienna exists, interest in visiting Vienna is low, inactive visitors	Low	Low	Define as non-target segment or launch image campaign to build entirely new image of Vienna

One was position 13, which is perceived as highly attractive among segment members who have more prior experience with Vienna. This represents a good starting point for strengthening the image within this group of tourists. In contrast, the market segments underlying the image positions which are dominated by perceptions concerning Prague and Budapest have no prior knowledge about Vienna. The map region strongly associated with Paris is similar to position 13, except for the perception of high prices. The underlying segment had a broad portfolio of alternatives in mind for the next city vacation, making these tourists very susceptible to changing their city destination the next time they travel, thus reducing their attractiveness for destination management to a certain extent.

The image positions constructed are highly profiled, and the market segments underlying the positions differ significantly in numerous characteristics, indicating that tourists' perceptions of European cities are far from homogeneous. The fundamental advantage of CPA as compared to step-wise procedures of market analysis is that sub-optimal decisions (sequentially dependent strategic marketing decision-making) are avoided.

Two limitations apply to using CPA. First, three-way data is required, a non-trivial condition requiring careful planning of the analysis for management decision support well in advance of the analysis itself (as early as questionnaire design). In addition, the number of objects that can reasonably be presented to the respondents is limited, calling for pre-analysis in selecting the stimuli. Second, the results emerging from CPA are not simple recipes. Instead, a large amount of market structure information is provided and subsequently has to be analyzed with care in order to arrive at analytically founded management decisions.

Besides the limitation of the CPA approach, the illustration provided in this article is not optimal because there was not a wide variety of background variables available to describe the segments underlying the perceptual positions in as much detail as would be required if CPA were used for managerial decision support. However, this is not a weakness of CPA but of the data set used for the real world application described.

Future work will include a systematic analysis of competition based on perceptual information, as well as a systematization of segmentation possibilities emerging from this framework.

NOTES

1. This of course is an arbitrary choice. The perspective of any of the city destinations could be chosen for the purpose of illustrating the managerial usefulness of CPA.

2. Although there is no rule that states how the proportion of data dimensions to sample size has to be, it obviously improves the insights derived if there is sufficient data to fill the space in as many dimensions as variables are used. Therefore the sample size of 226 is considered sufficient to illustrate the usefulness of CPA, but the authors wish to avoid setting bad precedence for too small sample sizes.

3. In order to determine the optimal number of prototypes (groups), preliminary calculations with different grid sizes were calculated. The 4×4 grid rendered the best relative results in terms of both heterogeneity and simplicity. Heterogeneity is calculated as sum of squared Euclidean distances of each data vector to the best representing prototype, divided by the total number of data points. Lower values thus indicate better results. The simplicity of the SOFM is calculated by the sum of squared Euclidean inter-prototype distances between adjacent prototypes. In general it is recommended to choose a larger number of prototypes in order not to lose valuable distinctions. If the grid turns out to be too detailed, merging of prototypes is possible without any sacrifice.

4. The authors are aware of the fact that computing Euclidean distance on the basis of ordinal data is a suboptimal choice, as it is not plausible to assume equidistant and equally equidistant representation of distances between the ordinally scaled values. The use of binary or metric data should be favoured when applying CPA for managerial decision making, a requirement which is best accounted for at the questionnaire design stage.

REFERENCES

Buchta, C., Dolnicar, S. & Reutterer, T. (2000). *A non-parametric approach to perceptions-based market segmentation: Applications*. Series: Interdisciplinary Studies in Economics and Management, Volume II. Springer-Verlag, Berlin.

Calantone, R.J., I. di Benedetto, A. Hakam & Bojanic, B.C. (1989). Multiple Multinational Tourism Positioning Using Correspondence Analysis. *Journal of Travel Research, 28*, 25-32.

d'Aspremont, C., Gabszewicz, J. & Thisse, J. (1979). On Hotelling's Stability in Competition. *Econometrica*, *47*, 1145-1150.

Day, G.S., Shocker, A.D. & Srivastava, R.K. (1979). Customer-Oriented Approaches to Identifying Product-Markets. *Journal of Marketing*, *43*, 8-19.

DeSarbo, W.S. and Jedidi, K. (1995). The Spatial Representation of Heterogeneous Consideration Sets. *Marketing Science, 14*, 326-342.

Dolnicar, S. (1997). *Erstellung einer psychographischen Taxonomie von Osterreich-Urlaubern unter Anwendung neuronaler Netzwerkverfahren.* Vienna: Service Fachverlag.

Dolnicar, S., Grabler, K. & Mazanec, J.A. (1999). A Tale of Three Cities: Perceptual Charting for Analyzing Destination Images, in: Woodside, A.G. et al. (eds.), *Consumer Psychology of Tourism, Hospitality, and Leisure.* New York: CAB International, 39-62.

Frank, R.E., Massy, W.F. & Wind, Y. (1972). *Market Segmentation.* Englewood Cliff: Prentice-Hall.

Gartner, W.C. (1989). Tourism Image: Attribute Measurement of State Tourism Products Using Multidimensional Scaling Techniques. *Journal of Travel Research*, *28*, 16-20.

Goodrich, J.N. (1978). The Relationship Between Preferences for and Perceptions of Vacation Destinations: Application of a Choice Model. *Journal of Travel Research*, *17*, 8-13.

Grabler, K., J. Mazanec & Wöber, K. (1996). Strategic Marketing for Urban Tourism: Analysing Competition among European Tourist Cities, in: Law, Ch.M. (ed.), *Tourism in Major Cities*, London: Mansell.

Grabler, K. (1997). Perceptual Mapping and Positioning of Tourist Cities, in: Mazanec, J. (ed.), *International City Tourism. Analysis and Strategy*, Pinter, London und Washington, 101-113.

Hauser, J.R. (1988). Competitive Price and Positioning Strategies. *Marketing Science*, *7*, 76-91.

Holbrook, M.B., Moore, W.L. and Winer, R.S. (1982). Constructing Joint Spaces from Pick-Any Data: A New Tool for Consumer Analysis. *Journal of Consumer Research*, *9*, 99-105.

Huber, J. (1988). APM system for adaptive perceptual mapping, software review. *Journal of Marketing Research,* 119-121.

Kohonen, T. (1984). *Self Organisation and Associative Memory.* New York: Springer-Verlag.

Manrai, L.A. & Manrai, A.K. (1993). Positioning European countries as brands in a perceptual map: An empirical study of determinants of consumer perceptions and preferences. *Journal of Euromarketing*, 2, 101-129.

Mazanec, J. & Strasser, H. (2000). *A Nonparametric Approach to Perceptions-Based Market Segmentation: Foundations.* Series: Interdisciplinary Studies in Economics and Management, Volume II. Springer-Verlag, Berlin.

Mazanec, J. (1994). Image Measurement with Self-Organizing Maps: A Tentative Application to Austrian Tour Operators. *Revue de Tourisme*, *49*, 9-18.

Mazanec, J. (1995a). Competition Among European Tourist Cities: A Comparative Analysis with Multidimensional Scaling and Self-Organizing Maps. *Tourism Economics*, *1*, 283-302.

Mazanec, J. (1995b). Positioning Analysis with Self-Organizing Maps: An Exploratory Study on Luxury Hotels. *Cornell Hotel and Restaurant Administration Quarterly*, *36*, 80-95.

Mazanec, J. (1999). Simultaneous Positioning and Segmentation Analysis with Topologically Ordered Feature Maps: A Tour Operator Example. *Journal of Retailing and Consumer Services, Special Issue on Marketing Applications of Neural Networks*, *6*, 219-235.

Mazanec, M. (1995). SOMnia 1.4.1, Revision A.

Moorthy, K.S. (1985). Using Game Theory to Model Competition. *Journal of Marketing Research*, *22*, 262-282.

Myers, J.H. (1996). *Segmentation and Positioning for Strategic Marketing Decisions.* American Marketing Association: Chicago.

Myers, J.H. & Tauber, E. (1977). *Market structure analysis.* American Marketing Association: Chicago.

Myers, J.H. (1992). Positioning Products/Services in Attitude Space. *Marketing Research A Magazine of Management & Applications*, *4*, 46-51.

Pike, S. (2002). Destination image analysis–a review of 142 papers from 1973 to 2000. *Tourism Management*, *23*, 541-549.

Steenkamp, J.-B.E.M. & van Trijp, H.C.M. (1996). Task Experience and Validity in Perceptual Mapping. A Comparison of Two Consumer-Adaptive Techniques. *International Journal of Research in Marketing*, *13*, 265-276.

Wedel, M. & Kamakura, W. (1998). *Market Segmentation–Conceptual and Methodological Foundations.* Boston: Kluwer Academic Publishers.

Woodside, A.G. & Lysonski, S. (1989). A General Model of Traveler Destination Choice. *Journal of Travel Research*, *27*, 8-14.

Index

© 2004 by The Haworth Press, Inc. All rights reserved.

For Product Safety Concerns and Information please contact our EU representative GPSR@taylorandfrancis.com Taylor & Francis Verlag GmbH, Kaufingerstraße 24, 80331 München, Germany

T - #0116 - 230425 - C0 - 273/210/7 - PB - 9780789025180 - Gloss Lamination